Resilience

The Science of Mastering Life's Greatest Challenges

Resilience

The Science of Mastering Life's Greatest Challenges

Written by

Steven M. Southwick

Glenn H. Greenberg Professor of Psychiatry, Posttraumatic Stress Disorder and Resilience
Yale University School of Medicine and Yale Child Study Center
Clinical Neurosciences Division, Department of Veterans Affairs National Center for PTSD
West Haven, CT, USA

Dennis S. Charney

Anne and Joel Ehrenkranz Dean, Mount Sinai School of Medicine
Executive Vice President for Academic Affairs, The Mount Sinai Medical Center
Professor, Departments of Psychiatry, Neuroscience, and Pharmacology and Systems
Therapeutics, New York, NY, USA

CAMBRIDGE
UNIVERSITY PRESS

CAMBRIDGE
UNIVERSITY PRESS

University Printing House, Cambridge CB2 8BS, United Kingdom

Published in the United States of America by Cambridge University Press, New York

Cambridge University Press is part of the University of Cambridge.

It furthers the University's mission by disseminating knowledge in the pursuit of education, learning and research at the highest international levels of excellence.

www.cambridge.org
Information on this title: www.cambridge.org/9780521195638

First published 2012
10th printing 2015

Printed in the United States of America by Sheridan Books, Inc.

A catalogue record for this publication is available from the British Library

Library of Congress Cataloguing in Publication data
Southwick, Steven M.
Resilience : the science of mastering life's greatest challenges / Steven M. Southwick, Dennis S. Charney.
    p. cm.
Includes bibliographical references and index.
ISBN 978-0-521-19563-8 (pbk.)
1. Resilience (Personality trait)   2. Adaptability (Psychology)
I. Charney, Dennis S. II. Title.
BF698.35.R47S68   2012
155.2′4–dc23   2012007345

ISBN 978-0-521-19563-8 Paperback

Contents

Acknowledgments

This book would not have been possible without the generous contributions of the many inspiring individuals who granted us permission to interview them and share portions of those interviews with our readers. These courageous men and women told us about extremely painful and trying experiences in their lives. Talking with us in depth about these experiences was extraordinarily difficult, but they chose to speak so that their stories and their insights might help others. Their stories and their advice make up the heart and soul of this book. It has been an honor and a privilege for us to interview and learn from these remarkable individuals. They have become our role models just as we hope they will become yours. They have taught us to look for light at the end of the tunnel; to view adversity as an opportunity for growth and wisdom; to live by our own highest moral and ethical standards; to foster strong personal relationships in which we both give and receive support; to rigorously train our physical, emotional, cognitive, and spiritual selves; and to assume responsibility for our own growth and resilience. They have shown us how to seek the very best in ourselves, and they have taught us that we are each far stronger and more resilient than we think.

We also wish to thank the editors and writers who helped to shape this book. Specifically, we acknowledge and express thanks to Lisa Berger, who partnered us in our early efforts to write about resilience. Lisa is an outstanding writer and editor. In addition, Cathy Shufro, Kara Baskin, and Marcia Southwick provided expert guidance in writing style and editing. We were also very fortunate to work with Elsa Peterson, who is an extremely talented scholar, writer, and editor. Elsa made enormous contributions to every aspect of the book – research, writing, and editing.

Many of our friends and colleagues helped us as we formulated ideas about resilience. They also reviewed drafts of the book and provided valuable suggestions and edits. We wish to thank Bernadette Lowthert, Jeanne Stellman, and Christina Baker, who reviewed and edited nearly all sections of the book. Paul Morrissey, Ron Duman, Eric Jackson, Jo Ann Thorp, Robb Pietrzak, Ann Graber, Catherine Chiles, and Lori Davis provided guidance and edits on specific chapters.

Finally, we wish to thank the many professionals at Cambridge University Press who edited and published this book.

SMS and DSC

Chapter 1

What is resilience?

Most of us at some point will be struck by one or more major traumas: violent crime, domestic violence, rape, child abuse, a serious automobile accident, the sudden death of a loved one, a debilitating disease, a natural disaster or war. If you are very lucky, then you have never encountered any of these misfortunes; but most likely you will someday. It is estimated that up to 90% of us will experience at least one serious traumatic event during our lives (Norris & Sloane, 2007).

Traumatic events throw our lives into turmoil in unpredictable ways; no two people will respond to them in exactly the same manner. For some, the stress of the event will become chronic, lasting for years. They may undergo a dramatic change in outlook, becoming sullen, demoralized, withdrawn, cynical, and angry. Some will become depressed or develop posttraumatic stress disorder (PTSD). Horrific, intrusive memories and nightmares will haunt them for days, months or even years, and they will feel unsafe in the world – hypervigilant – as if another serious danger lurks just around the corner. Some will take up drinking or drugs to numb their pain and dull their memories.

Nevertheless, many people will find ways to meet the challenge and continue with purposeful lives. For a period after their ordeal, they may become distressed, but in time they will bounce back and carry on. For some, it will be almost as if the trauma had never occurred. For others, the distress will persist, but they will find healthy ways to cope. Some survivors will even grow stronger and wiser because of their trauma. These survivors may report that their tragedy has helped them to appreciate life more, to become closer to family and friends, to find greater meaning, and sometimes to embark on a new mission in life. In the words of Elisabeth S. Lukas, a protegé of the neurologist, psychiatrist, and Holocaust survivor Viktor Frankl, "*The forces of fate that bear down on man and threaten to break him also have the capacity to ennoble him*" (1984).

Resilience after 9/11

On the clear, balmy morning of September 11, 2001, 45-year-old Jimmy Dunne was playing golf in New York's suburban Westchester County, looking forward to qualifying for the US Mid-Amateur Championship tournament. Along with the other golfers, he was stunned to learn that planes had crashed into the World Trade Center. Dunne's shock was intensified by the fact that his own company, the financial services firm Sandler O'Neill, was located at Two World Trade Center (the "South Tower"). As details of the damage became available, his fears were confirmed: the plane that struck the South Tower burst into flames on the 78th through 84th floors, trapping hundreds on the floors above (Dwyer *et al.*, 2002). Sandler O'Neill was on the 104th floor.

While Dunne watched television in disbelief, thousands of employees, visitors, police, firefighters, emergency medical personnel, and concerned bystanders were fighting to save lives while they struggled to understand what was happening. One Sandler O'Neill survivor, Karen Fishman, had arrived at her office in the South Tower about 8:45 that morning – moments before the first plane struck the North Tower and sent a massive, blinding ball of flame shooting through the air outside her office window. Shaking, she got up from her desk, stepped out into the hallway, and quickly found herself headed for the stairs with two colleagues who had announced, "We're getting the hell out of here" (Brooker, 2002, p. 56).

"I don't know why I left," Fishman said later. "I don't know that it was a conscious decision. It was instinct. So much depended on who you saw right at that moment." Several other Sandler O'Neill employees left, but others stayed in the office and made phone calls assuring family members and business associates that they were all right. Still, the horrors in the neighboring building had everyone so upset that CEO Herman Sandler told his workforce, "Whoever wants to leave can leave."

Fishman had reached the 64th floor when she heard an announcement that only the North Tower was affected and there was no need to evacuate the South Tower. But by then the stairwell was crowded, and turning back would have meant going against the tide of people headed down, so she continued.

Fishman was on the 62nd floor at 9:03 when United Airlines Flight 175 crashed into the South Tower. Forty-two stories above her, a Sandler O'Neill assistant was on the phone with her husband – "Oh, my God" were the last words he heard her say. A trader called his wife: "There is smoke everywhere. People are dying all around me" (Brooker, 2002, p. 57).

Survivors described how the building shook and twisted when the plane struck, causing paneling, duct work, and electrical wires to fall out of the walls and ceilings. The lights went out, and the building's sprinkler system activated in some areas, sending cascades of water down the pitch-dark stairwells as people groped their way down. Of course, neither Karen Fishman nor anyone else knew that the building was about to collapse. In a sense this was fortunate, for the evacuation was generally orderly and unhurried – some even commented later that they had paced themselves, aiming to lessen the risk of having to walk down dozens of flights with a sprained ankle (Clark, 2006).

Karen Fishman and another Sandler O'Neill employee, Mark Fitzgibbon, had reached street level and were making their way uptown at 9:59, when the South Tower collapsed. They were far enough away from the burning towers that the surrounding skyscrapers partially obscured their view. Like many who witnessed the event, they had no idea that the entire building was gone; they thought that they were seeing smoke from an explosion or a collapse affecting only the floors above the fire line.

Fitzgibbon called to Karen, "Look. The top of our building is gone." But she didn't look back (Brooker, 2002, p. 57).

A huge wave of ash and dust burst from the ruins and covered the area like a snow-fall. Stunned survivors fled by themselves or in groups, some running, some walking purposefully, others wandering as if in a fog. By 10:28, when One World Trade Center and the adjoining Marriott Hotel collapsed, news organizations had begun to report a possible terrorist connection, and other landmark buildings such as the United Nations were evacuated. Not knowing whether further attacks were immi-nent, New York Mayor Rudy Giuliani ordered the evacuation of lower Manhattan. This released a swelling tide of pedestrians into the streets as people attempted to get home. Transportation was severely crippled: the subway service was suspended, as were the PATH trains connecting Manhattan with New Jersey. Commuter buses stopped running, as all bridges and tunnels connecting Manhattan with the outer boroughs and with New Jersey were closed to non-emergency traffic. One survivor described taking a ferry homeward to New Jersey:

> … as we got parallel [to the World Trade Center site] we could look over and see that both towers were gone. It was just a surreal feeling. Disbelief. How could this happen? Of course, at the time we knew nothing about the planes being hijacked, nothing about the Pentagon, nothing about the plane going down in Pennsylvania, or the FAA getting all planes out of the air. We were completely in the dark. But we could look off to the Trade Center on our right and see that this building I had worked in for 27 years was gone. It was a staggering thought. There was silence. People just couldn't believe it. (Clark, 2006)

While these events were transpiring, Jimmy Dunne was on the phone, calling first his wife and then a series of friends and associates. He tried repeatedly to reach Chris Quackenbush, his business partner and closest companion; the two had been friends since childhood. And he kept trying to call his boss and mentor Herman Sandler, but could not reach him either. Had Chris and Herman made it out of the South Tower alive? After four or five hours without word on the whereabouts of Chris or Herman, Jimmy began to fear the worst. As painful as it was to imagine, perhaps his best friends and colleagues had been murdered by the terrorists. Perhaps he would never see them again.

Still, like so many others on that chaotic day, Jimmy held out hope and main-tained what he referred to as a "we are going to find them" state of mind. As he recalls, "There was a hope that there were people who had gotten out, gotten to a hospital, gotten somewhere and maybe they just couldn't make a phone call."

His hopes received a massive boost when he was told that a junior trader in the firm had been found.

> There was an intern who worked with us. He was terrific. His name was Kevin Williams. After I left the golf course I spoke to his father, who told me they found Kevin. And I was euphoric. I remember physical euphoria when I learned that Kevin was alive. It also meant that if they found Kevin, maybe they would find Chris and Herman and the others. I was euphoric. Absolute joy.

By mid-afternoon, Jimmy learned that surviving employees of his firm were gathering in a small office that Sandler O'Neill maintained in midtown. He decided to take the train into Manhattan and meet with them.

> I left for the train station with great hope. But on the way I received a call that I will never forget as long as I live. It was Kevin's father. He said, "Jimmy, Jimmy, they found Kevin Williams – but not our Kevin Williams." And I remember physically slouching down, almost collapsing. Fortunately there was a chair right there. I've never had anything like that happen before.

By the time the train arrived in Manhattan, however, Jimmy was surging with energy. He ran from Grand Central Station, headed toward the midtown office.

> And then I remember thinking, as soon as I get there everybody's gonna be looking at me, everybody's gonna be looking for direction from me. I want to set a very different tone, one of total calm. I remember I stopped running and I walked about four blocks before I got to the office.

Under normal circumstances, Jimmy saw himself as somewhat pessimistic. "I'm like the French Foreign Legion: I prepare for the worst and hope for the best." But on September 11, coming to terms with the news that the World Trade Center attack had been perpetrated by terrorists whose goal was to kill as many Americans as possible and create a sense of mass hysteria among the living, he remembered something his father had told him decades earlier. Jimmy and his father had been sitting together watching an Army–Notre Dame football game, and Notre Dame was crushing Army 40–7.

That's when Jimmy's father turned to him and said, "Now is the time that I would like to be a lineman on the Army squad."

Jimmy didn't understand.

> Why would anyone want to be on Army? They're being beaten 40–7! And we liked Notre Dame better than Army. Plus, being a lineman for Army, you'd be outweighed by something like 80 pounds. I can't think of a less desirable position to be in. So I asked my father, "why?" And I remember what he said like it was yesterday: "Because the guy on the other side of the line is gonna find out what I'm made of. I would wreak holy hell on that guy."

In his own way, after the destruction of September 11, that's what Jimmy did.

> The moment I heard what the terrorists wanted, I decided to do exactly the opposite. Osama Bin Laden wanted us to be afraid. I would show no fear. He wanted us to be pessimistic. I would be incredibly optimistic. He wanted anguish. I would have none of it.

The determination to "show them what I'm made of" served him well in the hours and days after the attacks, as the scope of the catastrophe became clear. As hard as he may have tried to prepare himself to face severe losses, the damage was unimaginable. Of 171 Sandler employees, 66 died (Kroft, 2001). Among them were Jimmy's close friends and fellow managing partners, Chris Quackenbush and Herman Sandler. In all, the deaths of the firm's workers left 46 widows and widowers, and 71 children under age 18 who had lost a father or mother. Furthermore, Sandler O'Neill was a small enough firm that its operations had been concentrated in the Two World Trade Center office. All of the company's paperwork and computer systems were destroyed. As *Fortune* magazine reported, "Every phone number of every person Sandler's traders had done business with over the years was vaporized" (Brooker, 2002, p. 60). Even more devastating was the loss of corporate memory.

Suddenly Dunne, who previously had shared responsibilities with Quackenbush and Sandler, was thrust into the role of chief executive and decision maker. The firm was so terribly crippled – should he simply dissolve it? If not, how could he possibly guide it to survival? Would an attempt to stay in business merely prolong the agony? How could so many traumatized employees manage to function and conduct business when they were grieving for their lost colleagues?

One of the first crucial decisions Dunne made was to "do right by the families" of those who had died (Nocera, 2006). He personally attended dozens of funerals and delivered eulogies for many. Despite the financial burden, comprising a third of the firm's working capital, Sandler O'Neill paid the salaries of the deceased employees through December 31, 2001 (McKay, 2002). The company paid bonuses and extended family health-care benefits for five years. In addition, the firm set up a fund for the education of the children who had lost a parent, and it provided five years of psychological counseling for all family members and for surviving employees.

Another of Dunne's crucial decisions was that he would find a way to carry on with business. If the firm failed, it could no longer support his colleagues and their families. Failure would also mean success for the terrorists. Although there were rumors – including a CNBC report – that the firm was closing, Sandler's operations never came to a halt. As much as Dunne felt the profound pain of his colleagues, he knew that the firm's only chance for survival was to rebuild immediately.

> Early on we got everyone together and they were in various levels of their pain. I said, "Look, everybody is re-evaluating their lives after 9–11." And I said, "That's fine. You can go ahead and re-evaluate your life. That's OK. And some of you may decide that coming to the city every day and chasing the dollar is not worth it, and that you should work in the post office and teach lacrosse. That's great. Some of you may want to go take a trip around the world. That's fine too. But I can tell you what I am gonna do. I'm gonna put on my Brooks Brothers suit every day and I am gonna come to work, and I am gonna rebuild this firm, and I am gonna pay for these benefits, and I am not gonna give in. That is what I have decided to do. Now for those of you who want to be doing the same thing, we have to be doing it *now*. And those of you who want to re-evaluate things and think differently, I wish you well. Go do it."

By September 17, the day the New York Stock Exchange reopened, the firm was set up in temporary office space donated by Bank of America and prepared to resume trading. Dunne and the other managers saw rebuilding the firm as a moral imperative. They were determined to honor their lost colleagues and make the trades that their colleagues no longer could. Several weeks later, after his first visit to Ground Zero, accompanying a colleague's widow who wished to view the site, Dunne commented to a co-worker, "… if I was determined before, I'm on fire now" (Brooker, 2002, p. 53). As founding partner Tom O'Neill told CBS's *60 Minutes,* "I don't think we appreciated the depth of [the terrorists'] hatred, but I think for every percentage that we might have underestimated them, I think they very much underestimated us" (Kroft, 2001). By the first anniversary of the attack, Sandler had hired 81 new employees and closed 59 deals, including 15 mergers worth $2.7 billion.

Although immersing himself in work was a healing influence for Dunne in many ways, the emotional toll was still vast. A year after the attacks, Dunne told National Public Radio's Scott Simon, "I'm better when I'm busy, but the very first thing I think about when I wake up in the morning and the very last thing I think about at night are those planes" (Simon, 2002). Then-Chief Operating Officer Fred D. Price, who had been away at a conference in Seattle on September 11, agreed:

> When you are busy and active you don't think about it, but when it's quiet, when you are driving alone, or on weekends when you get up in the morning, that is when I vividly miss [my colleagues]. … Some days, I feel bad and some days I feel good and I never know why … Weekends are tougher, and Sunday is my ugliest day. It's when I've got time on my hands. (Wayne, 2002)

The grief that Jimmy felt was unlike anything that he had experienced. Reflecting on the loss of his lifelong friend Chris Quackenbush and his mentor Herman Sandler, he likened it to the utter despondency that history tells us Thomas Jefferson experienced upon the death of his beloved wife Martha in 1782:

> It was absolute grief, the kind of grief that Thomas Jefferson talks about, grief without a point. I felt that kind of grief at Chris's funeral after I spoke, and when I went to see [Herman's widow] Suki Sandler. When other people talk about their grief, sometimes you don't even know what they're talking about. You don't really know what real grief is. Now I think I know. I think I have a sense about absolute grief. Those are the times I just broke down.

Five years later, *New York Times* reporter Joe Nocera interviewed Dunne and noted that "his eyes would well up while his voice would start to crack" when he talked about his partners (Nocera, 2006). Yet, far from being a sign of weakness, Dunne's heartfelt emotion was the driving force in his rescue of the firm. Jimmy Dunne personifies resilience in his unwavering determination to bounce back from the brink of despair, and to grow in the process, becoming a more compassionate, dedicated leader than he had been in the past.

How we became interested in resilience

Our interest in resilience evolved during nearly 20 years treating and studying trauma survivors who came to us for help with conditions such as depression and post-traumatic stress disorder. In our research, we examined the psychological, neurobiological, social and spiritual impact of having lived through overwhelming traumas such as combat, child abuse, physical and sexual assault, and disasters including the WTC disaster and Hurricane Ike (Charney *et al.*, 1993, 1996; Bremner *et al.*, 1993, 1999; Southwick *et al.*, 2006, 2007; Stellman *et al.*, 2008). We, and many other researchers, discovered alterations in psychological view of self and others, in the brain circuits that respond to frightening situations, and in feelings about one's purpose, meaning and place in the world. These alterations often had profound negative effects on the lives of our patients.

As we worked with traumatized individuals, we often wondered about survivors who seemed to somehow cope effectively with the negative effects of stress, those who did not develop stress-related symptoms, or who, if they developed symptoms, carried on successfully nevertheless. The term "resilient" (meaning having the capacity to bend without breaking, to return to an original shape or condition) described these survivors well. They had been "bent" by their traumatic experiences, but not broken.

Defining resilience

What is resilience? In the physical sciences, materials and objects are termed resilient if they resume their original shape upon being bent or stretched. In people, resilience refers to the ability to "bounce back" after encountering difficulty. The American Psychological Association defines it as "the process of adapting well in the face of adversity, trauma, tragedy, threats and even significant sources of stress – such as family and relationship problems, serious health problems, or workplace and financial stresses."[1] In his book *Aging Well*, Harvard University psychologist George Vaillant (2002) describes resilient individuals as resembling "a twig with a fresh, green living core. When twisted out of shape, such a twig bends, but it does not break; instead, it springs back and continues growing" (p. 285).

Resilience is complex, multidimensional and dynamic in nature (Bonanno, 2004, 2005; Carver, 1998; Layne *et al.*, 2007; Luthar *et al.*, 2000; Rutter, 1985). When faced with adversity, people tend to be more competent in some domains of their lives than in others, and during some, but not all, phases of their lives. For example, an individual may be remarkably sturdy in responding to adversity at work, but not so much in handling family or other interpersonal stresses. Or a person may demonstrate resilience to stress at a young age, but not as he or she grows older. It is important to note that healthy adaptation to stress depends not only on the individual, but also on available resources through family, friends, and a variety of organizations, and on the characteristics of specific cultures and religions, communities, societies, and governments – all of which, in themselves, may be more or less resilient (Southwick *et al.*, 2011).

---

[1] American Psychological Association Help Center. Accessed 12/4/09 at http://www.apahelpcenter.org/featuredtopics/feature.php?id=6&ch=2. It is worth noting that researchers have identified a coping style called hardiness which involves a constellation of personality characteristics associated with high performance under stressful conditions. These characteristics include commitment (the tendency to engage fully in life activities), perceived control (belief in one's ability to exercise control over life circumstances), and challenge (the tendency to view adversity as a challenge). See, for example: Kobasa (1979), Kobasa *et al.* (1982), Bartone (1999), Maddi (2005), and http://www.hardiness-resilience com/.

Researchers have developed various tests to measure resilience; among them are the Connor–Davidson Resilience Scale and the Response to Stressful Experiences Scale. These tests are self-report instruments with a 5-point Likert scale (strongly agree, agree somewhat, etc.) and include statements such as the following:

- During and after life's most stressful events, I tend to find opportunity for growth.
- I have at least one close and secure relationship that helps me when I am stressed.
- When there are no clear solutions to my problems, sometimes fate or God can help (Connor & Davidson, 2003).
- During and after life's most stressful events, I tend to calm and comfort myself (Johnson *et al.*, 2008).

Additional tests of resilience include the Dispositional Resilience Scale-15, which focuses on three dimensions – being fully engaged, having a sense of control over events, and being able to view adversity as a challenge – and the Resiliency Scale for Children and Adolescents, which assesses an array of attributes related to mastery, relatedness, and emotional reactivity (Bartone, 2007; Prince-Embury, 2008).

What makes some people resilient?

When we began our research we had many questions. Why do some survivors appear relatively unscathed by their trauma, while others develop debilitating disorders such as PTSD, depression and alcohol dependence? (For more information about PTSD, please see the Appendix.) And why do some survivors who develop trauma-related psychological symptoms continue to function well in spite of their symptoms? Do they differ genetically? Is there something unique about their nervous system? Have they been raised in a special manner? What about their personalities? Do they use specific coping mechanisms to deal with stress? And if we learn more about how they dealt with stress and trauma, will these lessons be helpful to PTSD patients and to the general public? Can the average person learn to become more resilient?

These were the questions that we asked ourselves as we began to investigate social, biological, psychological and spiritual factors associated with resilience to stress. And, of course, we also wondered whether these lessons would be helpful to us. Could we, ourselves, learn to become more resilient? We had many unanswered questions.

So we made a decision to search actively for answers to our questions about resilience. We knew that our task would be daunting, because anyone who has spent time studying human behavior, or investigating the nervous system and brain, under-stands that thoughts, feelings and behaviors are the complex products of genetic, biological, psychological, and social forces. Resilience is far more than a simple psy-chological trait or biological phenomenon. In order to truly understand it, researchers must approach it from multiple perspectives and examine it through a number of different scientific lenses. We did this by reviewing the available scientific research and popular literature on resilience, by initiating our own psychological and neuro-biological research on the topic, and by conducting in-depth interviews with a large number of highly resilient individuals (Southwick *et al.*, 2005).

To conduct these interviews, we needed to step out of our traditional clinical and research settings, and to go into the community and recruit people who had clearly demonstrated resilience in the face of extreme stress. We turned to three groups of highly resilient individuals: former Vietnam prisoners of war (POWs), Special Forces instructors, and civilian men and women who had not only survived enormous stress and trauma, but had somehow endured or even thrived.

We interviewed former Vietnam POWs

We began by conducting detailed and lengthy interviews with more than 30 former Vietnam prisoners of war. We chose to study former POWs for several reasons. First, the traumatic experiences they endured were extreme and of long duration; for some, the ordeal lasted for more than eight years. Second, because their captivity took place decades ago, we could examine how their lives had unfolded over many years after the trauma. Third, we believed that the former POWs were good role models and that their methods of coping with stress and trauma would be highly instructive for anyone facing or recovering from their own stressors.

Most of these former POWs were pilots who were captured when their planes were shot down over North Vietnam. After ejecting from disabled burning fighter jets flying at speeds of greater than 400 miles per hour, they parachuted into the jungle. There they were captured by North Vietnamese.

The North Vietnamese treated American prisoners as war criminals, not as prisoners of war protected by the Geneva Conventions. Often captured Americans were paraded through crowds of hostile villagers before being imprisoned, interrogated, beaten, and tortured. The largest and most infamous facility where POWs were held was Hoa Lo Prison in Hanoi, which the Americans sarcastically nicknamed the "Hanoi Hilton." Here prisoners were subjected to interrogation techniques like the "rope trick," in which both arms are tied behind the back and then gradually lifted higher and higher until one or both shoulders are pulled out of their sockets. At other times, guards wrapped a rope around the prisoner's throat, stretched the rope behind his back, and tied it to his ankles, so that if he relaxed his arched back, he would choke.

POWs were also starved. Typically, they were given meager portions of barely edible food: swamp grass or cabbage soup, a chicken head floating in grease, pumpkin soup, a piece of bread covered with mold, the hoof of a cow, an occasional tiny piece of pig fat, or a handful of rice that might be full of rat feces, weevils, or small stones. Even prisoners in solitary confinement rarely dined alone. Colonel Larry Guarino (1990, p. 45) describes his "dinner guests":

> A new civilian guard brought food, and as he set it down on the far bunk, a horde of hungry ants rushed out from the block mounts of the leg irons and swarmed into the tin plates. ... While eating, I was startled by two lightening-fast brown rats who darted around the cell and between my feet looking for food. ... I had more visitors. Arriving under the door were two huge scorpions ... The scorpions came in with raised stingers, but when they sensed my presence, they backed out into the cement channel where the pickings were presumably better. ... Mosquitoes by the hundreds lived under the cement bunks, where it was very

damp. I sat swinging my legs and swatting mosquitoes until my hands were swollen. Suddenly, I saw a huge gray-white, web-footed rat poking his head under the door. He was so big he couldn't get under the door to enter the cell. He sniffed about, showing me inch-long white fangs, then swirled his head under the door, still trying to get in. His tail was over an inch thick! No doubt this rat and his friends were the producers of the huge turds that covered the outside yard. What a disgusting and frightening creature. My heart pounded so, it was difficult for me to breathe, even as I told myself to calm down and take it easy.

In *Glory Denied: The Saga of Vietnam Veteran Jim Thompson, America's Longest-Held Prisoner of War*, Captain Thompson describes one of his "accommodations":

I was put into a horizontal cage maybe two feet wide, two feet high, and five feet long. There I was kept for four months, chained hand and feet. The leg irons were a nasty device, a U-bolt with a rusted rod through the back, much too small for American legs. Every time they put the thing on it took a chunk of flesh. This cage sat in the back room of a house in complete darkness. They had a bamboo wall around it so I saw nothing. I was not let out for exercise. For ten minutes a day I could use the latrine and wash up. Then they would stick me back in and put the leg irons back on. (Philpott, 2002, p. 147)

In this environment, it's not surprising that many POWs developed serious illnesses and were sick during much of their time in prison. They described skin infections, malnutrition, extreme weight loss, open untreated wounds, broken and dislocated bones, dysentery, malaria, depression and symptoms of posttraumatic stress, such as terrifying nightmares. Plagued by dysentery and needing to defecate dozens of times each day, some prisoners became severely dehydrated. Others described boils and skin diseases, where pus and blood attracted jungle flies and mosquitoes, and where maggots thrived.

All of the POWs we interviewed were deeply affected by their prison experience. A substantial number developed trauma-related depression and/or PTSD and experienced difficulty adjusting to civilian life. However, despite their wartime experiences, these former POWs went on to live productive lives after their release. In fact, many of them reported having a greater appreciation of life, closer connections with family, and a newfound sense of meaning and purpose because of their prison experience.

We interviewed Special Forces instructors

The second group of people we interviewed were members of the Special Forces (SF). The Special Forces is an elite command within the US Army. The Army selects these soldiers and trains them to be among the hardiest, most resilient men and women on the planet. In the world today, there is perhaps no group that is better conditioned to handle stress than are SF troops. They benefit from the US Military's constant refinement of its combat and training programs. SF soldiers are rigorously trained to deal with hardship and life-and-death situations. They're intelligent, agile, resourceful, and exceptionally well-prepared for covert missions related to reconnaissance, counter-intelligence, unconventional warfare, and foreign internal defense.

All of the SF members we interviewed were instructors. To become an instructor, one must first serve as an SF soldier. After completing tours of duty stationed around the globe, the instructor's job is to assess and train the next generation of elite soldiers. We chose to interview instructors in order to learn about their philosophy of training and about the actual principles and techniques they use to enhance resilience. These men had all served as instructors at the rigorous SERE course (Survival, Evasion, Resistance, Escape), which is designed to teach soldiers survival fieldcraft so that they can maneuver in enemy-controlled areas, escape detection, and return unharmed to friendly forces. They participate in a grueling war game with a well-equipped "enemy" while they have no food, water, or weapons. They learn how to live for several days with nothing but a knife and canteen and to overcome food aversions so they can eat snakes, insects, worms and dead animals. During the last segment of the course, trainees are taken captive and held in a mock POW camp. Here they are stripped of their uniforms and identity, and deprived of food and sleep. As SERE graduates who teach soldiers in this course, the SF instructors are real-life experts in how to cope with high levels of emotional and physical stress; in how to become emotionally and physically stronger.

Retired four-star general Henry Hugh Shelton, former Chairman of the Joint Chiefs of Staff, also talked with us about resilience. Early in his military career, he trained as an Army Ranger and later served as head of the Special Operations Command for all of the Armed Forces. He told us that his Ranger training gave him the tools that he needed to overcome the personal and professional traumas in his adult life.

Special Forces instructor Bruce Norwood described a mission that particularly stood out in his memory. He and his wife were living in Puerto Rico when his beeper went off one night and he was told to drive to his office immediately. Thirty minutes later, he and four team members were on board a Black Hawk helicopter, flying to Venezuela. As they approached their destination, in heavy rain and violent gusts of wind, the pilot directed the chopper's searchlight to the road below. There they could see scores of people being swept away by the torrential flood waters.

Once the pilot located a cluster of terrified survivors, Norwood and his colleagues slid down a rope while the Black Hawk hovered above. Norwood's left boot struck a firm but spongy object as he stepped onto the slippery terrain. It was an infant girl who had died in the flood.

> We worked for forty straight hours and saved hundreds of people, maybe as many as 1500. Most people don't know it, but at least 50 percent of our missions are humanitarian. They call us the Peace Corps with guns. Even when we're on a foreign international defense mission, the SF medics will go out to the front gate and treat whoever shows up. Some poor campesinos bring their dead baby that they carried across the mountains for three days, and they've never seen a doctor before. The SF medics will be out there five, six, seven hours a night on their off-time treating the locals. The engineers will go down to the nearest town and see what they can do for the schools, the churches. They'll put a new roof on. They'll build a new school, a new church.

We interviewed resilient civilians from many walks of life

The third group we interviewed consisted of civilian men and women who have gone on to lead productive and accomplished lives after experiencing severe psychological traumas, such as congenital medical problems, childhood sexual abuse, death of parents at an early age, abduction and rape, loss of a limb, and cancer.

Eleanor Jensen, for example, lost her parents in an automobile accident when she was eight. Eleanor remembers sitting with her sister on the front porch of their house, waiting to find out where and with whom they would live. After temporary placement with relatives, they were adopted by a childless couple who lived in another region of the country.

Soon Eleanor's new stepfather began to show "special" interest in her and started to touch her. One night, when her stepmother was out of the house, Eleanor's stepfather came into her room and asked her to sit with him. "He started feeling me, French kissing me. And I didn't know what was happening … I was still. Dead. A robot." The situation became chronic.

> My stepmother put a lock on my door, a screw and hook, and I could hear him come up the steps and scratch at the door. He would work on the lock with this little ruler until it opened. Then my stepmother tried a slide lock, and he'd work on it until he eventually got in, then a bolt lock, then a twist lock. There were about 4–5 locks on the door. I'd always be afraid to be home alone. One time when the dog got away and ran down the road and I was running after it, he drove in the car after me and told me to get in and I froze. I could not move my muscles. He said, "I'm sorry, I'm sorry, I won't touch you, I promise. Get in the car, I'll take you home." There was always this tension in being alone, and I'd panic.

As a teenager, Eleanor was sent to a boarding school where she was safe. Although the memories of abuse haunted her for years, she was eventually able to forgive her stepfather. Eleanor went on to become a highly respected nurse practitioner and psychotherapist specializing in treating posttraumatic stress disorder.

Additional examples of ordinary people who found constructive ways to cope with their trauma include, among others:

- Deborah Gruen, who, despite a serious congenital neurological condition, was valedictorian of her high school class, competed as a member of the Yale University Women's Varsity Swim Team, won bronze medals in the 2004 and 2008 Paralympics, graduated summa cum laude from Yale with a major in economics, and went on to pursue a law degree at Georgetown University.

- Elizabeth Ebaugh, who was kidnapped, raped, and thrown over a bridge into a freezing river only to survive and over the ensuing years who built a thriving clinical social work practice that focuses on holistic approaches to helping survivors of trauma and tragedy.

- Jerry White, who lost his leg to a landmine while hiking in Israel as a college student, and then slipped into depression. Years later he co-founded Landmine

Survivors Network and played a leading role in the International Campaign to Ban Landmines coalition, which was awarded the Nobel Peace Prize in 1997.

What we found: 10 resilience factors

During our interviews, we kept hearing a number of recurrent themes. Although their circumstances differed greatly, the resilient people we interviewed tended to use the same or similar coping strategies when confronted with high levels of stress. By conducting a detailed analysis of the interviews, we identified 10 coping mechanisms that proved to be effective for dealing with stress and trauma. Throughout the book we refer to these coping mechanisms as "resilience factors." In response to stress, all of the individuals we interviewed confronted their fears, maintained an optimistic but realistic outlook, sought and accepted social support, and imitated sturdy role models. Most also relied upon their own inner moral compass, turned to religious or spiritual practices, and found a way to accept that which they could not change. Many attended to their health and well-being, and trained intensively to stay physically fit, mentally sharp, and emotionally strong. And most were active problem solvers who looked for meaning and opportunity in the midst of adversity and sometimes even found humor in the darkness. Finally, all of the resilient people we interviewed accepted, to an impressive degree, responsibility for their own emotional well-being, and many used their traumatic experiences as a platform for personal growth.

We recognize that this list of what we call "resilience factors" (i.e. realistic optimism, facing fear, moral compass, religion and spirituality, social support, resilient role models, physical fitness, brain fitness, cognitive and emotional flexibility and meaning and purpose) is by no means definitive or complete and that other factors certainly contribute to stress hardiness. We focus on the above-mentioned resilience factors because they were the one most often described as crucial, and sometimes even life-saving, for the individuals we interviewed. In upcoming chapters we will discuss each of these factors in greater detail.

Most of us will never become a prisoner of war or step on a land mine, but we will inevitably face our own stressors, traumas, and tragedies. Today, for example, many people throughout the world face prolonged unemployment, financial distress, poverty, homelessness, separation from loved ones, medical and mental illness, and a host of other challenges. Fortunately, to withstand, overcome, and grow from these experiences, we don't need to have superior genes, take a "tough as nails" approach to life, or train with the Special Forces. But we do need to prepare ourselves, for life has a way of surprising us with adversity when we least expect it. As journalist Diane L. Coutu learned from her research on resilience for a *Harvard Business Review* article, top-level business executives invariably prize resilience in people they seek to hire. One CEO underscored its importance this way: "More than education, more than experience, more than training, a person's level of resilience will determine who succeeds and who fails. That's true in the cancer ward, it's true in the Olympics, and it's true in the boardroom" (Coutu, 2002, p. 47). We know of no better way to learn about tried-and-true methods for becoming more resilient than to listen to, be inspired by, and follow the advice of resilient people who have already "been there."

How resilient are we?

Where are we today? How resilient are we as individuals, communities, and societies? In the world today, as throughout history, millions of people who are exposed to stress and trauma respond with extraordinary resilience. Recent inspiring examples include individual, family, community, national and even international responses to tragedies such as the World Trade Center terrorist attack of 9/11, the 2004 Indian Ocean earthquake and tsunami, Hurricane Katrina, the Japan earthquake, tsunami, and resulting nuclear crisis, and the senseless mass killings in Norway.

Despite such impressive displays of strength and hardiness, some social critics point to recent trends in attitudes and behaviors that raise questions about the value that some societies places on building and maintaining resilience.

Consider these lifestyle statistics in the United States:

- About 40% of American adults engage in no regular physical exercise, and about half of the 60% who do exercise say their exercise is only moderate, as opposed to vigorous (Saad, 2008).

- Roughly one-third of American adults are obese (Body Mass Index (BMI) 30 or higher), and another third are overweight (BMI 25–29.9) (Centers for Disease Control, 2010).

- A 2003 study found that school physical education classes provide an average of just 25 minutes per week of vigorous activity for third-graders (Nader, 2003).

- Approximately one-third of Americans have abused or been dependent on alcohol at some time in their lives (Hasin *et al.*, 2007).

- The American Academy of Pediatrics (2001) recommends no more than 1–2 hours a day of total screen time (television, computer, etc.) for children aged 2 and older, and no screen time for children under age 2; but a 2010 Kaiser Family Foundation report found children spending an average of 7.5 hours per day watching television, playing video games, and using computers.

- A 2009 study found that 70% of US children have insufficient levels of Vitamin D, the "sunshine vitamin," which we get from being outdoors and which has a protective effect against cardiovascular problems (Kumar *et al.*, 2009).

In his 2003 book *The Progress Paradox: How Life Gets Better While People Feel Worse*, Brookings Institution fellow Gregg Easterbrook points out that while in material terms the Western standard of living has improved greatly in recent decades, our subjective well-being and happiness have declined. Psychologists Jean Twenge and W. Keith Campbell address an attitudinal change in *The Narcissism Epidemic: Living in the Age of Entitlement* (2009), pointing to a societal increase in a "me first" attitude, a lack of caring relationships, and a need for attention and material wealth that is somehow never satisfied.

Other authors – Robert Putnam in *Bowling Alone*, Christopher Lasch in *The Culture of Narcissism*, and David Riesman in *The Lonely Crowd*, to name a few – have expressed concern about the lack of social connections and community spirit in today's society. Dutch researcher Geert Hofstede, among other social psychologists, has categorized the US as a highly individualistic society, where becoming a "self-made" man or woman is more highly valued than contributing to the common good. While this individualistic spirit may have roots extending back to the early days of the American republic, it seems to be enacted in a more literal way today than in the past. According to the US Census Bureau (2006), the proportion of single-person households increased from 17% in 1970 to 26% in 2005. In 2005, only 1 in 10 of the nation's households contained 5 or more people, down from 1 in 5 in 1970. The decrease in household size has been accompanied by dwindling membership in service clubs, religious congregations, and workers' organizations. Psychologist Shigehiro Oishi (2010) refers to "duty-free friendships" as a byproduct of our decreased investment in interpersonal relationships. As *New York Times* columnist Roger Cohen wrote in 2010,

> Community – a stable job, shared national experience, extended family, labor unions – has vanished or eroded. In its place have come a frenzied individualism, solipsistic screen-gazing, the disembodied pleasures of social networking and the à-la-carte life as defined by 600 TV channels and a gazillion blogs. Feelings of anxiety and inadequacy grow in the lonely chamber of self-absorption and projection.

So how resilient are we? Are we becoming too self-absorbed and too ready to complain about the unfairness of life instead of equipping ourselves to take action to improve our lives and the lives of those around us? Are we adequately preparing ourselves, our families, our children, and our communities to weather the inevitable storms ahead and to thrive in times of stress and hardship?

Applying the science of resilience

In this book, we want to share with readers what we have learned from our interviews and from academic research about resilience. We believe that this book can benefit readers from all walks of life, including those who are currently coping with a trauma and those who have a loved one coping with a trauma; teachers, counselors, therapists, and medical professionals; and anyone who understands the need to prepare for the inevitable stresses and traumas of life.

We have organized the book into chapters focusing on specific resilience factors: facing fear, optimism, social support, and so on. Although these resilience factors overlap and interact with one another, we found it helpful to examine each one separately. The factors are described through the experiences and personal reflections of the highly resilient survivors whom we interviewed. Survivors also describe real-life methods for implementing, practicing and benefiting from the resilience factors. In addition to providing excerpts and insights from our interviews, we interweave the latest relevant scientific research on the topic. The evidence we cite comes from the fields of psychology, sociology, neurobiology and medicine. This evidence lends support to the strategies and recommendations for enhancing resilience that our interviewees described. It also helps to demystify the process of physical, cognitive, and emotional strengthening. There is a science behind resilience training, and by learning and practicing what is currently known, people can increase their ability to cope well in the face of stress and adversity.

Resilience and human physiology

Since resilience is fundamentally related to the experience and management of stress, throughout this book we refer to various parts of the brain, the nervous system, and the endocrine system: critical components of the stress response. We will discuss the following key brain regions:

- The amygdala, which is associated with fear and alarm; it plays a central role in fear conditioning and in triggering raw emotions and the "fight or flight" response.
- The prefrontal cortex, which is often referred to as the brain's "executive center," facilitates planning and rational decision-making; it helps to regulate emotions and acts to keep the amygdala (the "fear and alarm center") in check.
- The hippocampus, which plays a critical role in learning, forming new memories, and regulating the stress response; more so than many other brain structures, it is vulnerable to the effects of chronic stress.
- The anterior cingulate cortex, which plays an important role in our ability to focus attention, detect and monitor errors and conflicts assess the importance of emotional and motivational information and regulate emotions; it is connected both to the prefrontal cortex and the amygdala.
- The anterior insula, which is located in the fold of the cerebral cortex that marks the boundary between the frontal and temporal lobes; it is involved in many functions related to emotions, and aids in the sense of self-awareness.
- The nucleus accumbens, sometimes referred to as the "pleasure center," plays a central role in the brain's reward circuit; in association with the ventral tegmental area, it mediates the experience of reward and punishment, and is associated with the pleasurable effects of food, sex and drug abuse.

We occasionally also mention the limbic system. This term refers to the inner portion of the brain – located beneath the cortex – which is involved in emotion, memory, and other functions. It includes the amygdala, hippocampus, and a number of other structures and regions. Although the limbic system is technically neither a system nor a structure, the term provides a useful shorthand for referring to this area of the brain.

In addition to these brain regions, there are several other major systems in the body that respond to stress. One is the autonomic nervous system, which is composed of two parts: the sympathetic nervous system (SNS), which mobilizes the body under conditions of stress; and the parasympathetic nervous system, which conserves resources and maintains functioning under normal non-stressful conditions. Another major system is the hypothalamic–pituitary–adrenal axis (HPA axis), which responds to stress with a complex set of reactions involving the hypothalamus, the pituitary gland, and the adrenal glands.

Throughout the book we will also refer to various hormones and neurotransmitters that are involved in the stress response and resilience (McEwen, 2007; Southwick *et al.*, 2008):

- Cortisol is a stress hormone released through activation of the HPA axis. It produces energy by converting food into fat and glucose (a form of sugar). It also temporarily bolsters the immune system.

- Epinephrine, also known as adrenaline, is released by the adrenal glands under conditions of stress and accelerates heart rate, constricts blood vessels and dilates air passages as part of the sympathetic nervous system's fight-or-flight response.

- Norepinephrine, also known as noradrenaline, facilitates alerting and alarm reactions in the brain and is critical for responding to danger and for remembering emotional and fearful events.

- Serotonin is involved in the regulation of mood as well as sleep, appetite, and other functions.

- Dopamine is associated with pleasurable feelings and plays a key role in the reward systems of the brain. For this reason it is an important factor in cravings and addictive behaviors.

- Neuropeptide Y (NPY) is associated with decreasing anxiety and hastening return to baseline after the nervous system reacts to stress.

- Oxytocin, sometimes called the "love chemical," is associated with maternal behaviors, pair bonding, social communication, trust, social support, and anxiety reduction.

- Brain-derived neurotrophic factor (BDNF) acts to support the nervous system through the repair of existing neurons and growth of new ones.

Genetics

Although genes play a central role in how we respond to stress, research on the interface between genetics and resilience is in its infancy. Studies on twins have found that overall heritability of PTSD ranges from 32% to 38%, and DNA research is beginning to investigate how variations in our genes affect the way that we respond to stress. For example, recent evidence shows that the noradrenergic system's response to stress is influenced by variations of the alpha-2 adrenoreceptor gene. In a study of healthy volunteers, Alex Neumeister and colleagues (2005) found that volunteers with a specific variation of the alpha-2 adrenoreceptor gene (i.e. alpha-2cDel322–325-AR) had higher levels of norepinephrine at baseline, a greater increase in norepinephrine and anxiety when stressed, and a slower return of norepinephrine to baseline after termination of stress, compared to the other volunteers. The unusually robust activity of norepinephrine and the SNS in individuals with this genetic variation could make them more vulnerable to stress and thus less resilient.

The norepinephrine response to stress may also be affected by variations in the neuropeptide Y gene. In one study, individuals with a particular variation in the *NPY* gene, a variation that is associated with low production of neuropeptide Y, experienced greater activation of the amygdala and greater anxiety when exposed to threat-related stimuli compared to subjects without this gene variation (Zhou *et al.*, 2008). As noted above, neuropeptide Y is associated with decreasing anxiety and restoring calm after stress. When stress is high, neuropeptide Y is released and helps to inhibit the further release of norepinephrine so that the SNS does not "overshoot."

In addition to gene variants that affect the SNS, variants affecting the serotonin system, the dopamine system, and the HPA axis have also been investigated in relation to traumatic stress and resilience. Gene variants related to these symptoms may affect the relative efficiency of the stress response (Skelton *et al.*, 2011; Mehta *et al.*, 2011). In general, an optimal stress response activates rapidly in response to threat, rises high enough to respond appropriately to danger but not so high as to cause incapacitating anxiety and fear, and deactivates in a timely fashion. Hypoactive or hyperactive neurobiological stress systems tend to be maladaptive (Feder *et al.*, 2009).

It is important to emphasize that resilience to stress and susceptibility to develop PTSD undoubtedly result from complex interactions between multiple genes and multiple environmental factors rather than any single gene variant (Norrholm & Ressler, 2009).

Epigenetics

In fact, in recent years researchers have made gains in understanding exactly how the environment influences our genes through the study of epigenetics. A variety of internal and external environmental events (e.g. stress, social support, fears, etc) can trigger biochemical reactions (e.g. methylation) that then turn genes on or turn them off. These processes are dynamic and potentially reversible.

When a gene is "turned on" it directs the making of gene products (e.g. proteins). However, when a gene is "turned off" these gene products are no longer produced. In other words, various stimuli in our internal and external environment can initiate biochemical processes that either activate our genes or silence them.

For example, recent animal studies (Zhang, 2012) have shown that low levels of licking and grooming by a mother rat, the human equivalent of neglectful parenting, can cause increased susceptibility to stress throughout the life of her offspring. On the other hand, attentive maternal care, as reflected by high levels of licking and grooming, can contribute to later stress resilience. The effects of maternal licking and grooming appear to be mediated, in part, by epigenetic changes in gene expression. In research conducted in the laboratory of Michael Meaney, variations in maternal care have been associated with variations in expression of glucocorticoid receptors and hippocampal sensitivity to stress (Zhang, 2012). Similar epigenetic effects of maternal care – and other lifetime experiences – on later vulnerability or resilience to stress are likely to "hold up in humans" (Nestler, 2012).

A variety of environmental events, including stress, social interactions and drug use, can cause epigenetic changes in gene expression (Dudley, 2012). Although much remains to be learned, the rapidly expanding field of epigenetics may soon help us to better understand the origins of stress vulnerability and discover ways to manage it (Nestler, 2012). It may also help us to better understand resilience and the mechanisms by which training can enhance factors associated with resilience (e.g. exercise, social support, cognitive reframing). And as noted by psychopharmacologist Steven Stahl (2012), "psychotherapy can now be conceptualized not only by its classic psychodynamic principles, but also indeed as a neurobiological probe capable of inducing epigenetic changes in brain circuits, not unlike the ultimate actions of psychotropic drugs."

Neuroplasticity

In several chapters of the book we mention neuroplasticity. Neuroplasticity refers to "The ability of the nervous system to respond to intrinsic or extrinsic stimuli by reorganizing its structure, function and connections" (Cramer *et al.*, 2011). While many of us think of the brain as an organ that remains essentially unchanged during adulthood, neuroscientists have found that brain structure actually changes from moment to moment, hour to hour, day to day. Brain structure is neither fixed nor static but instead highly plastic, and like muscles in the body, the brain can be strengthened or weakened depending on how it is used. When cells in the brain are actively used, they transmit their messages more efficiently and form more connections with other cells. On the other hand, when brain cells are not stimulated, they die and are pruned away. As with other regions of the body, the well-known adage "use it or lose it" also applies to the brain.

What this means is that each of us, to some degree, has the power to change the structure and function of his or her brain. We can positively influence the way in which our brain develops, how efficiently it operates, and what skills it acquires. The key is activity. By repeatedly activating specific areas of the brain, we can strengthen those areas. In other words, by systematically following the advice of the POWs, Special Forces instructors, and other resilient women and men in this book, virtually anyone can become more stress-resilient. That's what we've tried to do. Both of us love challenges, and now when we find ourselves doubting our ability to overcome major obstacles, we often remember a conversation that we had with one of the former POWs, Special Forces instructors, or civilians whom we interviewed. And then we try to follow their advice by repeatedly imitating a specific attitude, style of thinking, emotion or behavior that helped them overcome their own stress and trauma. It helps us.

Bouncing back is a choice – but the choice is easier for some

When we began this project, we assumed that highly resilient people were somehow special, perhaps genetically gifted. We assumed that resilience was relatively rare, reserved for a select group of unique individuals. But we were wrong. Resilience is common (Masten, 2001). It can be witnessed all around us, and for most people it can be enhanced through learning and training. Millions of people all over the world exhibit resilience in their responses to challenging events and circumstances of all kinds. Most of us have been taught to believe that stress is bad. We have learned to see stress as our enemy, something that we must avoid or reduce. But the truth is, when stress can be managed, it tends to be very good and even necessary for health and growth. Without it, the mind and body weaken. If we can learn to harness stress it can serve as a catalyst for developing greater strength and even greater wisdom.

And yet we need to acknowledge that building resilience and bouncing back is easier for some than for others. Individuals who are temporarily (or, in some cases, permanently) unable to think clearly or regulate their moods will have difficulty putting into practice the advice in this book. For example, someone who is experiencing an episode of major depression will be handicapped by the profound sadness and sense of hopelessness, lack of energy and loss of interest in life that characterize this disorder. As another example, someone who has suffered a traumatic brain injury may have particular difficulties with cognitive strategies and/or emotional challenges. People with these kinds of serious conditions who want to practice the skills associated with resilience would certainly be advised to work with a professional who is trained in helping with their specific condition.

Even for people who do not suffer from severe medical and/or psychological conditions, the path to bounce back is steeper for some than for others. Those of us with resources such as financial security, a high level of education, an interesting and rewarding career, and strong social networks are able to leverage those resources, whereas people who lack resources may fall into what psychologist Stevan Hobfoll (2001) calls a "loss spiral." For example, if a family already under financial strain loses its primary breadwinner, the surviving family members may be forced to scramble for basic necessities such as food and a place to live at the same time that they are grieving; further, this struggle may potentially lead to additional traumas such as those associated with living in a high-crime neighborhood. In contrast, a financially secure family will have the resources to address their grief and loss in various ways (e.g. by paying for counseling, hosting a funeral to honor the loved one, and perhaps taking time off from work or school to re-evaluate their life priorities). One family that loses its home in a hurricane will have no place to live, while another family has the option to move in with relatives, and still another family will be fortunate enough to own a second house. Thus, while most of us can choose to fight back and attempt to re-right ourselves, some have access to resources that make it easier to do so. This does not mean we should give up if our resources are limited, but rather to recognize that we will likely have a more difficult road to travel. Understanding this may allow us to be more patient with ourselves.

We sincerely hope that the words and deeds of the generous individuals in this book will be as inspirational to you as they have been to us and that these individuals will serve as role models for you as you face the upcoming challenges of your life.

References

Alvarez, L. (2008). Nearly a fifth of war veterans report mental disorders, a private study finds. *New York Times*, April 18. Accessed 2/15/10 at http://www.nytimes.com/2008/04/18/us/18vets.html.

American Academy of Pediatrics (2001). Children, adolescents, and television. *Pediatrics*, **107**(2), 423–426.

American Psychiatric Association. (1994). *Diagnostic and statistical manual of mental disorders* (4th ed.). Washington, DC: Author.

American Psychological Association (2010). *The road to resilience.* Washington, DC: American Psychological Association. Accessed 6/25/2010 at http://www.apa.org/helpcenter/road-resilience.aspx.

Bartone, P. T. (1999). Hardiness protects against war-related stress in Army Reserve forces. *Consulting Psychology Journal: Practice and Research*, **51**(2), 72–82.

Bartone, P. T. (2007). Test–retest reliability of the Dispositional Resilience Scale-15, a brief hardiness scale. *Psychological Reports*, **101**(1), 943–944.

Bonanno, G. A. (2004). Loss, trauma, and human resilience: Have we underestimated the human capacity to thrive after extremely aversive events? *American Psychologist*, **59**, 20–28.

Bonanno, G. A. (2005). Resilience in the face of potential trauma. *Current Directions in Psychological Science*, **14**, 135–138.

Bremner, J. D., Southwick, S. M., Johnson, D. R., Yehuda, R., & Charney, D. S. (1993). Childhood physical abuse in combat-related post-traumatic stress disorder in Vietnam veterans. *American Journal of Psychiatry*, **150**, 235–239.

Bremner, J. D., Narayan, M., Staib, L. H., Southwick, S. M., McGlashan, T., & Charney, D. S. (1999). Neural correlates of memories of childhood sexual abuse in women with and without posttraumatic stress disorder. *American Journal of Psychiatry*, **156**, 1787–1795.

Brooker, K. (2002). Starting over. *Fortune*, January 21, 50–68.

Carver, C. S. (1998). Resilience and thriving. Issues, models, and linkages. *Journal of Social Issues*, **54**, 245–266.

Centers for Disease Control and Prevention. FastStats: Obesity and Overweight. Accessed 2/24/10 at http://www.cdc.gov/nchs/fastats/overwt.htm.

Charney, D. S., Deutch, A., Krystal, J. H., Southwick, S. M., & Davis, M. (1993). Psychobiological mechanisms of posttraumatic stress disorder. *Archives of General Psychiatry*, **50**, 294–305.

Charney, D. S., Nagy, L. M., Bremner, J. D., Goddard, A.W., Yehuda R., & Southwick, S.M. (1996). Neurobiological mechanisms of human anxiety. In B.S. Fogel, R.B. Schiffler, & S.M. Rao (eds.), *Neuropsychiatry* (pp. 257–278). Baltimore, MD: Williams & Wilkins.

Clark, B. (2006). A survivor's story. PBS Nova interview transcript. Accessed 3/9/10 at http://www.pbs.org/wgbh/nova/wtc/above.html.

Cohen, R. (2010). Op-Ed Columnist: The Narcissus society. *New York Times*, February 22.

Connor, K. M., & Davidson, J. R. (2003). Development of a new resilience scale: The Connor–Davidson Resilience Scale (CD-RISC). *Depression and Anxiety*, **18**, 76–82.

Coutu, D. L. (2002). How resilience works. *Harvard Business Review*, May, 46–55.

Cramer, S. C., Sur, M., Dobkin, B. H., O'Brien, C., Sanger, T. D., *et al.* (2011). Harnessing neuroplasticity for clinical applications. *Brain*, **134** (6), 1591–1601.

Dao, J. (2010). At War: Notes from the front lines: Presidential condolences and troop suicides. *New York Times*, February 1. Accessed 2/15/10 at http://atwar.blogs.nytimes.com/2010/02/01/presidential-condolences-and-troop-suicides/.

Dudley, K. J., Xiang Li, Kobor, M. S., Kippin, T. E., Bredy, T. W. (2011). Epigenetic mechanisms mediating vulnerability and resilience to psychiatric disorders. *Neuroscience and Biobehavioral Reviews*, **35**, 1544–1551.

Dwyer, J., Lipton, E., Flynn, K., Glanz, J., & Fessenden, F. (2002). 102 minutes: Fighting to live as the towers died. *New York Times*, May 26.

Easterbrook, G. (2003). *The progress paradox: How life gets better while people feel worse.* New York, NY: Random House.

Feder, A., Nestler, E. J., & Charney, D. (2009). Psychobiology and molecular genetics of resilience. *Nature Reviews*, **10**, 446–466.

Giller, E. (1999). What is psychological trauma? This article originated as a workshop presentation at the Annual Conference of the Maryland Mental Hygiene Administration, "Passages to Prevention: Prevention across Life's Spectrum," May 1999. Accessed 2/24/10 at http://www.sidran.org/sub.cfm?contentID=88&sectionid=4.

Guarino, Col. Larry (1990). *A POW's Story: 2801 Days in Hanoi*. New York, NY: Random House, 1990.

Hasin, D. S., Stinson, F. S., Ogburn, E., & Grant, B. F. (2007). Prevalence, correlates, disability, and comorbidity of DSM-IV alcohol abuse and dependence in the United States: Results from the National Epidemiologic Survey on Alcohol and Related Conditions. *Archives of General Psychiatry*, **64**(7), 830–842.

Hobfoll, S. E. (2001). The influence of culture, community, and the nested-self in the stress process: Advancing conservation of resources theory. *Applied Psychology: An International Review*, **50**(3), 337–421.

Jacobsen, L. K., Southwick, S. M., & Kosten, T. R. (2001). Substance use disorders in patients with posttraumatic stress disorder: A review of the literature. *American Journal of Psychiatry*, **158**, 1184–1190.

Johnson, D. C., Polusny, J. A., Erbes, C., King, D., King, L., Litz, B., *et al.* (2008). The response to stressful experiences scale (RSES). *Military Medicine*, **176**(2) 161–169.

Kessler, R. C., Sonnega, A., Bromet, E., Hughes, M., & Nelson, C. B. (1995). Post-traumatic Stress Disorder in the National Comorbidity Survey. *Archives of General Psychiatry*, **52**, 1048–1060.

Kobasa, S. C. (1979). Stressful life events, personality, and health: An inquiry into hardiness. *Journal of Personality and Social Psychology*, **37**, 1–11.

Kobasa, S. C., Maddi, S. R., & Kahn, S. (1982). Hardiness and health: A prospective study. *Journal of Personality and Social Psychology*, **42**, 168–177.

Kroft, S. (2001). Sandler O'Neill fights back. CBS News, October 4. Accessed 12/4/09 at http://www.cbsnews.com/stories/2001/10/04/60minutes/main313589.shtml.

Kumar, J., Muntner, P., Kaskel, F. J., Hailpern, S. M., & Melamed, M. L. (2009). Prevalence and associations of 25-hydroxyvitamin D deficiency in US children: NHANES 2001–2004. *Pediatrics*, **124**, e362. doi:10.1542/peds.2009–0051.

Layne, C. M., Warren, J. S., Watson, P. J., & Shalev, A. Y. (2007). Risk, vulnerability, resistance, and resilience: Toward an integrative conceptualization of posttraumatic adaptation. In T.K.M. Friedman & P. Resick (eds.), *Handbook of PTSD: Science and practice* (pp. 497–520). New York, NY: Guilford Press.

Litz, B. T. (2005). Has resilience to severe trauma been underestimated? *American Psychologist*, **60**, 262.

Lukas, E. S. (1984). *Meaningful living: A logotherapy guide to health*. New York, NY: Grove Press.

Luthar, S. S. (2006). Resilience in development: A synthesis of research across five decades. In D. Cicchetti & D.J. Cohen (eds.), *Developmental psychopathology, Vol. 3: Risk disorder, and adaptation*, 2nd edn (pp. 740–795). New York, NY: Wiley.

Luthar, S.S., Cicchetti, D. & Becker, B. (2000). The construct of resilience: A critical evaluation and guidelines for future work. *Child Development*, **71**, 543–562.

Maddi, S. R. (2005). On hardiness and other pathways to resilience. *American Psychologist*, **60**(3), 261–262.

Maguen, S., Lucenko, B. A., Reger, M. A., Gahm, G. A., Litz, B. T., Seal, K. H., *et al.* (2010). The impact of reported direct and indirect killing on mental health symptoms in Iraq War veterans. *Journal of Traumatic Stress*, **23**(1), 86–90.

Malik, M. L., Connor, K. M., Sutherland, S. M., Smith, R. D., Davison, R. M., & Davidson, J. R. T. (1999). Quality of life and posttraumatic stress disorder: A pilot study assessing changes in sf-36 scores before and after treatment in a placebo-controlled trial of Fluoxetine.

Journal of Traumatic Stress, **12**(2), 387–393. DOI 10.1023/A:1024745030140.

Masten, A. S. (2001). Ordinary magic: Resilience processes in development. *American Psychologist*, **56**, 227–238.

McEwen, B. S. (2007). Physiology and neurobiology of stress and adaptation: Central role of the brain. *Physiological Reviews*, **87**, 873–904.

McKay, M. J. (2002). '60 Minutes' looks at September 11. CBS News, September 5. Accessed 9/2/10 at http://www.cbsnews.com/stories/2002/09/05/60minutes/main520965.shtml.

Mehta D, Gonik M, Klengel T, Rex-Haffner M, Menke A, Rubel J, Mercer KB, Pütz B, Bradley B, Holsboer F, Ressler KJ, Müller-Myhsok B, Binder EB. (2011). Using polymorphisms in FKBP5 to define biologically distinct subtypes of posttraumatic stress disorder: evidence from endocrine and gene expression studies. *Archives of General Psychiatry*, **68**(9), 901–10.

Nader, P. R. (2003). Frequency and intensity of activity of third-grade children in physical education. National Institute of Child Health and Human Development Study of Early Child Care and Youth Development Network. *Archives of Pediatric and Adolescent Medicine*, **157**, 185–190. Accessed 2010 at http://aappolicy.aappublications.org/cgi/content/full/pediatrics;117/5/1834.

National Center for PTSD, Department of Veterans Affairs (2009). How common is PTSD? Accessed January 2009 at http://www.ptsd.va.gov/.

Nestler, E. J. (2012). Epigenetics: Stress makes it molecular mark. *Nature*, **490**, 171–172.

Neumeister, A., Charney, D.S., Belfer, I., Geraci, M., Holmes, C., Sharabi, Y., *et al.* (2005). Sympathoneural and adrenomedullary functional effects of alpha 2C-adrenoreceptor gene polymorphism in healthy humans. *Pharmacogenetics and Genomics*, **15**, 143–149.

Nocera, J. (2006). After 5 years, his voice can still crack. *New York Times*, September 9.

Norrholm, S. D., & Ressler, K. J. (2009). Genetics of anxiety and trauma-related disorders. *Neuroscience*, **164**(1), 272–287.

Norris, F. H. (1992). Epidemiology of trauma: Frequency and impact of different potentially traumatic events on different demographic groups. *Journal of Consulting and Clinmical Psychology*, **60**, 409–418.

Norris, F. H., & Sloane, L. B. (2007). The epidemiology of trauma and PTSD. In M.J. Friedman, T.M. Keane, & P.A. Resick (eds.), *Handbook of PTSD* (pp. 78–98). New York, NY: Guilford Press.

Occupational Safety and Health Administration, U.S. Department of Labor (2002). *A dangerous worksite: The World Trade Center*. Washington, DC: author. Accessed 3/12/10 at http://www.osha.gov/Publications/dangerous_worksite.pdf.

Oishi, S. (2010). The psychology of residential mobility: Implications for the self, social relationships, and well-being. *Perspectives on Psychological Science*, **5**(1), 5–21.

Ortiz, D. (2001). The survivor's perspective: Voices from the center. In E. Gerrity, T.M. Keane, & F. Tuma (eds.), *The mental health consequences of torture*. New York, NY: Kluwer Academic/Plenum Publishers.

Philpott, T. (2002). *Glory denied: The saga of Vietnam veteran Jim Thompson, America's longest-held prisoner of war*. New York, NY: Plume Books.

Prince-Embury, S. (2008). The Resiliency Scales for Children and Adolescents, Psychological Symptoms, and Clinical Status in Adolescents. *Canadian Journal of School Psychology*, **23**(1), 41–56. DOI: 10.1177/0829573508316592.

Rothbaum, B. O., Foa, E. B., Riggs, D. S., Murdock, T., & Walsh, W. (1992). A prospective examination of post-traumatic stress disorder in rape victims. *Journal of Traumatic Stress*, **5**(3), 455–475. DOI 10.1007/BF00977239.

Rutter, M. (1985). Resilience in the face of adversity: Protective factors and resistance to psychiatric disorder. *British Journal of Psychiatry*, **147**, 598–611.

Saad, L. (2008). Few Americans meet exercise targets: Self-reported rates of physical exercise show little change since 2001. Gallup, Inc., January 1 (press release). Accessed 2/24/10 at http://www.gallup.com/poll/103492/few-americans-meet-exercise-targets.aspx.

Simon, S. (2002). Jimmy Dunne gets back to business: Firm works to recover from unthinkable losses on Sept. 11. National Public Radio, September 7. Accessed 12/4/09 at http://www.npr.org/news/specials/091102reflections/jimmydunne/index.html.

Skelton K., Ressler K. J., Norrholm, S. D., Jovanovic, T., & Bradley-Davino, B. (2011). PTSD and gene variants: New pathways and new thinking. *Neuropharmacology* [Epub ahead of print].

Southwick, S.M., Vythilingam M., & Charney D. (2005). The psychobiology of depression and resilience to stress: Implications for prevention and treatment. *Annual Review of Clinical Psychology*, 1, 255–291.

Southwick, S. M., Gilmartin, R., McDonough, P., & Morrissey, P. (2006). Logotherapy as an adjunctive treatment for chronic combat-related PTSD: A meaning-based intervention. *American Journal of Psychotherapy*, 60(2), 161–174.

Southwick, S.M., Davis, L., Aikins, D. E., Rasmusson, A., Barron, J., & Morgan, C. A. (2007). Neurobiological alterations associated with PTSD. In M.J. Friedman, T.M. Keane, & P.A. Resick (eds.), *Handbook of PTSD: Science and Practice* (pp. 166–189). New York, NY: Guilford Press.

Southwick, S. M., Ozbay, F., Charney, D., & McEwen B. S. (2008). Adaptation to stress and psychobiological mechanisms of resilience. In B.J. Lukey & V. Tepe (eds.), *Biobehavioral Resilience to Stress* (pp. 91–115). Boca Raton, FL: CRC Press.

Southwick, S. M., Litz, B., Charney, D. S., & Friedman, M. J. (eds.) (2011). *Resilience and mental health: Challenges across the lifespan*. Cambridge: Cambridge University Press.

Stahl, S. M. (2011). Psychotherapy as an epigenetic 'drug': psychiatric therapeutics target symptoms linked to malfunctioning brain circuits with psychotherapy as well as with drugs.

Journal of Clinical Pharmacy and Therapeutics. June; 37(3): 249–253.

Stellman, J. M., Smith, R. P., Katz, C. L., Sharma, V., Charney, D. S., Herbert, R., et al. (2008). Enduring mental health morbidity and social function impairment in World Trade Center rescue, recovery, and cleanup workers: The psychological dimension of an environmental health disaster. *Environmental Health Perspectives*, 116(9), 1248–1253.

Twenge, J. M., & Campbell, W. K. (2009). *The Narcissism epidemic: Living in the age of entitlement*. New York, NY: Free Press.

US Census Bureau, Population Division, Fertility & Family Statistics Branch (2006). America's Families and Living Arrangements: 2005. Accessed 2/24/10 at http://www.census.gov/population/www/socdemo/hh-fam/cps2005.html.

Vaillant, G. E. (2002). *Aging well: Surprising guideposts to a happier life from the landmark Harvard study of adult development*. New York, NY: Little, Brown & Co.

Wayne, L., with Deutsch, C. (2002). It isn't easy, but Sandler thrives. *New York Times*, September 10. Accessed 1/22/10 at http://sandleroneillfamily.com/articles/nyt091002.htm.

World Health Organization (2006). Report of a workshop on tracking health performance and humanitarian outcomes. Accessed 11/22/09 at http://www.who.int/hac/events/

Zhang, T. Y., Labonte, B., Wen, X. L., Turecki, G., Meaney, M.J. (2012). Epigenetic mechanisms for early environmental regulation of hippocampal glucocorticoid receptor gene expression in rodents and humans. *Neuropsychopharmacology Reviews*, Sept 12. Doi: 10. 1038/npp.2012. 149. [Epub ahead of print]

Zhou, Z., Zhu, G., Hariri, A. R., Enoch, M. A., Scott, D., Sinha, R., et al. (2008). Genetic variation in human NPY expression affects stress response and emotion. *Nature* 452(7190), 997–1001.

Chapter 2

Optimism: belief in a brighter future

Optimism serves as a fuel that ignites resilience and provides energy to power the other resilience factors. It facilitates an active and creative approach to coping with challenging situations.

How do we define optimism? Optimism is a future-oriented attitude, involving hope and confidence that things will turn out well. Optimists believe that the future will be bright, that good things will happen to them, and that with enough hard work they will succeed. Pessimists, in contrast, see the future as dim. They believe that bad things will happen to them and doubt that they have the skills and stamina to achieve their goals. In other words, optimists and pessimists have very different expectations.

Can optimism be measured? Many researchers think so, and attempt to measure it with tools such as the Life Orientation Test (the LOT), a questionnaire that includes statements like "In uncertain times, I usually expect the best" and "I hardly ever expect things to go my way." The respondent rates each statement on a five-point scale ranging from "strongly disagree" to "strongly agree" (Scheier *et al.*, 1994).

Psychologists such as Shelley Taylor (1998) have identified two styles of optimism: dispositional optimism (also called trait optimism), which pervades the individual's outlook and tends to be stable from one situation to another; and situational optimism, in which the individual may feel hopeful and expect a favorable outcome in one situation but not in another. While some of the highly resilient people we interviewed for this book displayed trait optimism, for others optimism was more dependent on the situation. Still, they managed to build on whatever small glimmers of optimistic thinking they could find under adverse circumstances.

Of the many people we interviewed, perhaps the one who best exemplifies the spirit and power of trait optimism is Deborah Gruen. Her life story suggests the ways in which optimism can contribute to resilience, not only for the individual, but also for those around her.

Deborah's difficulties and challenges began at birth. In 1987 when Deborah was born, her father, Jeff, had just been appointed an Assistant Professor of Neonatology at the Yale Medical School. He was happily married with one healthy daughter named Michele; he was enjoying success at work and recently won a grant to fund his research; he was excited about the arrival of his second child. Several months earlier Deborah's mother, Susan, had been accepted to law school and was about to embark on a new career of her own.

The Gruens knew that their new baby would be a girl, and they had already picked the name Deborah. As a neonatologist, Jeff Gruen made certain that his wife received all of the finest in fetal testing, and Susan Gruen was meticulous in the care of her unborn fetus: she ate well, exercised regularly, took no medication, and avoided alcohol and cigarettes.

When Susan went into labor, Jeff drove her to the hospital, where her obstetrician and the other medical staff found no reason to expect anything other than a normal delivery and a healthy infant. But when Deborah finally emerged into full view, Jeff was stunned. He recalls,

> She had a large lipoma at the base of her spine, about the size of a half grapefruit. She had normal anatomy, but she didn't have normal posture from the waist down, and she was somewhat flaccid. There was some movement of her legs – but not a lot. She moved her hips and toes and feet, but it wasn't normal movement. It was never normal movement. I couldn't believe it. Disbelief – and I would say emotional shock, if there is such a thing.

Susan, still bleeding from the delivery, began crying. "What's going on?" she pleaded. "I need to know. What's going on?"

A pediatric radiologist was summoned for a CT, ultrasound, and an MRI. This was state-of-the-art medicine at the time, and the Gruens were lucky to be at a university hospital like Yale New Haven Hospital. A few hours later they knew: their new baby had a lipomyelomeningocele, a fatty tumor at the base of the spinal cord. Her vertebrae were malformed, and some were impinging on the spinal cord itself.

> The radiologist was concerned about the spinal cord so he calls Duncan, the neurosurgeon. Duncan looks at the scans and says, "We need to operate right now. The longer these vertebrae impinge, the more function she will lose." So your kid has to have surgery, and she's not even 12 hours old. We were just devastated. I didn't know what to do, so I went to see my section chief, Ian. I was standing there with Ian, and I just fell apart, sobbing. Susan is upstairs crying and screaming. They are telling me to do an operation. I don't even know Duncan. I mean, I know him professionally. I don't know what to do. I just don't know what to do. I am crying uncontrollably. Finally, Ian just hugged me.

The surgery was successful: once the spinal canal was widened by removing the impinging vertebrae, Deborah's condition improved rapidly. Still, there was no assurance that she would ever walk. There was a real possibility that that her condition would be degenerative, worsening year by year and putting her at risk for chronic problems such as impaired bladder and bowel functions. As a doctor himself, Jeff clearly understood that Deborah faced a long road ahead.

After two weeks in neonatal intensive care, Deborah came home. After a second operation, because her spine was so unstable, she was fitted for a "clam shell," a cast made of molded plastic with Velcro hinges that extended from her neck to the top of her thighs. The device restricted the movement of her torso, back, and hips. When her parents removed Deborah from the clam shell for short periods in order to bathe her, they were instructed to support her so that her back would remain as straight as possible. They were told to remain vigilant and resist the natural instinct to cuddle her into a fetal position. Susan remembers walking on eggshells, constantly worrying that she might lift or bend Deborah the wrong way and damage her baby's spinal cord.

For the first few days, Deborah cried nonstop. Concerned that she was in pain, her parents took her back to the hospital. It turned out they'd put her clam shell on upside down.

Jeff and Susan were overwhelmed at times, feeling helpless to make things better for their baby and deeply fearful about her future. Would she be rejected from preschool because she needed a walker? Would her physical disability prevent her from participating in everyday childhood activities? How would she feel about being short? Deborah was born in the autumn, a time when the Gruens customarily go apple-picking. Shortly after Deborah's birth, Susan wondered whether her new daughter would ever be able to pick apples with them. Jeff replied, "Of course she will. If she can't walk, I'll carry her."

When the infant Deborah was formally named and blessed at the synagogue, the rabbi ended his prayer with the words, "And may we all dance at her wedding." Susan whispered to Jeff, "I hope so."

To her parents' relief, Deborah began to develop normally in many ways: feeding, swallowing, smiling, and occasionally moving her legs. Months later, she had a second long but successful surgery to untether her spinal cord. Three weeks after the second surgery, however, just as the family was beginning to settle into a routine, Susan Gruen noticed several drops of clear fluid at the base of Deborah's back. She immediately called her husband, who suspected a cerebral spinal fluid leak, a potentially life-threatening situation. Deborah was rushed to the emergency room and admitted for her third surgery. "I was in the lab and I remember driving home, just screaming. I was on Interstate 95 and I was screaming," Jeff recalls.

> We worried about her every minute of every waking hour. We called each other two or three times per day. Susan would ask, "Do you think she will ever walk? Do you think she is going to be paralyzed?" I was really worried about her life in a chair. I was really worried about her kidneys and urinary infections; I was always worried about an asymptomatic UTI [urinary tract infection] and how would we know. An asymptomatic UTI can lead to pyelonephritis [kidney infection] and eventually kidney failure. I was also worried that she would be incontinent or have to be cathed. I didn't really want her in a chair. I worried about having to pick her up for the rest of her life and I worried that she would become dependent. I knew she would need multiple operations and there might be a mishap.

During the second and third hospitalizations, the Gruens received conflicting opinions about Deborah's need for a fourth surgery, a fusion of several thoraco-lumbar vertebrae that would further stabilize her spinal cord. She was only nine or ten months old, and some consultants believed she was too young for the procedure. They recommended postponing it for several years because she wasn't going to walk anyway, but others argued that the surgery should be done immediately. The Gruens agonized over the decision. Finally, they chose to have the surgery as soon as possible, even though the surgeon had never before performed this operation on a child as young as Deborah. Because HIV infections had become a major concern in blood banks, Jeff and Susan donated their own blood so that Deborah could safely receive emergency transfusions if needed. Eventually, at the age of five, Deborah required a fifth surgery.

With time, Deborah's condition stabilized. However, as expected, her physical growth and motor development were compromised.

> She never crawled. She dragged herself across the floor. And then she used a walker ... She had this little stand that the physical therapist made, like a box, and then literally strapped the kid into the stand. It locked her legs in, so she could start putting weight on her legs. It's a funny thing, the leg thing, because to us you don't really think about it, but to her using her legs requires active thought, even to this day.

Even though – or perhaps because – there were countless distressing and heart-breaking potential scenarios, the Gruens eventually learned not to fret about the future, but instead to help Deborah negotiate the present. Of course, negotiating the present wasn't always easy. They did their best to treat Deborah as they would any other child, just as they had treated Michele. But they also knew that Deborah was not like other children.

When Deborah was a preschooler, one of Susan's friends invited her to swim at the Ridgetop Club. Susan reluctantly agreed. She was apprehensive about how club members would respond to Deborah – who was able to walk only by using a pair of bright pink crutches – and how Deborah would respond to them. Would they stare at her, as happened so often in unfamiliar settings? Would the other kids welcome Deborah? Could she keep up with them? Susan recalls,

> So she got into the pool and as her mother, I'm dying, because, oh my God, everyone is looking at her. What's going to happen? Well, nothing happened. She swam, she did great, she gets out of the pool just like everybody else. Probably one of the kids picked her up, hugged her and then it was on to the next little game.

Looking back, Jeff and Susan reflect on how overwhelming the first five years of Deborah's life were for them as parents. When they weren't working, they spent most of their "free" time trying to keep their heads above water, trying to solve each new unexpected problem, one day at a time. Their primary goal, against all odds, was to help Deborah live as normal a life as possible. Their experience highlights the fact that traumas are family events; they affect everyone in the household. While young Deborah coped with her disability, life was also a challenge for those who loved her and wanted to do everything possible to help her grow and thrive.

Despite predictions that Deborah would never walk, she gradually learned to walk with two canes. And the invitation to the swim club turned out to be especially lucky: Deborah continued to swim, first for fun and then competitively. In 2004, at age 16, she traveled to Athens to compete in the Summer Paralympic Games, where she won the bronze medal in the 100-meter breast stroke. In 2005, this outgoing, gregarious and popular young woman was invited to swim on a number of prestigious NCAA swim teams, including those at Yale, Princeton, and Brown. Having the highest academic average in her high school class and being valedictorian, Deborah was awarded early admission to Yale University, where she majored in economics and competed on the Varsity Women's Swimming Team. Her speed at the 2008 Paralympics in Beijing earned her another bronze medal. By 2010, she had medaled in nearly a dozen international swimming competitions and set four world, pan-American, and American records in her class.

At age 18, she articulated her future ambition: "I am hoping to serve as a United States senator. I have my eye on Joe Lieberman's job." In the ensuing years, she continued to show potential to make that dream come true: she graduated summa cum laude and Phi Beta Kappa from Yale and was accepted to Georgetown University's school of law.

Emerging from such a rough beginning and living with such a severe lifelong disability, how has Deborah succeeded in so many areas of her life? The answer is complex and multi-faceted: her parents never gave up hope, provided unconditional love and support, treated Deborah like any able-bodied child, and expected others to do the same; her sister served as a powerful role model who protected Deborah only when absolutely necessary, at the same time pushing her to face her fears and achieve her goals; her friends never excluded Deborah from their activities, even if it meant waiting for her; and Deborah was inherently very bright and born into a highly accomplished family that valued ideas, moral and ethical principles, hard work, and community service. But perhaps most important, Deborah was and remains an optimist. In fact, her sister, Michele, has never heard Deborah complain about her disability. "She is just mentally tough. She walks around like you and me, like she has no problem. She has always been that way. I don't remember her ever having a problem with it."

Does Deborah have days when she feels down in the dumps? "Of course I do, but not because of my disability, maybe if I have a physics test tomorrow, but not because of my disability."

Blind optimism doesn't work

Contrary to popular belief, resilient optimists rarely ignore the negative in life by viewing the world through "rose-colored glasses." In their book *The Resilience Factor*, Karen Reivich and Andrew Shatté (2003) refer to this as "realistic optimism." Like pessimists, realistic optimists pay close attention to negative information that is relevant to the problems they face. However, unlike pessimists, they do not remain focused on the negative. They tend to disengage rapidly from problems that appear to be unsolvable. That is, they know when to cut their losses and turn their attention to problems that they believe they can solve.

Diane Coutu (2002) discusses the importance of paying close attention to negative information in the context of business success:

> That's not to say that optimism doesn't have its place: In turning around a
> demoralized sales force, for instance, conjuring a sense of possibility can be a very
> powerful tool. But for bigger challenges, a cool, almost pessimistic, sense of reality
> is far more important. ... Facing reality, really facing it, is grueling work. Indeed, it
> can be unpleasant and emotionally wrenching. (p. 48)

She goes on to observe that this flinty realism pays off when an organization needs
to overcome a major challenge or bounce back from a disaster. Assessing obstacles
realistically helps to surmount them.

Sandra Schneider, a psychologist at the University of South Florida, suggests that
realistic optimism is qualitatively different from the blind variety: "A realistic outlook
improves chances to negotiate the environment successfully, whereas an optimistic outlook places priority on feeling good. But are realistic and optimistic outlook
necessarily in conflict?" Schneider points out that in many cases, optimism and realism don't conflict with each other, but she writes "there remain numerous 'optimistic
biases' that do involve self-deception, or convincing oneself of desired beliefs without
appropriate reality checks" (2001, p. 250).

Many other researchers have documented examples of unrealistic optimistic
beliefs. Psychologist Tali Sharot of University College, London, and her colleagues
at New York University found, for example, that "people expect to live longer and be
healthier than average, they underestimate their likelihood of getting a divorce, and
overestimate their prospects for success on the job market" (2007, p. 102). This kind
of illusory superiority has been called the "Lake Wobegon effect" after the fictional
town created by author Garrison Keillor, where "all the children are above average."
Researchers have observed this effect in driving, among other behaviors; the popular book *Traffic: Why We Drive the Way We Do* includes a chapter titled "Why you're
not as good a driver as you think you are": "... if we were to ask ourselves, 'How's my
driving?' research has shown that the answer would probably be a big thumbs-up –
regardless of one's actual driving record" (Vanderbilt, 2008, p. 60).

It is not hard to see how excessive or unrealistic optimism can be detrimental, or
even dangerous. As noted by Justin Kruger and David Dunning of Cornell University
(1999), it tends to lead to "an underestimation of risk, an overestimation of ability, and
inadequate preparation." For an individual confronted with a major trauma like being
shot down and taken prisoner, being blindly optimistic could easily be the last mistake
he or she would ever make.

Admiral James Stockdale, one of the prisoners held by the North Vietnamese,
clearly recognized the dangers of blind, or "rosy" optimism. He shared his views in
a speech addressed to the Class of 1983 at the United States Military Academy, West
Point:

> We pretty much knew each other's outlook and most guys thought it was really
> better for everybody to be an optimist. I wasn't naturally that way; I knew too
> much about the politics of Asia when I got shot down. I think there was a lot of
> damage done by optimists; other writers from other wars share that opinion.
> The problem is, some people believe what professional optimists are passing

> out and come unglued when their predictions don't work out. … babbling
> optimists are the bane of existence to one under stress. (1984)

Humanitarian Hellen Keller likely would have agreed. Although her life was a testament to optimism, Keller was no Pollyanna. She believed that her own brand of optimism was the product of years of deprivation and hardship.

Born in 1880 in a small town in Alabama, Helen Keller contracted a life-threatening infection when she was 19 months old. Doctors at the time called it "brain fever"; it is now believed to have been scarlet fever or meningitis. She nearly died. When the fever lifted and Helen began to recover, her family rejoiced, not yet knowing that the illness had forever "closed her eyes and ears" (Keller, 1903b).

The next five years were marked by "outbursts of passion," screaming, daily (and sometimes hourly) temper tantrums and fits of violent and uncontrollable behavior. In 1887, when Helen's parents had reached their limit and seriously considered institutionalizing their daughter, Anne Sullivan came into Helen's life and "the light of love shone on me that very hour." With unwavering patience and persistence, Sullivan tackled the daunting task of teaching Helen to understand language and to communicate so that "the barren places between my mind and the minds of others blossomed like the rose" (Keller, 1903b).

If those around her had lacked hope, Helen might have lived a life of severe isolation. Without optimism, her parents wouldn't have hired a teacher, and Anne Sullivan would not have weathered her student's tantrums and would not have tried again and again to cultivate those "barren places."

The task was monumental. But with great effort and persistence, Helen eventually learned to associate words with objects, feelings, and concepts. Under Sullivan's creative tutelage, Helen rapidly learned to read raised letters, Braille, and to understand letters and words traced on her hand. Her progress was so rapid and extraordinary that within a few years she became a "phenomenon," receiving widespread publicity and meeting with numerous world dignitaries, including Alexander Graham Bell and President Grover Cleveland.

After four years of study at the Cambridge School for Young Ladies, Keller took, and passed, the entrance examinations for Radcliffe College. Doing so was an unexpected test of her resilience: Keller was informed only a day or two before the exam that the mathematical portion would be given in a style of Braille unfamiliar to her, so that she had to learn an entirely new set of symbols overnight. Nevertheless, she wrote,

> I do not blame anyone. The administrative board of Radcliffe did not realize
> how difficult they were making my examinations, nor did they understand
> the peculiar difficulties I had to surmount. But if they unintentionally placed
> obstacles in my way, I have the consolation of knowing that I overcame them
> all. (Keller, 1903b)

While at Radcliffe, Helen began to write about her life and her philosophy. In her essay "Optimism," she describes the superficiality and contingency of the type of happiness that people ordinarily seek: what she called "false optimism."

> Most people measure happiness in terms of physical pleasure and material possession. Could they win some visible goal which they have set on the horizon, how happy they would be! Lacking this gift or that circumstance, they would be miserable. If happiness is to be so measured, I who cannot hear or see have every reason to sit in a corner with folded hands and weep. (1903a, pp. 12–13)

And yet Keller saw herself as happy and optimistic, writing: "If I am happy in spite of my deprivations, if my happiness is so deep that it is a faith, so thoughtful that it becomes a philosophy of life, if, in short, I am an optimist, my testimony to the creed of optimism is worth hearing." Keller saw adversity as a prerequisite for real optimism.

> A man must understand evil and be acquainted with sorrow before he can write himself an optimist and expect others to believe that he has reason for the faith that is in him. I know what evil is. ... I can say with conviction that the struggle which evil necessitates is one of the greatest blessings. It makes us strong, patient, helpful men and women. It lets us into the soul of things and teaches us that although the world is full of suffering it is full also of the overcoming of it. My optimism then does not rest on the absence of evil, but on a glad belief in the preponderance of good and a willing effort always to cooperate with the good that it may prevail. I try to increase the power God has given me to see the best in everything and everyone, and make that Best a part of my life. (1903a, pp. 16, 17)

How does optimism increase resilience?

Barbara Fredrickson, a psychologist from the University of North Carolina, has developed what she calls the Broaden-and-Build model of positive emotions (2001). She begins by differentiating the functions of negative and positive emotions and notes that negative emotions such as anger, fear, and disgust help us survive by preparing us for danger. They do this by activating the sympathetic nervous system, which increases physiological arousal. This "fight–flight" reaction narrows our visual focus and tends to restrict our behaviors to those that are essential for attacking or fleeing.

Frederickson observes that positive emotions, in contrast, have been shown to reduce physiological arousal and to broaden our visual focus, our thoughts, and our behavior. When people experience positive emotions and an accompanying broadening of attention and behavior, their thinking tends to become more creative, inclusive, flexible, and integrative. Experiments have shown that inducing a positive mood (for example, by showing participants a funny movie or reading them a funny story) increases people's scope of attention, their ability to solve problems actively, and their interest in socializing and in strenuous as well as leisurely activities (Isen, 1990; Phillips *et al.*, 2002; Frederickson & Branigan, 2005). Thus, by broadening attention and action, positive emotions can contribute to our creativity, physical health, relationships with family and friends, our ability to acquire new knowledge, and our psychological resilience.

This capacity to broaden attention and build resources can help people cope with stress. The ability to step back from the maelstrom allows those who frequently experience positive emotions to look at stressful situations from multiple perspectives. Three coping mechanisms related to broadened attention include: positive reappraisal of trying circumstances; goal-directed, problem-focused coping; and the infusion of meaning into ordinary events. We will briefly discuss these coping mechanisms now, and elaborate on them later in the book.

First, when optimists broaden their attention, they increase their capacity to positively reappraise situations that initially appear to be negative. The process of reframing allows them to approach hardship as a challenge and to find opportunity embedded in adversity. Optimists who are realistic don't deny the difficulties they face, but they do tend to look for a silver lining.

Deborah Gruen is expert at positive reappraisal. When she received her "early acceptance" letter from Yale, she was ecstatic. Her long hours of studying and grueling workouts in the pool had paid off. Gaining acceptance to a college like Yale is no small feat, and the bar for early acceptance is even higher.

In the midst of her excitement, as she read and re-read the admissions letter, Deborah noticed a website that contained profiles of the applicants who had accepted early admission to Yale. Reading about the other students, she began to feel intimidated by their level of accomplishment and worried that she wouldn't be able to measure up against such high-powered classmates. But soon she reappraised the situation; she started to think about how interesting her new classmates were and how much fun it would be to get to know them.

A second characteristic of optimists is that they tend to cope with stress by actively employing strategies to solve problems. They gather information, acquire necessary skills, plan, set goals, make decisions, resolve conflicts, and seek social support. In a series of studies of individuals who were providing care to AIDS patients, researchers from the University of California at San Francisco found that positive emotion in caregivers was positively related to active problem-solving strategies, such as pursuing realistic and attainable caregiving goals. That is, the greater the optimism in the caregiver, the more he or she actively cared for patients (Folkman, 1997; Moskowitz *et al.*, 1996; Skelton *et al.*, 2009). Similarly, findings from a study of breast cancer patients conducted by researchers at the University of Miami suggest that optimistic patients who expect a positive outcome tend to embrace and actively pursue their treatment goals (Carver *et al.*, 1993).

In short, research has shown that optimism and positive expectations tend to promote active striving, while pessimism and negative expectations are associated with feelings of weakness and helplessness that may lead to unhelpful behaviors like, self-pity, resentment, denial and avoidance of problems.

A third characteristic of optimists is that they are more likely than pessimists to report that their lives are meaningful. A large body of research supports this observation. While it is widely believed that a sense of meaning and purpose enhances positive emotions and happiness, researchers have recently begun to ask whether it also works the other way – whether positive emotions and feelings of happiness can enhance one's belief that life has meaning. In a group of fascinating experiments, Laura King and colleagues (King & Hicks, 2009) from the University of Missouri examined the relationship between positive emotion, negative emotion, and meaning in life. Participants completed psychological rating scales that evaluated their sense of meaning and purpose in life and how much they experienced positive and negative emotions on a given day. The Purpose in Life scale evaluated the degree to which participants agreed or disagreed with statements such as "my personal existence is very purposeful and meaningful" and "I regard my ability to find meaning, purpose or a mission in life to be very great." The research team found that the greater the positive emotion on a particular day, the more life was experienced as being meaningful on that day.

In a separate experiment (King *et al.*, 2006), the team demonstrated that a sense of meaning in life could be increased by inducing a positive mood. In the laboratory, each participant read one of three mood-inducing scripts on a computer screen. Participants in the positive mood-inducing group read a script about being hailed as a hero after reuniting a lost child with her parents. Those in the negative-mood-enhancing group read about running a yellow light, crashing into another car and tragically killing a baby. The neutral script simply described a student's plans for the day. Results indicated that participants' judgments about meaning in life were enhanced only in the positive mood-induction group and not in the neutral or negative groups We will have more to say about the relationship between meaning in life and resilience in Chapter 11.

The findings in these experiments, in conjunction with those from numerous other studies, are consistent with Fredrickson's Broaden and Build Theory of Positive Emotions. In this theory positive emotions broaden the scope of attention, expand and open the individual's mind to new types of information, enhance cognitive flexibility, and increase the capacity to form creative and meaningful connections between elements of an experience. As a result, the optimist may be more likely than the pessimist to see the "big picture" and to view daily experiences within a larger framework of meaning.

Optimism is good for your physical and mental health

Optimism has widespread implications for physical and mental health. Numerous scientific studies have shown that optimists tend to be more satisfied with their lives and feel psychologically healthier than people who are not optimists (Affleck & Tennen, 1996; Chang *et al.*, 1997; Goldman *et al.*, 1996). It is also possible that optimism may protect against some of the negative effects of stress. For example, in a study of Israeli civilians who were exposed to SCUD missile attacks during the Gulf War, optimists developed fewer stress-related psychological illnesses, such as PTSD and depression, and used fewer medical services than did pessimists (Zeidner & Hammer, 1992).

Optimism has also been associated with better physical health in various populations, such as women with breast cancer (Carver *et al.*, 1993) and cardiac patients recovering from open heart surgery (Scheier *et al.*, 1989). In one study, heart transplant patients with positive expectations before surgery were found to be in better physical health after surgery than patients without positive expectations and, in a second study, optimistic patients were less likely than pessimistic patients to require re-hospitalization after coronary bypass surgery (Giltay *et al.*, 2006). In a third study, researchers from the Netherlands (Giltay *et al.*, 2006) studied 1000 elderly individuals over a period of 15 years and found that those who were optimistic had a significantly lower risk of dying from cardiovascular problems than those who were pessimistic.

Several classic research investigations have reported that optimists may live longer than pessimists. In a remarkable study involving 180 nuns from School Sisters of Notre Dame in Milwaukee, Deborah Danner and colleagues at the University of Kentucky examined the relationship between signs of good cheer and optimism at the time of initiation into the Sisterhood and subsequent length of life (Danner *et al.*, 2001). At the School Sisters of Notre Dame, it is customary for women to write a brief autobiographical sketch shortly before taking their vows of commitment to God and the Church. The researchers analyzed these autobiographical sketches, which the nuns had written decades earlier, by quantifying numerous variables within the sketches, such as degree of unhappiness, level of religious devotion, intellectual complexity of the sketch, and amount of positive emotion. Of all the variables, only positive emotion was related to longevity: 90% of nuns whose autobiographical sketches fell within the most cheerful quarter were still alive at age 85, compared with 34% of those in the least cheerful quarter; at age 94 the figures were 54% compared with 11%.

It is even possible that optimists have increased immunity to infectious diseases. In a fascinating experiment conducted by Sheldon Cohen, professor of psychology at Carnegie Mellon University, study subjects were required to live in a hotel for one week where they ate only what they were served by the research staff, were not permitted to leave the hotel, and did not have close physical contact with other research participants. On the first day of the experiment, all participants were infected with a cold virus. Consistent with a large body of research showing that positive emotions are associated with better health than are negative emotions, fewer participants assessed as having higher positive emotions developed colds. Those who did had fewer runny noses, less sneezing and congestion, and less mucus (Cohen *et al.*, 2003).

Further support for the relationship between optimism and immune function comes from a recent study by Susanne Segerstrom from the University of Kentucky and Sandra Sephton of the University of Louisville who measured academic optimism (i.e. expecting to do well in school), positive and negative emotional state, and cell-mediated immunity (i.e. immunity which protects against microbes that are living within hosts such as viruses) at five different points in time among students during their first year of law school. They found that changes in optimistic expectancies were accompanied by changes in immunity and this association was partly explained by changes in positive emotions (Segerstrom & Sephton, 2010).

Although researchers do not fully understand the mechanisms by which positive emotions benefit physical health, it is likely that the immune system and hormones, such as cortisol and growth hormone, are involved. It is also likely that optimists in general choose healthier lifestyles than do pessimists: they may adopt healthier eating patterns, exercise more, drink less alcohol, enjoy a more supportive network and be less likely to take drugs of abuse.

The neuroscience of optimism

Is there something special about the brains of people who are able to remain optimistic and hopeful in the face of extremely stressful life events? Scientists are beginning to elucidate the complex underlying neurobiology of positive emotions and optimism. Three brain regions that play a central role in optimism include: the prefrontal cortex; the amygdala; and reward systems involving the anterior cingulate cortex, ventral-tegmental area, and the nucleus accumbens (Feder *et al.*, 2009).

As we described in Chapter 1, the prefrontal cortex serves as the brain's "executive center"; it is essential for guiding behavior, regulating emotions, and understanding the difference between potential rewards and punishments. It is also essential for imagining the future and setting goals – functions that relate directly to optimism. The prefrontal cortex enables us to engage in optimistic processes like hoping for the best and imagining a bright future, anticipating and preparing to meet a challenge, and making plans to achieve and enjoy success.

The prefrontal cortex is also involved in learning. As we've said earlier, even though optimism has a substantial hereditary component, it can be augmented through learning. Even if you are a born pessimist, or a very limited situational optimist, you can teach yourself to increase optimistic thought. Research conducted by University of Wisconsin investigator Richard Davidson and colleagues has found that optimism is associated with high activity in the left prefrontal cortex, while depression is associated with low activity. This low level of left prefrontal activation is also associated with reduced activation of the brain's reward circuitry (i.e. nucleus accumbens) and decrease inhibition of the amygdala. This may help to explain why people who are depressed have difficulty sustaining positive emotions and inhibiting negative ones. (Heller *et al.*, 2009; Johnstone *et al.*, 2007)

The second brain area involved in optimism is the amygdala. Recall from Chapter 1 that the amygdala plays a role in triggering "raw emotions" such as fear or excitment. In this way the amygdala plays a role in our ability to experience positive emotions.

Areas of the brain involved in reward circuitry – the anterior cingulate cortex (ACC), ventral-tegmental area, and the nucleus accumbens – also appear to play a central role in optimism. These areas are associated with the rewarding effects of social attachment, eating, sex, and other pleasurable stimuli. Reward circuitry is generally active when we are engaged in behaviors that we enjoy. On the other hand, acute stress tends to reduce activity in these circuits (Nestler & Carlezon, 2006). The neurotransmitter commonly associated with reward is dopamine. Alice Isen and her colleagues at Cornell University (Isen, 1990) have found that dopamine improves cognitive flexibility and perspective-taking. These researchers believe that the broadened perspective and flexible cognitive style that accompany positive emotions may be related to increased dopamine in the brain's reward circuitry (Ashby *et al.*, 1999).

Psychologist Tali Sharot describes an experiment that she and her colleagues at New York University conducted to examine how the brain generates the positive bias that characterizes optimism. While undergoing functional magnetic resonance imaging (fMRI), participants were asked to imagine both positive and negative future events, such as "winning an award" or "ending a romantic relationship." When participants imagined a positive future event, activation of the amygdala and the ACC increased. The greatest activation of these regions occurred in participants with the highest scores on the LOT-R (Life Orientation Test-Revised), a measure of dispositional optimism.

In our own research with colleagues at the National Institutes of Mental Health (Vythilingham *et al.*, 2008), we recently investigated brain reward systems in highly resilient US Special Forces soldiers compared to healthy civilians. In one experiment we collected fMRI data while study participants performed a task in which they were instructed to press a button quickly enough to either win money or avoid losing money. When the civilian control subjects "won" money (or anticipated doing so), activity in reward centers and the prefrontal cortex (top-down control) increased. When they "lost" money, activity in these areas decreased. But in the brains of Special Forces soldiers, we observed equal activation of the reward systems whether they "won" or "lost" money in the task. The fact that the soldiers showed no relative reduction in reward center activity when they "lost" money suggests that the brain reward system of resilient individuals may be relatively impervious to stress or adversity. Perhaps people who are resilient tend to have a dopamine reward system that is relatively resistant to dopamine depletion and that functions well even under highly stressful conditions (Charney, 2004).

How optimists and pessimists think

By carefully analyzing thought patterns and spoken words, psychologists like Martin Seligman have found that pessimists and optimists have very different explanatory styles (ways of explaining bad and good events to themselves and others). When bad things happen to pessimists, they tend to believe that the negative consequences will last forever (permanence) and will intrude into many areas of their lives (universality). They commonly describe the event using words such as "always" or "never." Optimists, on the other hand, tend to respond to adverse events by viewing the consequences as temporary and limited in scope. They are more likely to use words such as "sometimes" or "lately." In addition, optimistic people tend to have an internal locus of control (Guarnera & Williams, 1987) – the belief that they can influence events in their lives.

For example, a pessimist whose romantic relationship falls apart might conclude that he will fail in all future romances (permanence), that his non-romantic as well as romantic relationships are doomed (universality), and that he inherently lacks some quality or skill needed to form lasting interpersonal bonds (external locus of control). When pessimists are challenged by stress, they tend to exaggerate their appraisal of threat, create negative self-statements, underestimate their capacities, and over-generalize the nature and extent of the problem.

In contrast, an optimist whose romance fizzles may conclude that he and his partner were not well suited for each other, that he has learned from the experience – making it more likely that his next romantic relationship will work out – and that he possesses the necessary qualities and skills to succeed in present and future relationships, both romantic and platonic. When threatened or challenged, optimists tend to minimize their appraisal of threat, create positive statements about themselves, and focus on their strengths.

Pessimists and optimists tend to employ opposite explanatory styles in good times as well as bad. In response to good events, pessimists often view their gains as temporary and specific to the particular event itself, while optimists generally anticipate long-standing and widespread benefits.

Are some people born more optimistic than others?

Is it possible that some of us are "born optimists"? The answer is complex, but it does begin with genetics. As we noted in Chapter 1, twin studies are one of the most productive methods for studying the heritability of personality traits such as optimism. If personality were solely determined by genes, then identical twins should have identical personality traits, because their genes are identical. This should hold true whether they have been raised together or apart – that is, in different environments and by different caretakers. However, it doesn't hold true. Instead, the results of many twin studies strongly suggest that only 30–50% of most personality traits are genetically transmitted, including optimism. That means that the other 50–70% depends on environment, including the efforts we make to reach our potential and maximize our positive experiences.

Scientists keep learning about genetic influences on behavior, personality, and emotions. A growing body of research has found that people with specific variations in their genes appear to be relatively protected from depression when they experience stressful or adverse events. For example, one promising area of inquiry involves the serotonin system that is known to play an important role in the regulation of mood.

We each inherit one of three variations of the serotonin transporter gene: a pair of short alleles (SS), one short and one long allele (SL), or a pair of long alleles (LL). In some studies, but not all, the SS variation was more likely to be found in people who developed depression after a range of stressful events compared to those with the SL or LL types (Caspi, 2002, 2003; Munafo *et al.*, 2008). Some researchers have referred to the LL version as a protection against depression in adverse circumstances.

However, the good news is that some social and environmental factors can alter the expression of the genetic code. There are many such gene–environment interactions. For example, in the case of the serotonin transporter gene, social support has been found to protect against stress-related depression, even in people with the SS version; Yale psychologist Joan Kaufman and colleagues (2006) found this to be true in foster children who had been severely maltreated. Our genetic makeup is not always our destiny: just as with many inherited tendencies – high blood pressure, for example, or a family history of diabetes – we may be able to take steps to decrease our risk of developing symptoms or possibly the disease itself.

Ways to become more optimistic

Deborah Gruen is what scientists might call a genetic optimist. For as long as she and her family members can recall, Deborah has been happy and confident that her future will be rewarding. But what about those of us who are not born optimists? If we did not inherit "optimism genes," is it still possible to become more optimistic? Fortunately, for most of us the answer is yes. For example, one way to increase optimism involves learning a set of cognitive skills that are part of what Martin Seligman (1998) has term "learned optimism." This does not necessarily mean that genetic pessimists can train themselves to become as optimistic as genetic optimists, but in many cases they can develop a more hopeful view of life and of the future.

Over the past several decades, social scientists and cognitive behaviorists have described two basic approaches to learning and enhancing optimism: increasing positive thinking and refuting negative thinking. With practice we can teach ourselves to think or insert positive thoughts. We can also teach ourselves not to dwell on negative thoughts. To do this we must learn to identify negative thoughts and then to challenge their accuracy.

War veteran Lew Meyer used the first of these approaches – increasing positive thinking – when his unit in Vietnam was overrun during the Tet Offensive. As a prisoner, he came to understand the importance of a positive attitude and a fighting spirit during times of high stress. Optimism didn't come naturally for Lew Meyer, but, he trained himself to become a positive thinker.

> We had this book in our house. My wife Gail read it and re-read it and quoted things and pushed me and pushed me. I started reading it. Then I ended up occasionally skimming through it and looking for a certain chapter … I started re-reading it in solitary.

The book was *The Power of Positive Thinking* by the Protestant minister Norman Vincent Peale, which has sold over five million copies since its publication in 1952 and has helped countless people learn to practice optimism. Meyer read Peale's classic before his experiences in Vietnam and he reconstructed it in memory during his four and half years in prison camps like Skid Row and Rockpile. He did so by spending hundreds of hours remembering and rehearsing meaningful passages like this one: "Without a humble but reasonable confidence in your own powers you cannot be successful or happy. But with sound self-confidence you can succeed. … self-confidence leads to self-realization and successful achievement" (p. 1).

While Peale believed that having faith in God and drawing strength from the divine were largely responsible for personal power and resilience, he also believed that our emotions and feelings are largely determined by our thoughts. He believed that when we think negative thoughts, we are likely to feel anxious, worried, angry, and sad; but if we think positive thoughts, we will tend to feel happy, energized, and peaceful. It is also possible that when we feel depressed or anxious we tend to think negative thoughts and that when we are happy we tend to think positive thoughts.

Peale knew that positive thinking does not come naturally to everyone. Many people must practice and systematically work at it, as did Lew Meyer. These are some of Peale's recommendations:

- Make a true estimate of your ability and then raise it 10%.

- Formulate and stamp indelibly on your mind a mental picture of yourself as succeeding. Always picture success no matter how badly things seem to be going at the moment.

- Practice positive and peaceful thinking by making a list of positive and peaceful thoughts and pass them through your mind several times each day.

- Practice the technique of suggestive articulation, that is, repeat audibly some positive, success-oriented and peaceful words.

- Do not build up obstacles in your imagination.

- Adopt an "I don't believe in defeat" attitude.

- Start each day by affirming positive, successful, peaceful, and happy attitudes and your days will tend to be pleasant and successful.

Two of Peale's other recommendations, to cultivate friendships with hopeful people and to avoid "worry conversations," bear special emphasis. Optimism and pessimism can both be "contagious," so it is often beneficial to intentionally surround ourselves with people who are positive, confident, and encouraging. Under adverse circumstances, people are best able to call upon their own resilience and keep their hopes up if people around them are doing the same.

Deborah Gruen may be a good example of the optimistic person with whom we would like to associate. A former neighbor and babysitter remembers Deborah's contagious optimism.

> Everything she did, she did with a smile. I can't remember her exact age, but Deborah had surgery on her back. I'm pretty sure she was having rods inserted along her spine to make her back straighter. Regardless of the type of surgery, it was a painful one. Jeff Gruen drove me up to visit her at Boston Children's Hospital. We were waiting in her room, and I remember that everyone was quiet, depressed and sad. No one was talking. Yet, as soon as Deborah was brought in, the entire room lit up. She was lying in a cart of some sort because she couldn't be in the sitting position, and she was so bandaged and fragile-looking. But once she started talking, you totally forgot that she had just had a

serious surgery. It was amazing. We spent the day in her hospital room as if we were hanging out at the picnic benches at Ridgetop Swim Club.

As Deborah's mother observed, "Deborah doesn't let other people get her down. She stays really positive. She is an uplifting person. I don't see how you can spend time with her and not get energized and uplifted."

Although Lew Meyer and many others swear by the teachings of Norman Vincent Peale, there is also evidence that we can build optimism by confronting negative thoughts and emotions. In fact, this practice is fundamental to cognitive behavioral therapies, which we will discuss in greater detail later in this book.

Many people make destructive statements about themselves (e.g. "How stupid can I be?") during trying times and setbacks, but psychologists Martin Seligman, Lisa Aspinwall, Albert Ellis, and others have observed that optimists are highly skilled at refuting and in some cases ignoring these negative statements. Optimists often employ a number of strategies and techniques that are taught in cognitive behavioral therapies. These techniques teach the learner to recognize automatic negative thoughts and then dispute those thoughts so that new, more positive patterns of thinking can replace the old negative ones. In essence, cognitive behavior therapy teaches people how to change their habitual automatic explanatory style (Aspinwall & Staudinger, 2002).

A healthy coping style can involve not only increasing positive thoughts and refuting negative ones, but also affirming the coexistence of both. In their research on positive and negative emotions, David Spiegel and colleagues from Stanford University (Speigel & Classen, 2000) have found that women with metastatic breast cancer benefit from a group therapy technique he has called "supportive-expressive therapy." This therapy requires the capacity to coactivate positive and negative emotions and then tolerate and withstand the resulting unpleasant tension. Squarely confronting, engaging, and grappling with the negative, as well as the positive, may facilitate the process of "working through" and possibly resolving or even transcending a major life stressor. Spiegel has observed that patients who actively use these techniques survive longer and experience better quality of life in the form of lower rates of anxiety and depression, and less physical pain. His work supports the views of James Stockdale and Helen Keller who describe the power of realistic optimism, which focuses on the positive without denying the negative.

One practical approach to enhancing optimism involves learning to recognize and modify your typical explanatory style. Developing these cognitive skills may also prove useful when dealing with adversity. Here are a few tips.

When something bad happens:

- Remember that these difficulties won't last forever. Take one day at a time. Where now there may only be pain, over time good things will return.

- Keep the adverse event or situation within its limits; don't let it pervade other areas of your life.

- Think of strengths and resources you can use to help deal with the problem.

- Notice what is good, for example, acts of kindness by those who recognize your struggle.

And when something good happens:

- Give yourself credit for whatever part you played in making it happen.
- Allow yourself to feel grateful for whatever part you didn't play in it – the efforts or generosity of others, or just simple good luck.
- Get the most out of it: think of ways to expand the scope and duration of the positive event or situation.

In his book *Authentic Happiness*, Martin Seligman discusses the importance of making a conscious choice to build a more positive explanatory style; he recommends responding to negative thoughts "as if they were uttered by an external person whose mission is to make your life miserable" (2002, p. 181). Sometimes it is helpful to ask yourself specific questions in order to refute negative beliefs. These may include:

- What is the evidence for this negative belief?
- Is there a less destructive way to look at this belief?
- What are the implications of this belief?
- Am I catastrophizing or exaggerating the potential negative impact of the situation?
- Am I over-generalizing, falsely assuming that this particular situation has broad implications?
- How useful is my pessimistic approach to the problem at hand?

The determinants of optimism are numerous and include genetic, developmental, neurobiological, cognitive, and social factors among others. Accordingly, in addition to modifying one's explanatory style, there are many other potential ways to enhance optimism and positive emotions including psychotherapy, medication, spiritual practices, increasing social support, and meditation among others. There remains a great need for multi-disciplinary research on the determinants of optimism and on ways to increase positive emotions.

A note of caution is in order. As we noted in Chapter 1, individuals who suffer pronounced alterations in mood, such as those with major depression, should seek help from a qualified professional who can assess and treat the mood disorder. Therapy for actual mood disorders often involves a combination of counseling and medication, such as antidepressants. Specific recommendations for diagnosis and treatment of depression are beyond the scope of this book. However, we hope readers will benefit from this discussion of optimism.

Is realistic optimism an important component of resilience? Yes. In fact, during an interview with a Special Forces instructor we asked, "Do Special Forces Soldiers tend to be pessimistic or optimistic?"

"Definitely optimistic," the instructor replied. "We can't afford to have a really negative pessimist on one of our teams because pessimism is infectious and brings everybody down ... All it takes is one guy getting excited and negative about something we can handle that causes other people to doubt the situation or the leadership ... If one of our guys is too pessimistic, we try our best to work with him, but if he can't get it right, then we remove him from the team. It's pretty simple really. If you want to be on one of our teams and you don't have optimism, then you better figure out how to get it."

References

Affleck, G., & Tennen, H. (1996). Construing benefits from adversity: adaptational significance and dispositional underpinnings. *Journal of Personality*, **64**, 899–922.

Ashby, F. G., Isen, A. M., & Turken, A. U. (1999). A neuropsychological theory of positive affect and its influence on cognition. *Psychological Review*, **106**, 529–550.

Aspinwall, L. G., & Staudinger, U. M. (eds.) (2002). *A psychology of human strengths: Fundamental questions and future directions for a positive psychology*. Washington, DC: American Psychological Association.

Carver, C. S., Pozo, C., Harris, S. D., Noriega, V., Scheier, M. F., Robinson, D. S., *et al.* (1993). How coping mediates the effect of optimism on distress: A study of women with early stage breast cancer. *Journal of Personality and Social Psychology*, **65**, 375–390.

Caspi, A., Sugden, K., Moffitt, T. E., Taylor, A., Craig, I. W., Harrington, H., *et al.* (2003, July 18). Influence of life stress on depression: Moderation by polymorphism in the 5-HTT gene. *Science*, **301**, 386–389.

Caspi, A., McClay, J., Moffitt, T., Mill, J., Martin, J., Craig, I., *et al.* (2002). Role of genotype in the cycle of violence in maltreated children. *Science*, **297**, 851–855.

Chang, E. C., Maydeu-Olivares, A., & D'Zurilla, T. J. (1997). Optimism and pessimism as partially independent constructs: Relations to positive and negative affectivity and psychological well-being. *Personality and Individual Differences*, **23**, 433–440.

Charney, D. S. (2004). Psychobiological mechanisms of resilience and vulnerability: Implications for successful adaptation to extreme stress. *American Journal of Psychiatry*, **161**, 195–216.

Cohen, S., Doyle, W. J., Turner, R. B., Alper, C. M., & Skoner, D. P. (2003). Emotional style and susceptibility to the common cold. *Psychosomatic Medicine*, **65**, 652–657.

Coutu, D. (2002). How resilience works. *Harvard Business Review*, May, 46–55.

Danner, D. D., Snowdon, D. A., & Friesen, W. V. (2001). Positive emotions in early life and longevity: Findings from the nun study. *Journal of Personality and Social Psychology*, **80**(5), 804–813.

Feder, A., Nestler, E. J., & Charney, D. (2009). Psychobiology and molecular genetics of resilience. *Nature Reviews*, **10**, 446–466.

Folkman, S. (1997). Positive psychological states and coping with severe stress. *Social Science & Medicine* (1982), **45**(8), 1207–1221.

Fredrickson, B. L. (2001). The role of positive emotions in positive psychology: The broaden-and-build theory of positive emotions. *American Psychologist*, **56**(3), 218–226.

Fredrickson, B., & Branigan, C. (2005). Positive emotions broaden the scope of attention and thought-action repertoires. *Cognition & Emotion*, **19**(3), 313–332.

Giltay, E. J., Kamphuis, M. H., Kalmijn, S., Zitman, F. G., & Kromhout, D. (2006). Dispositional optimism and the risk of cardiovascular death: The Zutphen

Elderly Study. *Archives of Internal Medicine*, **166**, 431–436.

Goldman, S. L., Kraemer, D. T., & Salovey, P. (1996). Beliefs about mood moderate the relationship to illness and symptom reporting. *Journal of Psychosomatic Research*, **41**, 115–128.

Guarnera, S., & Williams, R. L. (1987). Optimism and locus of control for health and affiliation among elderly adults. *Journal of Gerontology*, **42**(6), 594–595. doi: 10.1093/geronj/42.6.594.

Heller, A. S., Johnstone, T., Shackman, A. J., Light, S. N., Peterson, M. J., Kolden, G. G., *et al.* (2009). Reduced capacity to sustain positive emotion in major depression reflects diminished maintenance of fronto-striatal brain activation. *Proceedings of the National Academy of Sciences, USA*, **106**(52):224445–224450.

Isen, A. M. (1990). The influence of positive and negative affect on cognitive organization: Some implications for development. In N. L. Stein, B. Leventhal, & T. Trabasso (eds.), *Psychological and biological approaches to emotion*. Hillsdale, NJ: Lawrence Erlbaum Associates.

Johnstone, T., van Reekum, C. M., Urry, H. L., Kalin, N. H., Davidson, R. J. (2007). Failure to regulate: counterproductive recruitment of top-down prefrontal-subcortical circuitry in major depression. *Journal of Neuroscience*, 15;27(33):8877–8884.

Kaufman, J., Yang, B. Z., Douglas-Palumberi, H., Grasso, D., Lipschitz, D., Houshyar, S., *et al.* (2006). Brain-derived neurotrophic factor-5-HTTLPR gene interactions and environmental modifiers of depression in children. *Biological Psychiatry*, **59**, 673–680.

Keller, H. (1903a). *Optimism: An essay*. New York, NY: Thomas Y. Crowell.

Keller, H. (1903b). *The story of my life*. New York, NY: Doubleday.

King, L. A. & Hicks, J. A. (2009). The detection and construction of meaning in life events. *Journal of Positive Psychology*, **4**, 317–330.

King, L. A., Hicks, J. A., & Krull, J., & Del Gaiso, A. K.. (2006). Positive affect and the experience of meaning in life. *Journal of Personality and Social Psychology*, **90**, 179–196.

Kruger J., & Dunning D. (1999). Unskilled and unaware of it: How difficulties in recognizing one's own incompetence lead to inflated self-assessments. *Journal of Personality and Social Psychology*, **77**, 1121–1134.

Moskowitz, J. T., Folkman, S., Collette, L., & Vittinghoff, E. (1996). Coping and Mood during AIDS-Related Caregiving and Bereavement. *Annals of Behavioral Medicine*, **18**(1), 49–57.

Munafo, M. R., Brown, S. M. & Hariri, A. R. (2008). Serotonin transporter (5-HTTLPR) genotype and amygdala activation: A meta-analysis. *Biological Psychiatry*, **63**, 852–857.

Nestler, E. J., & Carlezon, W. A. (2006). The mesolimbic dopamine reward circuit in depression. *Biological Psychiatry*, **59**, 1151–1159.

Peale, N. V. (1952). *The power of positive thinking*. Englewood Cliffs, NJ: Prentice-Hall.

Phillips, L. H., Bull, R., Adams, E., & Fraser, L. (2002). Positive mood and executive function: Evidence from Stroop and fluency tasks. *Emotion*, **2**, 12–22.

Reivich, K., & Shatte, A. (2003). *The resilience factor: Seven keys to finding your inner strength and overcoming life's hurdles*. New York, NY: Broadway Books.

Scheier, M. F., Carver, C. S., & Bridges, M. W. (1994). Distinguishing optimism from neuroticism (and trait anxiety, self-mastery, and self-esteem): A reevaluation of the Life Orientation Test. *Journal of Personality and Social Psychology*, **67**(6), 1063–1078.

Scheier, M. F., Matthews, G. L., Owens, J. F., Magovern, G. L., Lefbvre, R. C., *et al.* (1989). Dispositional optimism and recovery from coronary artery bypass surgery: The beneficial effects of physical and psychological well-being. *Journal of Personality and Social Psychology*, **57**, 1024–1040.

Schneider, S. L. (2001). In search of realistic optimism: Meaning, knowledge, and warm fuzziness. *American Psychologist*, **56**(3), 250–263.

Segerstrom, S. C., & Sephton, S. E. (2010). Optimistic expectancies and cell-mediated immunity: The role of positive affect. *Psychological Science*, **21**(3), 448–455.

Seligman, M. E. P. (1998). *Learned optmism: How to change your mind and your life*. New York, NY: The Free Press.

Seligman, M. E. P. (2002). *Authentic happiness: Using the new positive psychology to realize your potential for lasting fulfillment*. New York, NY: Free Press.

Sharot, T., Riccardi, A. M., Raio, C. M., & Phelps, E. A. (2007). Neural mechanisms mediating optimism bias. *Nature*, **450** (October 24), 102–115.

Skelton K, Ressler KJ, Norrholm SD, Jovanovic T, Bradley-Davino B. (2011). PTSD and gene variants: New pathways and new thinking. *Neuropharmacology* [Epub ahead of print].

Spiegel, D., & Classen, C. (2000). *Group therapy for cancer patients: A research-based handbook of psychosocial care*. New York, NY: Basic Books.

Stockdale, J. B. (1984). *A Vietnam experience*. Stanford, CA: Hoover Institution.

Taylor, S. E. (1998). Optimism/pessimism. Summary prepared by Shelley Taylor in collaboration with the Psychosocial Working Group. University of California at San Francisco. MacArthur Research Network on SES & Health. Accessed 7/8/09 at http://www.macses.ucsf.edu/research/psychosocial/optimism.php.

Vanderbilt, T. (2008). *Traffic: Why we drive the way we do (and what it says about us)*. New York, NY: Alfred A. Knopf.

Vythilingam, M., Nelson, E. E., Scaramozza, M., Waldeck, T., Hazlett, G., Southwick, S. M., *et al.* (2008). Reward circuitry in resilience to severe trauma: An fMRI investigation of resilient special forces soldiers. *Psychiatry Research: Neuroimaging*, **172**(1), 75–77.

Zeidner, M., & Hammer, A. L. (1992). Coping with missile attack: resources, strategies, and outcomes. *Journal of Personality*, **60**, 709–746.

Facing fear: an adaptive response

Fear is ubiquitous. No one escapes its grip. Fear even strikes individuals who are widely admired for their courage. South African dissident Nelson Mandela reported that during his years of imprisonment and struggle against oppression, "I learned that courage was not the absence of fear, but the triumph over it. I felt fear myself more times than I can remember, but I hid it behind a mask of boldness. The brave man is not he who does not feel afraid, but he who conquers that fear" (1995, p. 622).

For some people, fear is constricting and even paralyzing, while for others it is energizing and serves as a catalyst for growth. Fear, whether we allow it to diminish us or enlist it as an ally, has an enormous impact on how we conduct our lives. To become more resilient, sooner or later we will need to face our fears. In this chapter, we will discuss the importance of fear, its neurobiological underpinnings, and ways to manage and even take advantage of it.

The science of fear

We begin this chapter with science because it will deepen your understanding of the survivor stories that follow. When we encounter something that frightens us, we react with the urge either to defend ourselves or to run away. This "fight-or-flight" response was first described by Harvard physiologist Walter Cannon in the early twentieth century. Cannon observed that, without any conscious effort on our part, our body mobilizes us to fight or to flee. Fear does us a great favor: it prepares us to react to danger.

The fight–flight response is mediated, in part, by a group of chemicals called catecholamines (which include epinephrine, norepinephrine, and dopamine). These chemicals are released by the nervous system in response to perceived danger. Catecholamines shut down blood flow to the digestive system, which slows during dangerous situations, and instead shunt blood to the heart and skeletal muscles, which are needed for fighting or fleeing. Our reflexes sharpen and blood flow to capillaries decreases. This reduces bleeding if we are wounded.

In the brain, the catecholamine norepinephrine stimulates multiple brain regions including the amygdala and helps us to orient toward potentially dangerous stimuli, and then zero in on the most threatening stimulus in our immediate environment, such as a weapon or an attacker's fist. Increased levels of norepinephrine in the amygdala also enhance encoding and consolidation of memory, which makes memories that occur during dangerous situations especially strong and sometimes unforgettable.

To demonstrate the importance of norepinephrine in the formation of memories for arousing and traumatic events, Larry Cahill and James McGaugh at the University of California, Irvine, studied a group of college students and showed them a series of photographic slides. Some of the slides were neutral in content while others showed a traumatic event (a young child being hit by a car) (Cahill *et al.*, 1994). A week later, the college students came back for "surprise" memory testing. The students remembered the traumatic slides better than the neutral ones. Why? The researchers hypothesized that traumatic slides stimulated arousal, and an increase in norepinphrine in the amygdala, and that this norepinephrine enhanced memory consolidation.

To test this hypothesis, McGaugh and Cahill conducted a second experiment (McGaugh, 2000). They divided students into two groups and gave the first group a drug called Propranolol, which blocks norepinephrine. Propranolol is commonly used to treat high blood pressure. They gave the second group of students a placebo sugar pill. Both groups then viewed the same series of neutral and traumatic slides. As in the first study, the participants returned a week later for surprise memory testing. As predicted, the placebo group remembered the slides showing trauma better than the neutral slides, presumably because viewing the traumatic slides caused an increase in arousal and norepinephrine which in turn caused an increase in memory consolidation. The Propranolol group, however, remembered the traumatic slides no better than the neutral slides – apparently because the drug had blocked the action of the norepinephrine which had been released upon viewing the slides of trauma.

In light of these studies, we ourselves decided to evaluate further the effects of norepinephrine on memory (Southwick *et al.*, 2002), but we took a different approach: rather than blocking norepinephrine while subjects viewed this same series of slides, we increased norepinephrine shortly after the subjects had finished viewing the slides. We gave half of the volunteers a medication that briefly increases the body's release of its own norepinephrine. The others received a placebo pill. As expected, subjects with the greatest increases in norepinephrine remembered both neutral and traumatic slides better than did subjects with less robust increases in norepinephrine. Taken together, these and many other studies provide support for the finding that people remember emotionally arousing events better than emotionally neutral events, and that norepinephrine plays an important role in strengthening memory for these emotionally arousing events.

Fear conditioning

Not only do people tend to remember emotionally arousing and traumatic events better than emotionally neutral events, but they also tend to remember the context in which arousing events occur (LeDoux, 1996, 2002). The brain's limbic system links the fear that accompanies a traumatic event to sights, sounds, odors, time of day, weather conditions, and other ordinarily neutral stimuli that are present during the frightening event. These contextual stimuli can then become fear-conditioned cues capable of triggering fear by themselves and now serve as predictors of potential danger because of their association with a previous danger. Because the linking of fear with contextual stimuli occurs in the limbic system, we may not be consciously aware that these contextual stimuli can trigger a fear response on their own (LeDoux, 1996).

For example, imagine that you are walking through a park near your home, a place where you've frequently taken pleasant and relaxing walks. This time, however, someone runs up behind you, holds a knife to your throat, grabs your wallet, shoves you to the ground, kicks you, and runs away. The park that you once enjoyed visiting now becomes a fear-conditioned stimulus. From now on, each time you walk near the park, its newly formed association with danger makes you feel anxious. In fact, you may become afraid of all parks, not just this one.

This process, known as classical conditioning, is familiar to those who know the story of Russian physiologist Ivan Pavlov and his dogs. Seeking to study digestion in dogs, Pavlov measured their saliva flow when they were fed meat powder. He began to notice that the dogs salivated even before being fed, as soon as they heard the sound of the researcher's footsteps approaching their cages. The footsteps had become associated with meat powder so that the footsteps themselves now elicited salivation. Classical conditioning works similarly in humans: we have a response (in this case a negative response, fear) when we are exposed to formerly neutral stimuli (such as the sights, smells, and sounds of a park) that have been paired with a traumatic event (i.e. being attacked).

A friend of ours, John, was mystified by a personal experience that involved fear conditioning. One spring, John noticed that every time he walked outdoors into his garden, he immediately began to feel both afraid and nauseated. When he walked back into the house, the fear and nausea rapidly dissipated. This sequence lasted for a few weeks, and then one day it just stopped; walking into the garden no longer bothered him. John remained baffled until one evening, months later, when he suddenly identified the trigger for his fear and nausea: the song of a particular type of migrating bird that passed through his town for several weeks each spring. But why would birdsong trigger anxiety and such an unpleasant reaction? Because a year earlier, John had been diagnosed with cancer and was receiving chemotherapy. Naturally, he was frightened by the cancer and the chance he might not survive, and like many patients, he suffered from nausea as a side effect of the chemotherapy. Each time he came home from a treatment, he sat in the garden hoping to ease his anxiety and recover from his nausea. At that time of the year, the migrating birds were singing in his garden. At a purely unconscious level, John's limbic system formed an association between the bird songs and his feelings of fear and nausea.

Returning to the example of the assault in the park, suppose you were attacked on a hot and humid day. In the days, weeks, months and even years after the attack, you might find yourself unaccountably feeling anxious every time the weather is hot and humid. In our own research, we have observed this phenomenon in veterans who had narrowly escaped death during combat. Years later, they, too, may feel afraid when the weather resembles the weather on the day that they risked death, yet unable to explain why they feel afraid. Anniversary reactions can operate in a similar way. The survivor may feel anxious on the anniversary of a traumatic event without consciously associating his current anxiety with the original trauma, and may try to explain his or her mood based on something else that is occurring in the present.

Why does the brain have a mechanism to strengthen memory for dangers and the conditions under which the dangers occur? The answer is survival. An organism that remembers a past danger (through enhanced consolidation) can recognize a similar potential danger in the future, and respond accordingly. Similarly, the organism that remembers the context or stimuli that were associated with a past danger (through fear conditioning) will react to similar stimuli as if a danger is present again. In other words, the neutral stimuli that have been transformed into fear-conditioned stimuli now serve as predictors of potential danger. And, of course, the animal or person that can predict danger is likely to survive and pass on its genes.

Memory formation for dangerous events and associated fear-conditioned stimuli occurs quickly and tends to be very durable. In fact, these memories may last a lifetime. Joseph LeDoux, a pioneer in the neurobiology of fear, puts it this way,

> If an animal is lucky enough to survive one dangerous encounter, its brain should store as much about the experience as possible, and this learning should not decay over time, since a predator will always be a predator. In modern life, we sometimes suffer from the exquisite operation of this system, since it is difficult to get rid of this kind of conditioning once it is not longer applicable to our lives, and we become conditioned to fear things that are in fact harmless. Evolution's wisdom sometimes comes at a cost. (2002, p. 124)

Can we prevent or undo fear conditioning?

Once we live through a terrifying experience, does that mean that we will be haunted by fear-conditioned memories of the experience for the rest of our lives? Fortunately, no. The story of Al DeAngelis' skydiving trip provides an example of how "getting back on the horse" right away can alter memory consolidation.

On Memorial Day, in 1989, 26-year-old DeAngelis and several friends drove to a small airport in northwestern New Jersey for an afternoon of skydiving. None of them had ever been skydiving before, so to prepare for "static-line jumping" (parachuting without a partner), they had each trained for 4–6 hours to learn how to leap out of a plane, deploy a parachute, and land without injury.

When they arrived at the airport, they were surprised at the condition of their airplane. The exterior was patched together, and although it was built to carry 8–10 passengers, the interior had no seats. As Al put it, "It was no Cessna." However, nobody had promised them a luxury plane, so they began to joke and laugh about the V.I.P. accommodations as they assembled their gear. They boarded the plane along with the pilot and a jump master, sat on the floor, and waited for takeoff. However, despite numerous attempts, the engine failed to turn over. Finally the pilot called air traffic control and requested a jump start. "So they bring a truck to jump-start the plane … It was a big joke," Al recalls. "'Oh my God, they're going to jump-start our plane. I just can't wait to get out.' We were kidding around." Eventually, the engine started and the plane took off, but before it reached cruising altitude, an enormous explosion shook the plane. Within seconds, Al and his friends were covered with oil, and the cabin had filled with smoke.

> I couldn't even see the guy next to me or in front of me. As soon as this happened, the pilot screamed "Mayday!" He was trying to get control of the plane, but I guess the motor wasn't operating properly and it threw a rod; it actually blew a part of the motor out along with the hydraulics and electronics. … The jump master was totally panicked, screaming and running back and forth – that's why I remember it so vividly, because I thought of all the people in the plane, he is the one who is supposed to be the calmest.

When some of the smoke inside the cabin briefly cleared, Al could see the jump master opening the side door of the plane. Al remembers thinking, "I'm either going to burn to death or get thrown out of the plane." Somehow, in spite of the chaos and blinding smoke, the pilot, who had spent years flying large jets for a major airline, successfully landed the burning plane in a rural field. After what seemed like an eternity, the plane finally came to a stop and everyone, including the pilot, jumped out and took off running away from the wreckage.

> As soon as we got away from the plane, we didn't really say anything to each other; we were just standing around; we were scared. … The pilot had a pack of cigarettes – I guess he is a smoker, and I have never even had a cigarette in my life. I took one of his cigarettes. I smoked that thing probably in two breaths, I was so nervous. The pilot was so scared he couldn't light his cigarette, he was shaking so much. We all had bumps and bruises, but nobody was seriously hurt.

A police helicopter soon landed on the site, and fire trucks and ambulances arrived. After Al and his coworkers were medically evaluated by EMTs, they were offered an ambulance ride to the nearest hospital. But each of them refused; all they wanted was a ride back to the airport so they could get their cars and drive home.

> As we were driving back to the airport, I started getting really nervous, and I got nervous to the point where I started to shake a little bit. So we got to the airport, and I told my friends, "I am going up on the next flight." I said, "If I don't go up on this next plane, I am never going to get in an airplane again, let alone skydive again." They thought I was crazy.

When Al told the sky-diving company that he wanted to go up again in the next available plane, they were amazed but agreeable.

> When they began to put the parachute on me, I started to shake so much that my knees – like in a cartoon or in a movie – were quivering to the point where I couldn't stand. So I sat down on a table and they strapped the chute on me while my knees were shaking. I was trying not to. I did not want them to see it; I was wearing a jumpsuit, but I was shaking. … Then they gave us a few minutes, and I kind of got myself together so that I could stand up.
>
> As I was walking towards this airplane, which, again, looked a little shady, the new pilot jokingly said, "I heard you guys were in a crash. I don't think we'll get in another one." You know, kidding around, trying to ease my mind. … So

> I got on the plane, and as we started to taxi and take off, I am telling you, I could not wait to get out of that plane. I never felt so motivated in my life. I just wanted to get to the door and jump out. And sure enough, I did it, and when I landed, it was probably the greatest feeling that I have had in my entire life. I did it and got it out of the way.

Al DeAngelis went on to a successful career as a forensic detective in Monmouth County, New Jersey, where he has routinely faced danger and fear. He has worked in uniform and undercover, on narcotics squads and SWAT (Special Weapons And Tactics) teams. As a young man he learned one of the most important lessons in facing fear: when you're bucked off a horse – or a plane – get back on as soon as possible.

Why was Al DeAngelis able to leave his terrifying outing feeling good? Research shows that new memories remain unstable or malleable for a short period of time immediately after the event. During this unstable period, memories are being encoded and consolidated into long-term storage through a mechanism that involves the synthesis of proteins. In rats, this malleable period of memory consolidation may last no longer than an hour or two. In humans the period appears to be longer. If we intervene during this window of time when the new memory is "unstable," it may be possible to alter consolidation of the memory.

Our colleague, Roger Pitman at Harvard Medical School, conducted an experiment addressing this theory, extending the research by James McGaugh that we described earlier. In 2002, Pitman intervened with accident victims who came into an emergency room. Beginning within six hours after the trauma, these patients took either a placebo or the drug Propranolol for 10 days. Recall that Propranolol is known to block the increase of norepinephrine that naturally occcurs at and around the time of a traumatic event. Pitman and his colleagues hypothesized that taking Propranolol shortly after the trauma would interfere with consolidation, making the memory less emotionally arousing and upsetting in the future.

At an assessment three months later, the Propranolol-treated patients showed no difference in level of PTSD symptoms compared to patients who received a placebo; however, they did have significantly reduced physiological reactions (heart rate, skin conductance) upon listening to a recorded account of their own traumatic experience. These findings are encouraging for possible medical interventions in the future aimed at decreasing the potency of traumatic memories. However, it is important to note that studies using medication to decrease the intensity of traumatic memories are in their infancy; currently there are no medications approved by the Food and Drug Administration to alter emotionally arousing and fear-related memories.

As we saw in the story of Al DeAngelis, encoding and consolidation can be altered immediately after an event without the use of medication. But what happens if you don't get back on the horse right away? Does there come a time when it is too late? The answer appears to be no. Until recently it was believed that once a memory has been consolidated into long-term storage it remains essentially permanent. However, newer research suggests that every time a memory is retrieved, it once again becomes unstable for a brief period of time until it is re-consolidated. This unstable period provides another window of time during which the memory may be updated and transformed. Research in animals and more recently in humans holds promise for both pharmacologic (e.g. Propranolol) and behavioral (e.g. extinction training) interventions aimed at modifying fearful memories shortly after a trauma, or later, even years later, when fearful memories are retrieved and re-consolidated (Hartley & Phelps, 2010; Brunet *et al.*, 2008; Schiller *et al.*, 2010; Quirk *et al.*, 2010).

The neuroscience of extinction

The process of overcoming a learned fear is called extinction (LeDoux, 1996, 2002). It involves the brain structures that we discussed earlier (the amygdala, prefrontal cortex (PFC), hippocampus). To extinguish a fear-conditioned memory, one must be exposed to the fear-inducing stimulus in a safe environment, and this exposure needs to last long enough for the brain to form a new memory which conveys that the fear-conditioned stimulus is no longer dangerous in the present environment. Brain imaging findings suggest that extinction may involve a strengthening of the capacity of the PFC to inhibit amygdala-based fear responses (Phelps *et al.*, 2004).

Several approaches to treating anxiety disorders such as PTSD and phobias have been shown to be effective in promoting extinction. In essence, these therapies encourage the patient to confront the fear and anxiety head on. To understand why such treatments are effective, it is important to note that avoidance is a hallmark of anxiety disorders. Although it is natural for trauma survivors to avoid situations that remind them of the original trauma and that make them anxious, avoiding such situations prevents them from updating ot transforming their fear-based learning and memories. This is why many successful psychotherapies involve some form of confronting the fear.

One of these therapies, known as flooding or direct exposure therapy, requires prolonged exposure to the memory of the traumatic event. In her book *Stress and Trauma*, Patricia Resick (2001) describes the therapy as consisting of "extended exposure to moderate or strong fear-producing cues. In addition to confronting fear cues in imagination, flooding also involves confrontation with the conditioned fear cues *in vivo*" (p. 153). In the imagination component, patients are asked to recount the traumatic experience with eyes closed and in as much detail as possible, describing sights, sounds, smells, and sensations, as well as what they were thinking and feeling. These sessions are recorded and the client then listens to the recording repeatedly on subsequent days. In the in-vivo component, clients "gradually confront safe situations that evoke moderate levels of anxiety and then follow up with confrontations of more fearful situations" (p. 153).

Just as we saw earlier with the use of Propranolol to prevent the consolidation of fear-conditioned memories, researchers are also developing pharmacological methods designed to facilitate extinction of traumatic memories. Because extinction involves new learning, and the protein molecule known as the NMDA receptor is critical to learning, Barbara Rothbaum and colleagues at Emory University have combined the NMDA receptor partial agonist D-cycloserine (DCS) with exposure therapy. DCS is a drug that activates the NMDA receptor, which then enhances learning of the new memory. Rothbaum hypothesized that the combination of exposure therapy and DCS would speed up the process of extinction, and their findings supported this hypothesis: patients taking DCS showed significantly faster improvement, with fewer sessions than were necessary for subjects taking placebo.

A related treatment approach is eye movement desensitization and reprocessing therapy (EMDR). In EMDR, the patient is asked to remember the trauma in detail while visually tracking the therapist's finger as it moves back and forth (Resick, 2001). It was initially proposed that lateral eye movements would facilitate the mental processing of the trauma. However, studies by Roger Pitman and others suggest that exposure is the key therapeutic element and that the eye movement component may not be crucial.

Cognitive Processing Therapy (CPT) is another therapeutic technique that involves confronting fear. It uses the Socratic method of teaching, in which the teacher poses questions and the student, by answering them, learns new ways of understanding. Cognitive Processing Therapy focuses on emotions such as anger, humiliation, shame, guilt, and sadness, which trauma survivors often experience in addition to fear and anxiety. It is not uncommon for trauma victims to believe, for example, that they could have done something to prevent the incident or acted more heroically to minimize harm, even if in reality such actions would have been impossible. They tend to blame themselves and to imagine that others blame them as well. For example, a crime victim may have unrealistic beliefs such as, "I shouldn't have gone to the ATM that night." Using CPT, the therapist asks questions aimed at helping the patient to arrive at the more realistic conclusion that he or she could not have predicted that a robber would choose that particular ATM on that particular evening, and that the fault lies with the thief, not with the victim.

Another related technique involves helping trauma survivors understand when and why various fear-conditioned stimuli make them feel anxious and afraid in their current life. For example, as mentioned earlier, a trauma survivor may feel anxious at the same time every year but not understand why. By becoming aware that the brain unconsciously associates this time of year with a traumatic event that occurred during the same season or on the same day of the year in the past, the survivor is better able to anticipate current and future "anniversary reactions." They are better able to interpret and understand the origin of emotions that previously may have been confusing and sometimes overwhelming. Our friend John's experience with birdsong provides a good example. Once he became consciously aware of the connection between birdsong, nausea, and anxiety, he was better able to understand and anticipate this yearly reaction. John believes that this understanding has provided him with an increased sense of control because now when the birds return, he can remind himself that "this anxiety that I am feeling now is not related to anything that is happening to me in the present but instead to the circumstances of the past when I was worried about my cancer." Similarly, other cues associated with a trauma can be brought to consciousness – certain sights, sounds, odors, weather conditions. Emerging laboratory evidence has shown that becoming consciously aware of an unconscious fear-conditioned association may help to inhibit or reduce feelings of fear related to the conditioned cue (Jovanovic & Norrholm, 2011). It may be that with conscious awareness one can appraise the current situation as no longer dangerous, a process that is likely to facilitate prefrontal cortical inhibition of the amygdala.

However, you don't necessarily have to undergo therapy to transform or extinguish a fearful memory. The experience of our good friend Janine Solejar provides a relevant example. Solejar coped with longstanding fear when she literally got back on a horse after a long hiatus. She recalls:

> I was 14 and we had just gotten a horse for Christmas named Macy. One Sunday my sister brought Macy out in our driveway so the whole family could take turns riding. I had taken riding lessons for a few years, and had been told horses can tell if you're scared, but I always said I wasn't afraid of horses at all. I felt very confident as the older sister, so I decided to ride down the street instead of just staying in the yard.
>
> Apparently Macy saw this as a chance to escape – or maybe she was having a fear response of her own? Anyway, she took off at a trot, then a canter, and then a full-out gallop. I tried to pull the reins and yell "Whoa!" as I'd been taught, but it didn't work with Macy. She just kept running faster and faster. A car went by and spooked her even more. At that point I was totally panicked. Neighbors who saw it happen said the reins were flapping loose and I was yelling, "Oh, no! Oh, no!" Finally, after what seemed like forever, Macy lunged in a mud puddle and I fell off. Landing on the pavement felt like a great relief to me. A man who had been working in his yard ran over and asked if I was all right. I started reciting my name and address, like an automated·recording.
>
> That night we were watching TV and "Bonanza" came on. Someone jumped on a horse and started galloping away, and I started shrieking and put my hands over my eyes and had to get up and run out of the room, I had such an overwhelming feeling of panic seeing that man on the galloping horse. Of course I knew in my head that he was an actor and it was all just staged for TV, but at the gut level that didn't matter, I was sure he was going to fall off and I didn't want to have to watch. I was afraid of all horses after that.

Although Janine's traumatic experience lasted only a few minutes and didn't result in any permanent injury, she continued to fear horses and reminders of horses for several years. However, like Al DeAngelis, Janine Solejar found a way to confront her fear without medical intervention, but she didn't seek it out, and it didn't happen until several years after the mishap.

> When I was 17, I was visiting some friends, Ruth and Barbara, who had a horse named Danny that they assured me had always been very gentle and was now quite old and didn't even have any teeth anymore. They encouraged me to try riding again, saying they would lead Danny around by the reins. I was shaking so badly I had trouble mounting, and then I think I just sat there kind of frozen while Ruth and Barbara walked Danny around their garden for about 10 minutes.

> I was still pretty shaky when I got off, but after that I was OK around horses. I was
> even able to enjoy riding again. To this day, more than 40 years later, I still feel fear
> when I relive the memory of the runaway, but it doesn't paralyze me anymore.

Janine formed a new memory of riding a horse, a memory in which being on the horse was a safe experience. This new memory then successfully competed with the fearful memory of her earlier, traumatic experience.

Feeling fear is only human

Although in this chapter we emphasize the value of surmounting one's fears, at this juncture we do want to acknowledge that fear is inevitable; at times everyone feels afraid.

In a 2007 book, *In Extremis Leadership: Leading as if Your Life Depended On It*, Col. Thomas Kolditz, head of the Department of Behavioral Sciences and Leadership at the United States Military Academy at West Point, points out that fear is largely a chemical reaction. It's a natural bodily process, it doesn't signify weakness. Journalist Sebastian Junger came to understand overwhelming fear while embedded with US troops in Afghanistan. He is the author of books such as *War*, *A Death in Belmont*, and *The Perfect Storm*, and co-director of *Restrepo*, a documentary film about the Afghan war. He is known for his hands-on coverage of military combat, high-risk civilian occupations, and other life-threatening situations. Although Junger seems relatively compatible with high-stress situations, he nevertheless admits to moments of sheer terror, such as the time that he and a colleague, an Iranian-born photographer, were pinned down in a foxhole in Afghanistan as Taliban missiles pelted the surrounding hillside.

> There was nothing exciting about it, nothing even abstractly interesting. It
> was purely, exclusively bad. … No matter how small the odds were, the idea
> that I could go straight from life to nonexistence was almost unbearable. …
> Bravery – the usual alternative to fear – also held no appeal, because bravery
> could get you killed. It had become very simple: It was their war, their problem,
> and I didn't want any part of it. I just wanted off the hill. (2001, pp. 207–208)

Eventually Junger and the photographer got their wish to get "off the hill." It came in the form of a order to abandon their position and run for their lives. As they ran, Junger recalls,

> Mainly there was the sound of my breathing: a deep, desperate rasp that ruled
> out any chance of hearing the rockets come in. … Ten minutes later it was over:
> we sat behind the next ridge and watched Taliban rockets continue to pound
> the hill, each one raising a little puff of smoke, followed by a muffled explosion.
> From that distance they didn't look like much; they almost looked like the kind
> of explosions you could imagine yourself acting bravely in. (2001, p. 208)

Don't let fear hang around for too long

As Junger notes, his experience of intense fear was fleeting. But what happens to a person when fear persists for long periods of time? Imagine yourself as a soldier in combat, exposed to one danger after another, day after day, for months or even years. Or suppose you are a woman in an abusive marriage. Because of your life circumstances, you live with fear day in and day out. In such circumstances, chronic stress and fear can wear you down mentally and physically. As the Canadian endocrinologist Hans Selye described some 50 years ago, repeated exposure to such threats will eventually lead to exhaustion. Chronic fear is counterproductive.

When fear, stress, or hypervigilance continue unabated for a long period of time, the effects can be serious. In a patient information article entitled "Stress and Your Health," Bruce McEwen and Robert Sapolsky (2006) describe the symptoms that can occur with chronic stress:

- stomach upsets and diarrhea,
- overeating,
- weakening of the immune system,
- insomnia,
- decreased interest in physical activity,
- decreased sex drive,
- anxiety and depression.

Through its tendency to increase blood pressure, heart rate, cholesterol and triglycerides, blood sugar, and appetite, chronic stress can even lead to an increased risk of heart disease.

Recent evidence (Arnsten, 2009) suggests that prolonged stress can damage the PFC and the hippocampus. Damage to either of these brain areas can make it more difficult to shut off the fear response (Lang *et al.*, 2009), and leaves the person feeling anxious and afraid much of the time. Thus, while fear can benefit us in the short run, unabated fear can harm us.

Practical applications: learning to face fear

In order for soldiers in the Special Forces to accomplish their missions and avoid the negative consequences of prolonged stress, learning to face fear is essential. Tim Cooper, Gordon Smith, and Mark Hickey, instructors in the Special Forces SERE School, believe that we can all learn to face our fears by using a number of tested techniques. Some of these techniques focus on thinking, while others focus on behaviors. Even if you have no plans to join the military, these techniques will be useful when facing your own fears or perhaps recovering from a traumatic experience.

View fear as a guide

For Sergeants Cooper, Smith, and Hickey, to master fear one must first accept it, even welcome it. Rather than appraising fear as something to avoid, these men have trained soldiers to view fear as normal, as a guide and even as an opportunity to grow. When afraid, they focus on their goal or mission,

Fear is normal. You try to tell the student that throughout life, you'll experience fear in some form or fashion; but the difference between that and panic is control. You let your fear guide you. You respect it. I mean, I got bit by a snake, a copperhead. OK, not a smart move, but I'm not going to panic because that's just going to make the symptoms worse.

From a neuroscience perspective, under normal non-stressful conditions, moderate levels of catecholamines such as norepinephrine enhance functioning of the prefrontal cortex. However, when brain catecholamine levels rise too high, they tend to take the PFC "off-line," meaning that the PFC no longer adequately inhibits the amygdala. At that point the fight–flight response predominates and the individual may panic and become impulsive.

Cooper intuitively understands the difference between fear and panic.

You can control fear. I can almost even use it for my benefit. But with panic, I can't control it. And if I let fear get so big that it turns into panic, then that's when it immobilizes me, keeps me from doing what I need to do.

When Cooper notes that fear can "almost be your friend," he is pointing out that moderate levels of fear (and moderate levels of catecholamines) may actually sharpen focus and decision-making. And when he cautions against letting fear "get so big that it turns into panic," he means that panic (excessively high levels of catecholamines) can dramatically compromise prefrontal cortical functioning and rational decision-making. During combat, soldiers sometimes refer to this compromised cognitive state as "the fog of war," which means stress-related loss of mental clarity and rational decision-making.

View fear as an opportunity

In addition to viewing fear as a helpful warning and guide, medic and SF instructor Mark Hickey believes that fear is good because it keeps him on his toes and serves as a platform for developing courage, self-esteem, and a sense of mastery. When Hickey experiences fear, he often thinks, "I'm scared, but I can learn from this," or "This is a test that's going to make me stronger." During dangerous missions or training exercises, he feels "apprehension and excitement mixed with fear," and as he puts it,

I think that fear is good because it keeps you sharp. They say when you don't become afraid at all, that's when mistakes start happening, when you take things for granted. When you still have that little bit of fear, you recheck your equipment. You make sure things are as they should be.

Indeed, a certain amount of fear is adaptive.

Focus on the goal or mission

When a person faces fear, excessive focusing on potential negative or catastrophic scenarios can be harmful because precious time and resources are wasted fretting about the unknown. Instead, SF instructors teach soldiers to focus on goals and on the mission of the group when they are grappling with fear.

Cooper recommends that soldiers ask themselves,

> What are my goals? What is my mission? What is the mission of my group? In order to meet my goals and accomplish my mission, I know that I must make a choice: either back down and fail, or face this fear and forge ahead. It's that simple.

When Cooper advises a frightened trainee who is about to make his first night parachute jump from 20,000 feet, he tells the trainee to concentrate on his or her own personal goals and remember that he or she is part of a team with a shared mission:

> Look, I need you out there right now. You need to be helping me, I need you involved in this. Don't worry about it, dude, I'm afraid too. This is an unnatural act for humans; otherwise we'd all be flying to work, we'd all be flying home. Bottom line is: I understand your nervousness … But you have to think, there's a bigger task, there's a bigger goal and it's bigger than you and it's bigger than me. We have to go out and get a job done. And I need you as a part of this, so, come on – let's you and I go ahead and knock this out.

The SF instructors we interviewed also recommend a number of behaviors that they have found helpful in dealing with fear. These include acquiring as much information as possible about what is feared, learning and practicing the skills necessary to face the fear, developing a plan and a back-up plan, confronting fear in the company of a friend or colleague or spiritual presence whenever possible, and taking a calculated leap of faith.

Acquire information about what is feared

The former Navy pilot and Vietnam POW Al Carpenter observes that fear is often associated with the unknown:

> A big part of true fear is the fear of the unknown, when you don't know what's gonna happen to you. You can't anticipate, but you think it's gonna be horrible. But most of the scenarios that we, as combat pilots, might face, we have already learned about from other people [instructors and colleagues], from our own experiences, or whatever. So we were prepared.

Becoming a successful member of a fighter pilot squadron or an SF team requires seemingly endless didactic classroom work addressing a wide array of topics, which is necessary for optimal performance during complex, challenging, and often dangerous missions. The goal is to expose soldiers to as many potential mission scenarios as possible so that they won't be surprised or overwhelmed by the unknown. The military believes that knowledge is power. To master fear successfully, first learn as much as possible about what is feared.

Learn and practice the skills necessary to master the fear

In addition to acquiring information about what is feared, it is important to learn and practice the skills that are needed to master the fear. Whenever possible, those skills should be practiced repetitively until they become automatic or second nature, what psychologists call achieving automaticity.

West Point instructor Col. Thomas Kolditz advises,

> Of all the autonomic responses to the adrenalin rush – including heart rate, respiration, skin conductivity, and muscle tension – the one that we can best control consciously is respiration. Deep, controlled breathing is largely incompatible with the other elements of the fear response. Physical relaxation can get you to the point where mental relaxation, and therefore outward focus, can be re-established and maintained. (2007, p. 122)

When we asked former POW pilots about how they felt while ejecting from fighter jets that had burst into flames while traveling hundreds of miles per hour, we were surprised that many of them did not recall feeling afraid. Instead, they remember responding almost "automatically" to a checklist of skills they had mastered during countless hours of training, where they had practiced mock ejection scenarios so many times that an actual real-life ejection required little thought. Lt. Al Carpenter describes his ejection over North Vietnam:

> It was the back end of the aircraft that was ablaze. I really needed to take care of myself, get out of there. … So I started climbing very rapidly. I was at full power, still on fire. My intention was to climb to about 9000 feet, shut the engine down purposely, hope that the fire would go out, and try to get a re-light and possibly I could get back to the ship.
>
> Well, that was a pretty optimistic approach. But it was the only game in town at that point. On my way to 9000 feet, passing about 5500 feet, the airplane lurched … I lost my oxygen. I lost all my electrical power. I deployed my emergency generator and I got electrical power back and then I lost it again, and then basically all I had were pressure instruments. Nothing else was working. The control stick went full forward and right. My right rudder pedal slammed full forward. The plane lurched sideways and started to roll right. What had happened really is that the tail burned off, and it started to turn and that caused me to start a slow rudder roll. Well, I was headed up and I was climbing at a pretty good rate. … The aircraft continued to roll all the way to inverted.
>
> And there's something about most aviators, we just really don't want to eject inverted, 'cause you have visions of becoming a lawn dart. I had already stowed all the stuff, with my kneeboard, my flashlight, and anything that might hurt me on the way out. I waited for the airplane to become upright. I looked down at the airspeed just before I punched out: it was at 550 knots and climbing very rapidly. I'd already ejected a couple of months before that, in August, back at the ship at 200 knots, and that was a nice, calm deliberate ejection. No problem.
>
> But this one was just incredibly violent. Incredibly violent. When the canopy went off, the noise outside was just incredible. It was like lying on train tracks with a freight train going over you. … And as the seat fired and I went up the rails, I could feel this knife edge come down across me, which was the air blast on my body. You know how fast these things are happening. And still the mind becomes so acutely aware, you just compress everything and get it in slow-motion.

Then your training kicks in and you determine what you're going to do next. Well, I was now floating in the chute. I opened my eyes to assess the situation and my first reaction was, I lost my vision. It was totally black. I knew that my eyes were open, but I had absolutely no vision whatsoever. And in the race that your mind goes through trying to make sense out of all of this, I first thought, well, maybe my optic nerves have been severed. How would that happen? Who knows? And then the next thought was, well, maybe I've lost my face 'cause the pain was so incredible all over, I had no idea what might be damaged.

So I thought, well, I have to survive so we'll just go on. And the first thing you do after you eject from a jet like that is reach up and get rid of your oxygen mask. So I reached up with both hands but felt incredible pain in one shoulder. Finally, I hit something that was very hard and smooth and felt like it was wet.

Yup. I've wiped off my face. But for some reason, I went around to the side, I guess to see if I still had ears or something, and here's my oxygen mask. Boy, that was a good feeling. I grabbed the ear piece of my helmet, and I pulled it around and, bingo, I could see. It was like the Wizard of Oz, you know, everything becomes Technicolor for Dorothy. But that was one of the best feelings of my life. So then I knew why I couldn't see. My eyes had been encased in the helmet ear piece.

For most people, such a situation would evoke paralyzing fear, but not for Carpenter. When asked if he felt afraid or terrified, he replied,

Not really, I was just taking care of business. ... Now, I know that sounds like an oversimplification, but it's the absolute truth. ... You don't get fearful. You get tense. You tighten up. And all your senses are alert and you're aware that you need to do your best job. And it's not that you're not afraid, but you're not overcome with fear. We had trained a great deal. ... you just do it. How conscious are you driving down the road of every movement that you make? You're not, because that's training through experience. It's that kind of a thing.

Face fear with friends or colleagues

Most people find it easier to face fear when they are accompanied by other people, particularly those whom they know and trust. (We will discuss this concept of social support in greater depth in Chapter 6.) Confronting fear with others tends to help in a variety of ways. It may increase our ability to make a realistic appraisal of the feared situation. It may also reduce physiological stress responses, such as elevated heart rate and blood pressure, hyperventilation, and stomach "butterflies." With supportive friends or colleagues by their side, people tend to feel more confident and are better able to cope with problems by finding constructive solutions rather than by avoidance. It is much easier to jump out of a plane, rappel down the face of a cliff, go to the hospital for a cancer biopsy, begin the first day of college, or challenge political injustice when you are doing it with a colleague, friend, or a loved one.

Face fear with spiritual support

Religious or spiritual support can also provide the perspective and strength needed to face one's fears. (We will discuss the power of spirituality further in Chapter 5.) For General Hugh Shelton, fear is no match for God.

> If you're getting ready to do something really dangerous, like jump out of an airplane at 30,000 feet in the middle of the night, having a strong faith in God is very important. When the bullets are flying, if you're scared to death that you are going to die because you're worried about what comes after life on this Earth, I think that takes away from your confidence. I was always confident that God was by my side: he was there when I went out of the airplane; he was there when the bullets were flying. It bothered my wife that I was never afraid of dying. Do I want to die? No, but I wasn't worried about it. I was worried about the people on the left and right and the people I was entrusted to care for, but not about myself.

Elizabeth, a social worker who was kidnapped, raped, and thrown off a bridge, also uses spiritual insight to fight fear. She has mastered this technique.

> I see fear as energy. I try to come into the body and feel where it is lodged, and breathe into it and allow it to flow. If it is not moving, I turn to my spiritual practices, which include chanting, meditation, body movement and yoga, to help the stuck energy move. Once it is moving, the essential self underneath – the inner spirit – is more accessible and the fear has no more power over me. Making the decision to turn and face my fear rather than repress or run from it is half the battle. I believe we all have the capacity to do this; however, we need to know that we have the choice.

While Elizabeth is not a Buddhist, her approach resembles the Buddhist practice of mindfulness in which emotions and fear are faced head on. Mindfulness involves observing one's thoughts and emotions without judging them. In his book *Mindfulness in Plain English*, the Buddhist monk Bhante H. Gunaratana (2002) notes that mindfulness and meditation require attention to reality and resemble Elizabeth's practice of going toward the fear. Gunaratana writes:

> Meditation is running straight into reality. It does not insulate you from the pain of life but rather allows you to delve so deeply into life and all its aspects that you pierce the pain barrier and go beyond suffering. …
> In order to observe our fear, we must accept the fact that we are afraid. We can't examine our own depression without accepting it fully. The same is true for irritation and agitation, frustration and all those other uncomfortable emotional states. You can't examine something fully if you are busy rejecting its existence. (pp. 25, 139)

To deal with fear, Gunaratana writes,

> Observe the fear exactly as it is. Don't cling to it. Just watch it rising and growing. Study its effect. See how it makes you feel and how it affects your body. When you find yourself in the grip of horror fantasies, simply observe those mindfully. Watch the pictures as pictures. See memories as memories. Observe the emotional reactions that come along and know them for what they are. Don't try to repress the memories or the feelings or the fantasies. Just step out of the way and let the whole mess bubble up and flow past. It can't hurt you. It is just a memory. It is only a fantasy. It is nothing but fear. (p. 108)

Thich Nhat Hanh, the Vietnamese Buddhist monk who was nominated for the Nobel Peace Prize in 1970 for his role in the Paris Peace Talks, recognizes that all of us are afraid. "Fear is always there within us: the fear of getting old, the fear of getting sick, the fear of dying, the fear of being abandoned by our loved ones. It is very human to be fearful and to worry about it" (Hanh, 2003, p. 148).

However, he also understands that hiding from fear is not the answer.

> If you try to run away, instead of confronting or embracing your ill-being, you will not look deeply into its nature and will never have the chance to see a way out. That is why you should hold your suffering tenderly and closely, looking directly into it, to discover its true nature and find a way out. (Hanh, 2000, p. 84)

> The Buddha advised us to invite these fears to the upper level of our consciousness, recognize them and smile at them. To do so was the daily practice for monks and nuns in the time of the Buddha, as it is for monks and nuns now. Every time your fear is invited up, every time you recognize it and smile at it, your fear will lose some of its strength. When it returns to the depth of your consciousness, it returns as a smaller seed. That is why the practice should be done every day, especially when you are feeling mentally and physically strong. (Hanh, 2003, p. 148)

Get someone or an organization to push you

But facing fear is never easy, even with the help of friends or colleagues. As a result, organizations that specialize in overcoming fear, such as the military, have developed a host of methods to "coax" or "encourage" their members. Tim Cooper says that Special Forces training is designed to overcome fear.

> Just about every course will have something that bothers somebody at some time. And they'll try to push you through that. They'll be screaming, yelling in your face ... calling you all types of names and talking about your mom ... basically trying to physically push you over the wall, without touching you. They don't give you any space to retreat. It's all designed to get you to force yourself past the fear. Then once you go through it, they'll congratulate you and pat you on the back and tell you, "Good boy." And once you go over the edge and you're doing fine, you look back and say, "You know, it wasn't a problem."

Special Forces instructor Mark Hickey has a similar approach: "I can say from my own experience that after you do one thing and conquer it, the next thing is a little bit easier, whereas if you let the first one knock you out, it's going to be even harder to try to overcome the next one."

Just as the military designs its training to strengthen members and foster growth by pushing its members beyond their current level of comfort, numerous civilian organizations do the same. Examples include Outward Bound Wilderness Expeditions, police and fire academy training, high school and college athletic teams, and intensive educational programs (e.g. law school, medical school).

Fear is ubiquitous. No one escapes its grip. But what is the best way to deal with it? The bottom line: the best way around fear is through it. To conquer fear one must face fear. That's what resilient people do.

References

Arnsten, A. F. T. (2009). Stress signaling pathways that impair prefrontal cortex structure and function. *Nature*, **10**, 410–422.

Brunet, A., Orr, S. P., Tremblay, J., Robertson, K., Nader, K., & Pitman, R. K. (2008). Effect of post-retrieval propranolol on psychophysiologic responding during subsequent script-driven traumatic imagery in post-traumatic stress disorder. *Journal of Psychiatric Research*, **42**(6), 503–506. Epub 2007 Jun 22.

Cahill, L., Prins, B., Weber, M., & McGaugh, J. L. (1994). β-Adrenergic activation and memory for emotional events. *Nature*, **371**, 702–704.

Gunaratana, B. H. (2002). *Mindfulness in plain English*, expanded and updated edition. Somerville, MA: Wisdom Publications.

Hanh, T. N. (2000). *The path of emancipation: Talks from a 21-day mindfulness retreat*. Berkeley, CA: Parallax Press.

Hanh, T. N. (2003). *No death, no fear: Comforting wisdom for life*. New York, NY: Riverhead Trade.

Hartley, C. A., & Phelps, E. A. (2010). Changing fear: The neurocircuitry of emotion regulation. *Neuropsychopharmacology*, **35**(1), 136–146.

Jovanovic, T., & Norrholm, S. D. (2011). Neural mechanisms of impaired fear inhibition in posttraumatic stress disorder. *Frontiers in Behavioral Neuroscience*, **5**, 1–8.

Junger, S. (2001). The lion in winter. In *Fire*. New York, NY: W. W. Norton.

Kolditz, T. A. (2007). *In extremis leadership: Leading as if your life depended on it*. Hoboken, NJ: John Wiley & Sons.

Lang, S., Kroll, A., Lipinski, S. J., Wessa, M., Ridder, S., Christmann, C., *et al.* (2009). Context conditioning and extinction in humans: Differential contribution of the hippocampus, amygdala and prefrontal cortex. *European Journal of Neuroscience*, **29**(4), 823–832.

LeDoux, J. E. (1996). *The emotional brain*. New York, NY. Simon and Schuster

LeDoux, J. E. (2002). *Synaptic self: How our brains become who we are*. New York, NY: Viking.

Mandela, N. (1995). *The long walk to freedom*. New York, NY: Back Bay Books.

McEwen, B. & Sapolsky, R. (2006). Stress and your health. *Journal of Clinical Endocrinology & Metabolism*, **91**.

McGaugh, J. L. (2000). Memory: A century of consolidation. *Science*, **287**, 248–251.

Phelps, E. A., Delgado, M. R., Nearing, K. I., & LeDoux, J. E. (2004). Extinction learning in humans: Role of the amygdala and vmPFC. *Neuron*, **43**, 897–905.

Quirk, G. J., Pare, D., Richardson, R., Herry, C., Monfils, M. H., Schiller, D., *et al.* (2010). Erasing fear memories with extinction training. *Journal of Neuroscience*, **30**(45), 14 993–14 997.

Resick, P. A. (2001). *Stress and trauma*. Hove: Psychology Press Ltd.

Schiller, D., Monfils, M.-H., Ledoux, J. E., Phelps, E. A., Raio, C. M., & Johnson, D. C. (2010). Preventing the return of fear in humans using reconsolidation update mechanisms. *Nature*, **463**(7277), 49–53.

Southwick, S. M., Davis, M., Horner, B., Cahill, L., Morgan, C.A., Gold, P.E., *et al.* (2002). Relationship of enhanced norepinephrine activity during memory consolidation to enhanced long-term memory in humans. *American Journal of Psychiatry*, **159**, 1420–1422.

Moral compass, ethics, and altruism: doing what is right

In an age of moral relativism, situational ethics, and social Darwinism, it may seem irrelevant to talk about "moral compass." Some believe that over the past century, psychology, with its focus on the unconscious, has transformed what once were moral judgments into non-judgmental assessments of behavior, sometimes to the point where individuals are absolved of personal responsibility for the choices they make. However, concerns about the loss of moral responsibility are not new. Throughout history social critics have decried the decay in moral values, especially among members of the young generation.

Is the moral climate in today's society really worse than that of our parents' or grandparents'? Perhaps. In her book *A Better Man*, author Kelly H. Johnson argues that "in addition to the perennial trials of peer pressure, hormones and popularity, young men must now grapple with a media-saturated culture that places enormous emphasis on physical appeal, material wealth and celebrity status" (Johnson, 2009). Power, money, sex, and violence are glorified while values such as courage, integrity, and kindness are often ignored. Former Secretary of Education William Bennett made headlines by publishing books entitled *The Book of Virtues* and *Moral Compass* because they stood out as some of the only contemporary resources for parents, educators, and others wishing to instill moral values in today's youth.

In our interviews, we found that many resilient individuals possessed a keen sense of right and wrong that strengthened them during periods of extreme stress and afterward, as they adjusted to life following trauma. Also altruism – selflessness, concern for the welfare of others, and giving to others with no expectation of benefit to the self – often stood as a pillar of their value system, of their "moral compass."

Morality and ethics are complex topics; they have been debated and expounded upon over the centuries by many esteemed philosophers and religious leaders. We are certainly not proposing to compete with such authorities. However, we have found that many resilient individuals articulate a core set of moral principles and strive to adhere to them. In this chapter we argue that actively identifying your core values, assessing the degree to which you are living by these values, and challenging yourself to adopt a higher standard can strengthen character and build resilience.

Epictetus at the Hanoi Hilton

James Bond Stockdale, the independent candidate for Vice President of the United States in 1992, was a highly decorated veteran; he received two Distinguished Flying

Crosses, three Distinguished Service Medals, two Purple Hearts, and the Congressional Medal of Honor. He was also president of the Naval War College, a senior fellow of the Hoover Institute, and the holder of eight honorary degrees. Midway through his naval career, in the spring of 1960, Stockdale received orders to enroll in a master's degree program in International Relations at Stanford University. There he took a philosophy course called "The Nature of Good and Evil" with readings that included works by Plato, Aristotle, Socrates, Koestler, and Dostoevsky. Stockdale's professor was a military veteran himself, and on the last day of the course he gave Stockdale a gift: a copy of *Enchiridion*, a manual for the combat officer written in AD 50 by the Greek philosopher Epictetus. The professor explained to Stockdale, "I think you might find this useful."

Epictetus, the son of a Roman slave, was sold into slavery himself at age 15. According to legend, after being chained, beaten, and crippled for life, he was sold to a man who would later murder the Roman emperor. Over the next 10 years, Epictetus served as an apprentice to the best Stoic teacher in the empire and eventually gained his freedom, becoming a highly respected and well-known philosopher.

Stockdale was puzzled by the parting gift and wondered how the teachings of a classical stoic philosopher could apply to his life as a fighter pilot. But trusting in the wisdom of his professor, he kept the copy of *Enchiridion* by his bedside at each of his duty stations, on every ship he sailed. He read and reread it, studying it and trying to practice its messages about the importance of discipline, self-control, endurance and perseverance, virtue and moral character, courage, toughness tempered by compassion, pursuit of one's goals, attempts to be the very best, and dignity in the face of deprivation and suffering. However, Stockdale did not fully appreciate its value until September 9, 1965. On that day his plane was shot down over Vietnam.

Parachuting from his crippled fighter jet, Stockdale struck the ground with enough force to fracture a bone in his back and severely damage his leg. Still, even though he could not stand on his injured leg for years, he drew strength and inspiration from the words of Epictetus: "Lameness is an impediment to the body but not to the will." According to Epictetus, one can never be the victim of another – only the "victim" of himself.

> When I ejected from that airplane in 1965, I left my world of technology and entered into the world of Epictetus. I was alone and crippled; self-reliance was the basis for daily life. The system of values I carried with me into this realm was to be tested by my captors. The payoff was my self-respect. I would keep it or it would be torn from me and used as leverage against my senses of purpose and stability. (Stockdale, 1984, p. 4)

For the first four years as a prisoner, Stockdale lived in solitary confinement because the North Vietnamese knew that he was a commanding officer and they wanted to prevent him from giving orders to the other prisoners in the Hanoi Hilton. Stockdale was rarely isolated, however, because he shared walls with other American POWs and communicated using the tap code, a system in which prisoners tapped messages to one another on prison walls.

As the senior ranking officer at the Hanoi Hilton, Stockdale knew that it was his duty to retain command over his fellow POWs and to provide them with leadership, direction, inspiration and military orders. For guidance, he initially turned to the Military Code of Conduct, which states that the American chain of command will remain in effect for those who are captured or imprisoned; that captured soldiers will divulge only name, rank, serial number, and date of birth; that they will resist by all means available; and that they will make every effort to escape.

Some POWs supported adherence to a strict interpretation of the Code of Conduct, advocating death before giving up classified information. Stockdale did so as well until he was forced to face reality. In the fall of 1965, the North Vietnamese first began to use torture during their interrogations of American prisoners. In late October of that year, Stockdale received detailed descriptions of North Vietnamese brutality from Lt. Rod Knutson, the first fellow POW to be tortured in North Vietnam.

Like Stockdale, Knutson had strong beliefs about moral behavior, but instead of Epictetus, he cited his father as a key source of those beliefs.

> I grew up in Billings, Montana. In third grade a friend of mine and I stole mail from a neighbor's mailbox and threw it into a fish pond. We didn't know there was a check inside one of the envelopes. Later that day, my father confronted me. He picked me up under my armpits, set me on the kitchen counter, and planted his big old palms on either side of my hips. He got his nose about six inches from my face and said, "I'm going to stop right here and look you in the eye and see if you can earn my trust and confidence. And if you tell me the truth, it will be different than if I just punish you. I want you to tell me what you did with Mrs. Chase's mail and what you did with her check."
>
> So after a long wait during which he didn't blink or move, I finally said, "Yeah, I took it and I tore it up and we threw it in the fish pond." He looked at me for a minute, and then, after putting his arms around me, thanked me for telling the truth. Then, he jerked me off the counter and marched me across the street to Mrs. Chase. I had to apologize and volunteer to clean her fish pond for the next five years.
>
> Anyway, while I was in prison, a Vietnamese interrogator would be right there, nose to nose with me, asking me questions, saying I had to answer. And my old dad was standing right there, too. ...
>
> By the time they got me to Hanoi, to the Hoa Lo Prison, I was in pretty bad shape, pretty beat up. I couldn't get out of the truck when they untied me. They pulled me out, just threw me like a sack of beans on the pavement, and then picked me up and dragged me inside and put me in an interrogation room. When I wouldn't answer any questions beyond name, rank, serial number, and date of birth, a guard stationed behind me took a rifle butt and smacked it into the side of my head. I was knocked off my chair, and I went sprawling across the floor. After the interrogation, they put me in a cell about the size of a table. On either side was a concrete pallet about 18 inches wide. At the foot of the concrete pallet, there was a set of leg stocks built into the concrete, two little shallow cut-out areas and a steel bar that swung over the top and locked.

The cell was filthy. I can't even describe how filthy it was. It had a toilet bucket that was rusted, full of feces and urine and flies. A rat was in the cell, trying to carry off a crust of bread. I called outside my cell door to see if there were any other POWs, and a guard came and smashed me in the face – I wasn't allowed to make any noise.

The next morning, a guard came to the cell with eleven questions on a sheet of paper. He jammed the pen in my hand and pointed to the paper. I just shook my head at him and said, "No, I'm not going to do that." He roughed me up and handed me the paper again. This time I said, "You want me to sign this? You want me to sign this? OK, I'll sign it!" I rammed the pen through the paper and tossed it aside. That sounds very John Wayne, but it led to a torture session that lasted five days.

They beat me with fists and a club, until my backside was just hamburger. Blood was splattering everywhere. They tied my arms behind my back, which is one of their favorite torture tricks. They use thin line and tie it into your muscle, cutting off all circulation to your lower arms. Your hands puff up like a rubber glove that's been blown into a balloon. They never let me up to go to the bathroom, so I was lying in my own bodily fluids. When they did finally let me up, well, I couldn't get the flight suit off, and I couldn't stand up or sit down. A thick scab, which had previously been my rear end, had attached itself to my flight suit, and everything was welded together.

Knutson withstood nearly 16 consecutive days of brutal torture, but ultimately he felt profound despair over having told the North Vietnamese more than the "basic four": name, rank, serial number, and date of birth. Although Knutson fabricated facts about his family and background, he nevertheless felt devastated and guilt-ridden over having "broken."

When some prisoners heard that Knutson had "broken," they thought he was weak. Stockdale, however, understood that Knutson's torture signaled a frightening change in how the North Vietnamese were to treat American POWs and he also recognized that other prisoners did not really understand the horrific nature of Knutson's ordeal.

Now, Stockdale faced a major dilemma that was to preoccupy him for the remainder of his prison term. The Military Code of Conduct was clear, and as a Navy officer, Stockdale was bound by military law to uphold the Code and to order his men to obey it. But after hearing about Knutson's torture, Stockdale now knew that the Code would be impossible to follow; every POW, no matter how tough or determined, had his breaking point and under torture would eventually provide more information than the "basic four." As the senior ranking officer, what guidelines should he provide his fellow POWs? How should he advise them to deal with torture? Stockdale turned to Epictetus and Stoicism.

Stoic philosophy is largely focused on personal control, reducing vulnerability, and living by a set of time-honored standards that promote dignity, even under the harshest of conditions. At the core of personal control is the ability to differentiate that which is within your control from that which is beyond it. Stockdale put it this way:

> … a Stoic always keeps separate files in his mind for (A) those things that are "up to him" and (B) those things that are "not up to him." Another way of saying it is (A) those things that are "within his power" and (B) those things that are "beyond his power." Still another way of saying it is (A) those things that are within the grasp of "his Will, his Free Will" and (B) those things that are beyond it. … In short, what the Stoics say is "Work with what you have control of and you'll have your hands full." (Stockdale, 1995, p. 190)

For Stockdale, "station in life" generally belongs in category B because often we have little or no control over it. One moment, Stockdale recalls, he was "on top," the admired commander of over 1000 men and over 100 pilots, "confident" and "self-satisfied," a man who thought he had "found every key to success," but within minutes of being shot down he became "an object of contempt" and a "criminal" in the eyes of the North Vietnamese. In a matter of minutes, your station in life "can be changed from that of a dignified and competent gentleman of culture to that of a panic-stricken, sobbing, self-loathing wreck …" (Stockdale, 1995, p. 228).

Stockdale knew this firsthand because he too had been tortured. As a senior officer and vocal resister, Stockdale was regularly singled out for interrogations. Over the course of his four years of solitary, Stockdale was brutally interrogated on 15 occasions, and at times was forced to provide information. He recounts in his book *In Love and War* (Stockdale & Stockdale, 1990) that after one extended round of torture he became so depressed that he attempted suicide by cutting his wrists with a shard of broken glass.

His own experience with torture taught Stockdale to avoid creating unrealistic expectations and standards that could never be met. When prisoners fell short of their own expectations, Stockdale offered support, compassion, and forgiveness. Even when a POW resisted admirably and provided only information that was useless or of relatively little value, he typically felt ashamed, believing that he had betrayed himself, his fellow prisoners, and his country. For example, Admiral Robert Shumaker remembers the first time he divulged any information to the North Vietnamese. After relentless torture, Shumaker could hold out no longer.

> My first experience [with divulging information] was just crushing – tears and sobbing. Not so much from the physical abuse, but from the realization that you hadn't lived up to your own expectations and the military's expectations of you. And I guess somewhere along the line you learn to become street smart and you learn to lie and you remember your lies and it's just kind of a departure from the American and George Washington dream of always telling the truth. (Stockdale, 1995, p. 187)

Stockdale knew that the suffering arising from starvation, harsh living conditions and physical pain paled in comparison with the agony of shame. He wrote that "a shoulder broken, a bone in my back broken, a leg broken twice were peanuts by comparison ... Shame is heavy, a heavier burden than any physical wounds ... the thing that brings down a man is not pain but shame" (Stockdale, 1995, p. 199).

In terms of the categories "A" (what is up to you) and "B" (what is not up to you), Stockdale recognized that the torture endured by Rod Knutson, Bob Shumaker, and so many others belonged in category B, because it was not up to them, not within their power and not within the grasp of their free will. However, according to Stoic philosophy, each man did bear responsibility for those things that were within his power and the grasp of his free will. In her book *Stoic Warriors: The Ancient Philosophy Behind the Military Mind*, Nancy Sherman, a Professor at Georgetown University and the inaugural holder of the Distinguished Chair in Ethics at the United States Naval Academy, discusses this Stoic imperative.

> We are to continue to meet challenges, take risks and stretch the limits of our mastery. We are to continue to strive to the best of our efforts to achieve our ends. We are to push our agency to the limit. In this case, the message is one of empowerment. But at the same time, we are to cultivate greater strength and equanimity in the face of what we can't change. We must learn where our mastery begins, but also where it ends. (Sherman, 2005, p. 3)

Stockdale thought deeply about how best to advise his fellow prisoners. Debates over how to interpret the Code and how to deal with torture became a regular and at times heated topic on those occasions when prisoners were able to communicate with one another. With Epictetus as his guide, Stockdale carefully weighed opposing viewpoints and gradually developed a set of rules that incorporated many of the basic values of Stoicism. Stockdale knew that "a structured set of values supporting a basic tenet of self-respect was fundamental to the performance of these men," and his goal was to make certain that the men "returned home with their heads held high" (Stockdale, 1984, p. 4).

Stockdale developed a set of rules that formed the acronym BACK US: B stood for bowing. Prisoners should never voluntarily bow in public. Refusing to do so would show the world that American prisoners had not been defeated, and if prisoners were visibly forced to bow by the North Vietnamese, any observer would see that US prisoners were being mistreated according to the Geneva Conventions. A – air. Stay off the air, refuse radio interviews and tape-recorded messages or confessions. C – crime. Never use the word "crime" and never admit to having committed a crime against the North Vietnamese people. K – don't kiss 'em goodbye when we eventually get released. Never give the impression that the North Vietnamese were civilized in their treatment of prisoners and never show gratitude for any treatment by the North Vietnamese, even if granted early release from prison for medical reasons. US – Unity over self.

Although the BACK US code was composed of specific rules, the rules took into account the reality of prison life. This is what Stockdale expected – for his men to resist to the best of their physical and moral capacity, to endure torture before divulging information, to tell their fellow prisoners how they had been tortured and what information they had revealed, and to make their torturers "begin all over again the next day." No one was to accept special favors from the North Vietnamese and no one was to accept early release unless all prisoners were released at the same time.

Fellow POW Steve Long described the implementation of the BACK US code:

> You had to be real careful in accepting things. They'd offer you a bath and you were very prone to accepting the bath but you learned that you shouldn't do that unless everybody gets a bath. Most of us were offered early release. The Vietnamese would tell us, if you give us information, then maybe we'll release you early. You'll go home in maybe thirty days. Well, our rules were no one accepts early release. Nobody goes home until we all go home.

South African leader Nelson Mandela provides a parallel example in his autobiography, *The Long Walk to Freedom*. In 1976 Jimmy Kruger, the country's Minister of Prisons, paid Mandela a visit on the infamous Robben Island, where Mandela had served 12 years of a life sentence on charges of sabotage and conspiracy. As Mandela describes it,

> He came armed with a specific offer. … If I recognized the legitimacy of the Transkei government [one of the so-called bantustan homelands for black South Africans] and was willing to move there, my sentence would be dramatically reduced. I listened respectfully until he had finished. First, I said, I wholly rejected the bantustan policy, and would do nothing to support it, and second, I was from Johannesburg, and it was to Johannesburg that I would return. Kruger remonstrated with me, but to no avail. A month later he returned with the same proposal, and again I turned him down. It was an offer only a turncoat could accept. (Mandela, 1995, pp. 481–483)

The 9/11 terrorist attacks as a moral imperative

Recall from Chapter 1 the story of Jimmy Dunne, the only surviving managing partner at the investment firm Sandler O'Neill & Partners. As Dunne and his colleagues rebuilt the firm, they were motivated by the belief that it was morally incumbent upon them to bring the firm back from the brink of destruction. As University of Pennsylvania researcher Steven F. Freeman and colleagues described it, "The firm, once an instrument, as one owner described it, 'for feeding the mouths of families,' became a moral enterprise: to honor the dead, care for both the family members of the deceased as well as the living, and deny the terrorists a victory. … Moral purpose was a motivational factor in and of itself, spurring on the efforts of the partners and employees, as well as customers, suppliers, volunteers and other sources of external help" (Freeman *et al.*, 2004, p. 73). The workers were "selling not just for themselves but for their dead colleagues. … any commissions generated by a client of a deceased Sandler employee would go to that employee's estate" (Brooker, 2002, pp. 60–61).

Outsiders displayed a spirit of cooperation unusual in the traditionally cutthroat Wall Street culture. Other investment firms donated office space and computers, and referred business to Sandler O'Neill. Overall, "a newly found moral purpose invigorated an entire community …" and the recovery effort became a "'virtuous circle' in which effort, opportunity, hope, and motivation created an upward spiral of confidence and performance" (Freeman *et al.*, 2004, pp. 72, 73).

Sandler O'Neill was by no means the only firm that felt this way. Many throughout Wall Street and the entire New York City business community believed that recovering and thriving would send a powerful message to the terrorists. The "virtuous circle" extended throughout the New York metropolitan region, inspiring businesses of all kinds to "show their stuff," recover from the economic losses of 9/11, and possibly even go on to achieve greater successes than they had enjoyed before the attacks.

One person's morality may be another person's evil

While most of the world's religions and cultures uphold a core set of moral principles having to do with truth, respect for human life, and treating others as we would like to be treated, people of good conscience can disagree on what is, and is not, moral and ethical. Diane Coutu makes this point with regard to organizations in her *Harvard Business Review* article, citing the values promoted among employees of businesses such as the Phillip Morris tobacco company. "Companies can hold ethically questionable values and still be very resilient," she writes. "Philip Morris has very strong values, although we might not agree with them – for instance, the value of 'adult choice.' But there's no doubt that Philip Morris executives believe strongly in its values, and the strength of their beliefs sets the company apart from most of the other tobacco companies" (Coutu, 2002, p. 52). As another example, someone might admire the resilience and moral courage of the many military veterans we describe in this book, even if that person were opposed to war.

A pacifist who has written eloquently about the Vietnam War and the complex dynamics of living out one's nonviolent beliefs while honoring the sacrifices of POWs and other veterans is a woman whose name is anathema in some military circles: the musician Joan Baez. Lampooned in the Doonesbury comic strip as "Joanie Phoanie," Baez has used her talents to support nonviolent movements directed toward wars, desegregation, and rights of workers. She was instrumental in establishing the US chapter of Amnesty International and has advocated for gay rights, environmental causes, and abolishing the death penalty.

In 1972, after several years of outspoken opposition to the Vietnam draft – for which she had twice been arrested – Baez was asked to join ex-Brigadier General Telford Taylor, Episcopal priest Michael Allen, and antiwar activist veteran Barry Romo on a visit to Hanoi arranged by a peace group called The Liaison Committee. The purpose of their visit was to deliver Christmas mail to American POWs and to express a spirit of friendship between the people of the United States and the people of North Vietnam.

Such a visit by Americans behind enemy lines was considered relatively safe because there had been no combat activity in North Vietnam for many months. On the third night of their two-week visit, however, the delegation was taken by surprise when their hotel lost electricity, sirens sounded, and guests were ushered into a bomb shelter beneath the building where they remained for days. As they later learned, this was the beginning of the 11-day Operation Linebacker II, more commonly known as the "Christmas bombing" – the largest heavy bomber strikes launched by the US Air Force since the end of World War II. Baez later described the destruction she witnessed when she was allowed to leave the hotel.

> There was a man weeping to himself, and a surviving family moving about their small area like zombies. Everywhere were headbands of white cloth, the symbol of mourning for a relative. … I saw a woman sitting on a small heap of rubble, pounding her fists on her thighs and crying with a despair that was ferocious. She would go from a wail to a moan to almost a growl, then sob wretchedly from her island of misery. … Here was a shoe, here a half-buried little sweater, a piece of broken dish jammed into the earth, a book lying open, its damp pages stuck together. … On the other side of a thirty-foot abyss I saw [another] woman bending low to the ground singing a strange little song as she hobbled back and forth over an area of ten or twelve feet of ground. … [I asked the interpreter] what she was singing. … Oh, heaven and earth. Such depths of sadness cannot exist. I crumpled to the ground and covered my face and sobbed. That woman's boy lay somewhere under her feet packed into an instantaneous grave of mud, and she, like a wounded old cat, could only tread back and forth over the place she'd last seen him, moaning her futile song. "Where are you now, my son?" (Baez, 1987/2009, pp. 217–218)

The experience served as the inspiration for Baez's 1973 album, entitled "Where Are You Now, My Son?" Yet Baez was not one to follow the "leftist party line" as some might have expected; by 1979 she was speaking out in opposition to the Communist regime that now governed Vietnam, putting her at odds with many former compatriots in the antiwar movement.

Decades later, Baez wrote of an encounter with four Vietnam veterans who were picketing one of her concerts.

> Their signs were uncomplimentary at best … but that is not the point. They have stories to tell that have not been heard: stories of real bravery, of deep sorrow, violence, killing, and death. We who have not experienced what they have can never understand their dilemma, and have no right to stand between them and the honor, respect, and compassion they deserve.
>
> I, of course, opposed the Vietnam War. I oppose all wars. I do not expect most people to understand that fact, certainly not the four soldiers who stood in front of me with signs reading "Joan Baez, Soldiers don't kill babies, liberals do" and "Joan Baez gave comfort & aid to our enemy in Vietnam & encouraged them to kill Americans!" However, the anger and disrespect they have mistakenly placed upon me is far less compromising than that which was placed upon them when they returned from the jungles of Vietnam. (Baez, 2009)

After she approached the veterans and had a conversation with them, Baez writes,

> We each had unique reactions to this bizarre confrontation, which dared to become genuine communication. Mine was one of sorrow at their unresolved

struggle, their rage, and the amount of time they'd spent trying to get their lives back. At their request I autographed their signs (on the back). I also dedicated a song to them during our concert that evening. Even though they continued to picket for a brief while, I felt I had made four new friends and come closer to mutual understanding. (Baez, 2009)

Morality requires courage

To our knowledge, Admiral James Stockdale and Joan Baez never met. We can only imagine that they would have disagreed about war and a host of other topics. However, we can also imagine that they would have seen eye-to-eye on the importance of living and standing by one's deepest held values. The moral values that Stockdale treasured and relied on to bolster his resilience have been admired over the centuries by nearly every world culture. However, they are not easily acquired because they all require courage. Taking his guidance from Plato and Aristotle, Stockdale defined courage as "endurance of the soul" (Stockdale, 1995, p. 16). It is "the measure of a man's ability to handle fear" (Stockdale, 1978, p. 2) and it must "be exercised in the presence of fear" (Stockdale, 1984, p. 56). Without fear, there can be no courage. Stockdale understood this, and while he respected the physical courage of soldiers who march into battle or pilots who land on aircraft carriers in stormy seas, he was most impressed by what many philosophers have called "moral courage."

Rushworth M. Kidder, who directs the Institute of Global Ethics, defines moral courage as "standing up for values ... the willingness to take a tough stand for right in the face of danger ... the courage to do the right thing ... the quality of mind and spirit that enables one to face up to ethical challenges firmly and confidently without flinching or retreating" (Kidder, 2006, p. 72). Moral courage serves as the backbone for all of the great virtues. In fact, the eighteenth-century English diarist Samuel Johnson described it as "the greatest of all virtues; because, unless a man has that virtue, he has no security for preserving any other" (Boswell, 1791). Former POW and Presidential candidate John McCain asserts, "without courage all virtue is fragile: admired, sought, professed, but held cheaply and surrendered without a fight" (McCain, 2004, pp. 38–39).

Kidder divides moral courage into three components (p. 42). First, we must believe in and commit to a core set of moral values and principles. Second, we must recognize that by standing up for these principles we are likely to face danger. The danger may take many forms: physical threat, loss, rejection, shame, or disappointment. Third, to be morally courageous we must be willing to endure that danger and do what we know to be right, even if it means loss, disapproval or shame.

In Stockdale's mind, Rod Knutson easily met Kidder's criteria for moral courage, even though he "broke" and gave the North Vietnamese more than the "basic four" pieces of information. Knutson confronted fear and behaved honorably by taking as much punishment as possible and ultimately disclosing only fictional information. In retrospect, Knutson proved to be one of the toughest, most defiant and resilient of all the Hanoi Hilton prisoners.

Altruism and resilience

On January 2, 2007, a 50-year-old Navy veteran and construction worker named Wesley Autrey and his two daughters were waiting for a train in New York's 137th Street subway station, when a man standing near them on the platform collapsed and fell onto the train tracks. As passengers on the platform watched in horror, the headlights of an approaching train became visible in the tunnel. Making a split-second decision, Mr. Autrey jumped onto the tracks and lay on top of the victim, who was writhing in an apparent seizure. Telling him to lay still, Autrey pressed himself and the victim down between the tracks. Although the train's engineer slammed on the brakes, five cars passed over the men before the train screeched to a halt. Miraculously, although Autrey's coat was torn by the passing train, neither man was seriously injured. Autrey told the *New York Times*, "I don't feel like I did something spectacular; I just saw someone who needed help. I did what I felt was right" (Buckley, 2007).

Heroic acts like that of Mr. Autrey, where one individual makes a sacrifice or takes a risk for the benefit of another, are examples of altruism. Social science research has shown that altruism is associated with resilience, positive mental health and well-being in people with and without mental disorders. For example, in a study of 2016 members of the Presbyterian Church, Schwartz and colleagues (2003) found that positive mental health (but not physical health) was most common among church members who either helped others or received help from others. Importantly, giving help was even more strongly associated with positive mental health than was receiving help. During World War II, a phenomenon known as "required helpfulness" was first described in citizens who cared for the immediate needs of others after aerial bombardments. Those who performed personally satisfying tasks that were viewed by others as socially necessary developed fewer trauma-related mood and anxiety symptoms than expected. Further, in a 1979 study, Stanley Rachman found that altruistic individuals with pre-air raid psychological syndromes reported a decrease in their symptoms after bombardments. Carolyn Schwartz and Rabbi Meir Sendor (1999) reported similar findings among individuals with multiple sclerosis; in this case, those who were trained to deliver peer support by providing an empathic ear to fellow patients with multiple sclerosis experienced significant improvement in well-being.

In 2003, a team of University of Massachusetts researchers led by Carolyn Schwartz reported that altruism, or what some call social interest, was associated with better life adjustment, better marital adjustment and less hopelessness and depression. Receiving help from others and giving help to others both predicted better mental health although giving help to others was a stronger predictor. Further, they found that social interest moderated life stress and predicted physical health status. They theorized that the association between social interest, better mental health, and reduced stress may be related to a shift in attention from the self to others, enhanced self-confidence and self-acceptance, a reframing of one's own disease experience and greater perceived meaning in life.

Altruism also appears to foster resilience among children who have survived highly stressful environments. In a longitudinal study of physically abused Israeli children, Hanita Zimrin and colleagues (1986) found that those children who adapted well over time were more likely to assume responsibility for someone else, like a sibling or a pet, than were those who fared poorly. Similarly, in Emmy Werner's (1992) classic study of children living in poverty on the Hawaiian island of Kauai, children who helped others in a meaningful way (e.g. assisting a family member, a neighbor, or some other community member) were most likely to lead successful lives as adults.

The neuroscience of altruism and other moral behavior

For centuries, the scholars studying ethics and morality were mostly philosophers and religious thinkers. Recently, however, psychologists, anthropologists, and neuroscientists have begun to investigate the potential role of evolution and brain function in shaping and maintaining moral standards and societal values.

A large body of scientific evidence from infant research, ethology (the study of animal behavior), and experimental psychology suggests that altruism has had an important influence on behavior throughout human history, and that it represents a complex interplay of environmental and genetic influences. For example, among native South American forager-horticulturalists, those individuals who produce and share more food than average are rewarded during times of hardship (e.g. illness, accidents, disease) by receiving greater quantities of food from a larger number of people than those who produce and share below-average amounts of food. Yakov Shapiro (1994) proposes that this practice, which has been called "reciprocal altruism," has many benefits and rewards, including enhanced reputation and power, greater mating opportunities, and privileged access to resources when the community faces catastrophic stress.

Author Michael Shermer further argues for "the evolutionary origins of moral sentiments." He writes, "As a species of social primates, we have evolved a deep sense of right and wrong to reward reciprocity and cooperation and to attenuate selfishness and free riding. On the constitution of human nature are built the constitutions of human societies" (Shermer, 2011).

As part of a new field called neuroethics, neuroscientists are examining how the brain processes moral thinking and decision-making. A number of questions lie at the heart of this new science. Are moral and ethical values hard-wired into our brain? What regions of the brain are involved in moral and ethical decision-making, and are any of these areas associated with resilience? Has morality, or some aspect of morality, been passed down through our DNA because it improves chances for survival? Can moral thinking and ethical behavior be enhanced by behavioral or pharmacological interventions and, if so, does enhanced morality increase hardiness and resilience to stress?

Neuroscientists have recently begun to investigate brain mechanisms involved in social cooperation and altruism by observing research participants as they play specially designed games while their brain is being imaged in an fMRI scanner. An often-used game for this research is known as the Prisoner's Dilemma. It involves a scenario in which two players, isolated from each other, must each decide whether to betray the other player in exchange for a greater or lesser penalty. This research has found that mutual cooperation consistently activates brain regions (e.g. the dopamine nucleus accumbens system) that are known to be involved in the processing of reward. Thus, it appears that mutual cooperation, but not selfish behavior, tends to activate dopamine reward systems, which may leave the individual feeling good and wanting to repeat similar cooperative behaviors. Perhaps, through natural selection, the survival value of cooperation and group cohesion have been reinforced by the rewarding activation of dopamine systems.

This possibility is supported by a number of twin studies that demonstrate strong heritability of prosocial behaviors such as cooperativeness, empathy and altruism (Rushton, 2004). Further, a recent genetic study of 101 healthy volunteers reported that subjects with a specific polymorphism (i.e. variation) of a gene (the catechol-o-methyltransferase gene) that affects dopamine activity, donated twice as much of the money, which they had just earned in two challenging computer experiments, to a poor child from a developing country compared to subjects without this specific polymorphism (Reuter *et al.*, 2010). While this finding is intriguing, it is important to note that complex constructs and behaviors such as altruism are influenced by many different genes.

In studies on personal values, researchers have also found that thinking about and affirming one's values can diminish perceptions of threat, reduce defensive responses to threatening information, and decrease rumination after failure. Focusing on personal values has even been found to buffer physiological and psychological stress responses during a challenging laboratory test. In a study involving college students, J. David Creswell and colleagues at the University of California (2005) found that those who reflected on and affirmed their own most important personal values immediately prior to a stressful laboratory test had significantly lower responses of the stress hormone cortisol compared to students who reflected on and affirmed values that were not personally important to them.

In a 2001 fMRI study, Joshua Greene and colleagues used a classic test of moral reasoning, the "runaway trolley" dilemma,[1] to examine which brain regions (i.e. regions of the brain dedicated to reasoning, such as the PFC, versus regions of the brain involved in processing emotion, such as the limbic system) become activated when wrestling with a moral dilemma. This dilemma involved two different scenarios. In the first scenario, research participants were asked to imagine themselves watching a runaway trolley roll down a track toward five strangers, who would be killed if the trolley struck them. The participant had the ability to flip a switch and divert the trolley onto another track, where one person (also a stranger) was standing. If the switch was flipped, one person would be killed instead of five. Most participants said that it was morally right to flip the switch. However, in the second scenario, the

---

[1] Dilemma originally designed by Philippa Foote and Judith Jarvis Thomson (Greene *et al.*, 2001).

participant was asked to imagine him- or herself standing on a footbridge next to a stranger and that five people were trapped below in the path of an oncoming runaway trolley. Pushing the stranger onto the track was the only way to save the other five people. Even though the end result of the two options would have been the same (i.e. one person dies and five survive), most participants said they would refuse to push the stranger into the path of the trolley. Compared with the first decision, whether or not to flip the switch, the second decision, whether or not to actively kill someone, involved far more emotional processing and significantly greater blood flow in limbic brain regions. The same areas of the brain that become activated during grief or fear became activated during the decision to deliberately kill the one stranger even though it meant saving the lives of five other people. This study suggested that when emotional areas of the brain become activated, emotion may win out over logic and reasoning.

We might speculate that resilient individuals, when wrestling with moral dilemmas, tend to activate cortical brain regions to a greater degree than non-resilient individuals, and as a result make difficult moral decisions that are based on reason and emotion rather than emotion alone.

Sometimes there are no good choices

It is important to realize that moral choices often involve dilemmas, some even more wrenching than the one posed by the trolley experiment. The runaway trolley scenario is hypothetical, but in real life, trauma survivors are sometimes faced with far worse situations. Sometimes there is no "right" or "better" choice.

A torture survivor interviewed by Sister Dianna Ortiz recounts being subjected to the unimaginable:

> A father remembers not only his own horror and humiliation but also that of his teenage daughter and 9-year-old son, all of whom were detained by the military. "I was given another choice; I rape my daughter or the guard does it. ... I could not violate my own daughter. ... I lowered my eyes in shame. ... One guard held my face up, forcing me to watch this horrible scene. ... When they were through, they forced me to do what they had done to her. ... What kind of men are they? What kind of a father am I?" (Ortiz, 2001, p. 18)

Like the Vietnam POWs who "broke" under torture, and like many other trauma victims, a father who has survived such a horrific experience will understandably be haunted by memories and questions of "what else could I have done?" even when there were no viable alternatives. It is important to acknowledge that in some situations there may be no optimal "moral" choices, and that individuals may exhibit resilience simply by retaining a modicum of sanity after having been subjected to unspeakable terror, hardship, or humiliation.

Training for moral compass

Is morality (or moral courage) innate, or can it be learned? This is a question that scholars have struggled with for centuries. While some doubt that morality and the courage to live by one's values can be taught, others believe that it can. Gus Lee, a former corporate whistleblower and later US Senate ethics investigator, writes in his book *Courage: The Backbone of Leadership* that "courage is not something with which we are born. ... Courage is a learned quality, an acquirable set of skills, a practiced competence. It's like boxing, except it's easier, it smells better, and it causes fewer nosebleeds" (Lee, 2007, p. 4).

If I want to develop my moral courage, where do I begin? In his book *Moral Courage*, Rushworth Kidder outlines a three-step process. First, I must perform a candid self-assessment by examining myself, openly and honestly. We all have core values and beliefs. What are mine? Which are the most important to me? Am I living by these principles and values? Am I falling short, and where? Am I motivated to change? Do I have the courage to do so?

This self-assessment is only the first step. Next, Kidder recommends that I discuss these questions with highly principled people whose ethics I admire. These discussions can then help me to recognize and analyze the numerous situations in life where my actions have moral implications, and to honestly evaluate the risks and dangers involved in defending my core values.

In the third step, I practice my moral values and try to uphold them in challenging situations. I need to remain vigilant because it is so easy to relax one's values, make compromises, and take short cuts As noted by Gus Lee, I must "confront the seduction of avoidance." By repeatedly doing what I know to be right, and by taking a stand, I solidify my moral compass, and grow stronger. As Aristotle wrote in his *Nicomachean Ethics*, "We become just by doing just acts, temperate by doing temperate acts, brave by doing brave acts."

But where should we begin? John McCain (2004) states it simply: "Do the duty before me." That is, there is no need to search far and wide for situations that require moral courage: these situations surround each of us every day of our lives.

What about our children? How do we teach them moral courage? One effective approach is the Giraffe Project, whose motto is "moving people to stick their necks out for the common good." This project has developed a Heroes Program for students in grades K-12. As of 2007, it had recorded the stories of more than 900 "Giraffes" and reached more than 30,000 students in the US and abroad (through Giraffe Service Club International). Students listen to or read the stories, tell similar stories about heroes in their own community and, finally, "become the story" by identifying a need in their community and working to address it though a service-learning project. For example, at the Wildwood School in Mountain Lakes, New Jersey, students and parent volunteers have completed projects with the Valerie Fund at Morristown Memorial Hospital, the Montville Animal Shelter, and the New Jersey Battered Women's Shelter. Active participation in these projects teaches children firsthand about the joy of giving and the strengthening effects of altruism. These projects then become a source of inspiration for other children and adults (Whang, 2010).

In summary, adherence to our own moral compass and resilience are often inextricably linked to one another. We can become more faithful to our moral compass by taking an inventory of our most closely held beliefs and values, by learning from the writings and examples of ethical men and women, by discussing our beliefs with people whose values we respect, and then by practicing our values, particularly during times of adversity. Step by step we can build our moral courage. When we most need to do the right thing, we will be ready.

References

Baez, J. (1987/2009). *And a voice to sing with: A memoir*. New York, NY: Simon & Schuster.

Baez, J. (2009). Joan's Corner: Notes from Joan. Idaho Falls. Blog post, updated 08/14/09. Accessed 3/29/10 at http://www.joanbaez.com/joanscorner.html.

Boswell, J. (1791). *The life of Samuel Johnson, LL.D.* London.

Brooker, K. (2002). Starting over. *Fortune*, January **21**, 50–68.

Buckley, C. (2007). Man is rescued by stranger on subway tracks. *New York Times* (January 3). Accessed 9/3/10 at http://www.nytimes.com/2007/01/03/nyregion/03life.html.

Coutu, D. (2002). How resilience works. *Harvard Business Review*, May, 46–55.

Creswell, J. D., Welch, W. T., Taylor, S. E., Sherman, D. K., Greunewald, T. L., & Mann, T. (2005). Affirmation of personal values buffers neuroendocrine and psychological stress responses. *Psychological Science*, **16**, 846–851.

Freeman, S. F., Hirschhorn, L., & Maltz, M. (2004). The power of moral purpose: Sandler O'Neill & Partners in the aftermath of September 11th, 2001. *Organization Development Journal*, Winter, pp. 69–81.

Greene, J. D., Sommerville, R. B., Nystrom, L. E., Darley, J. M., & Cohen, J. D. (2001). An fMRI investigation of emotional engagement in moral judgment. *Science* **293**(5537), 2105–2108.

Johnson, K. H. (2009). *A better man: A book of positive role models for 21st century boys… and the adults who love them*. Richmond, VA: Brandylane Publishers, Inc.

Kidder, R. M. (2006). *Moral courage*. Harper Paperbacks.

Lee, G. (2007). *Courage: The backbone of leadership*. San Francisco, CA: Jossey-Bass.

Mandela, N. (1995). *The long walk to freedom*. New York, NY: Little, Brown & Company.

McCain, J. (2004). *Why courage matters*. New York, NY: Random House.

Ortiz, D. (2001). The survivor's perspective: Voices from the center. In E. Gerrity, T.M. Keane, & F. Tuma (eds.), *The mental health consequences of torture*. New York, NY: Kluwer Academic/Plenum Publishers.

Rachman, S. (1979). The concept of required helpfulness. *Behaviour Research and Therapy*, **17**, 1–6.

Reuter, M., Frenzel, C., Walter, N. T., Markett, S., & Montag, C. (2010). Investigating the genetic basis of altruism: The role of the COMT Val158Met polymorphism. *Social Cognitive and Affective Neuroscience*, **6**, 662–668.

Rushton, J. P. (2004). Genetic and environmental contributions to pro-social attitudes: A twin study of social responsibility. *Proceedings of the Royal Society London*, **271**, 2583–2585.

Schwartz, C. E., Meisenhelder, J. B., Ma, Y., & Reed, G. (2003). Altruistic social interest behaviors are associated with better mental health. *Psychosomatic Medicine*, **65**, 778–785.

Schwartz, C. E., & Sendor, M. (1999). Helping others helps oneself: Response shift effects in peer support. *Social Science & Medicine*, **48**(11), 1563–1575.

Shapiro, Y. (1994). A reconsideration of altruism from an evolutionary and psychodynamic perspective. *Ethics & Behavior*, **4**(1), 23–42.

Sherman, N. (2005). *Stoic warriors: The ancient philosophy behind the military mind*. New York, NY: Oxford University Press.

Shermer, M. (2011). The science of right and wrong. *Scientific American*, **304**, Issue 1.

Stockdale, J. B. (1978). *Naval War College Review*, Volume **31**.

Stockdale, J. B. (1984). *A Vietnam experience: Ten years of reflection.* Stanford, CA: Hoover Institution.

Stockdale, J. B. (1995). *Thoughts of a philosophical fighter pilot.* Stanford, CA: Hoover Institution.

Stockdale, J. B., & Stockdale, S. B. (1990). *In love and war: The story of a family's ordeal and sacrifice during the Vietnam years* (Third Edition). Annapolis, MD: Naval Institute Press.

Werner, E. E. and Smith, R. S. (1992). *Overcoming the odds: High risk children from birth to adulthood.* Ithaca, NY and London: Cornell University Press.

Whang, O. (2010). The Giraffe Program. Blog post, The Giraffe Heroes Project. Accessed 9/3/10 at http://www.giraffe.org/in-new-jersey-200707266/.

Zimrin, H. (1986). A profile of survival. *Child Abuse and Neglect*, **10**, 339–349.

Chapter 5

Religion and spirituality: drawing on faith

Many people turn to religion or spirituality as a way to cope with hardship or trauma. Some find solace in formal religious services, while others seek inspiration and strength through private spiritual practices that help them to connect with God or to find their place in the universe.

In her 2009 book *The Journey Home*, psychologist Ann Graber articulates the distinction and relationship between religion on the one hand and spirituality on the other. She observes that "People may change their religion, but they retain their inherent spirituality." Graber defines religion "as a path to God, the Source of Being" and spirituality "as that essential human endowment in which direct experience of God can take place" (2009, p. 19). Whether or not one considers oneself to be religious, there is no denying the importance of religion and spirituality in American culture and in other cultures around the globe. Among Americans, a 2007 Gallup poll found that 92% believe in God or a universal spirit, 81% believe in heaven, and 70% believe in the devil and in hell (Newport, 2007). The US Army includes the spiritual dimension as one of the core strengths in its Comprehensive Soldier Fitness (CSF) program.

In some areas of the world, religion and spirituality are even more influential than in the United States. For example, Dr. Samoon Amad, a colleague of ours from the Department of Psychiatry, New York University, returned from a series of journeys to the mountains of Pakistan where he interviewed survivors of the devastating October 2005 earthquake. Dr. Amad found religious belief among survivors to be the single most powerful force in explaining the tragedy and in explaining survival.

In our interviews with highly resilient individuals, time and again we were told about the powerful effects of spirituality or religion, particularly during times of high stress. For social worker Elizabeth Ebaugh, it was years of practice in spiritual traditions that saved her emotional life as she faced a life-threatening trauma and its aftermath.

Will I live to see the sun come up?

It was 9 p.m., and Elizabeth was returning home from work. The previous day, she had attended a Gestalt therapy training program which focused on synthesizing Eastern spiritual philosophy and Western psychological insights. As part of the experiential training, she was held down by two other participants and then instructed to fight free. The goal of the exercise was to experience a freeing of her personal power which was trapped inside. She had also just completed a 10-day cleansing fast designed to help purify body and soul.

On her drive home, Elizabeth stopped to buy groceries. When she returned to her car with groceries in hand, she noticed a man sitting in a pickup truck in the parking space next to hers. She thought he looked a bit suspicious, so she hurried along, trying to focus simply on getting into her car and driving away. But when she put her grocery bag on the front passenger seat and turned to close the car door, there he was: crouching beside her, holding a hunting knife, ready to take the wheel.

Elizabeth wasn't new to trauma. As a social worker, she had treated many patients who suffered with symptoms of posttraumatic stress disorder. For years she had volunteered as a counselor for a child abuse and crisis telephone hot line. She knew how to negotiate with angry and hostile clients, so she wasn't particularly afraid, at first. Besides, the man looked scraggly and homeless; she thought he probably just needed money.

Using her negotiating experience, she began to bargain with her assailant by suggesting that the two of them drive to an ATM where she would withdraw cash for him and then return to the parking lot where he would leave her and go his own way. At first, he seemed agreeable. He drove her car to the bank, she withdrew cash from the ATM, and they headed back to the parking lot. Elizabeth remembers picturing herself sitting at home, telling her friends about her adventure.

However, as they approached the supermarket, Elizabeth's captor had a change of heart. He took a sharp right turn and drove to a remote section of the parking lot. He parked, then cuffed Elizabeth's hands behind her back. Now, she was truly frightened. She screamed and kicked. He told her to shut up. She tried to reason with him, but he ignored her and began to drive. Hours and miles went by, and Elizabeth started to lose hope.

The kidnapper told Elizabeth that he was not going to hurt her and that he would soon let her go.

> And I was holding onto that. Every time he stopped the car, I thought he was going to let me out. So it was hope, disappointment, hope, disappointment throughout the night.

At 1:00 in the morning, after driving aimlessly, he stopped at a convenience store just outside the city limits. At last, Elizabeth thought, she could escape. But the relief quickly turned to fright when he tied her hands to the steering wheel. As he entered the store, Elizabeth pounded the car horn over and over, hoping to attract attention. No one responded. Now she feared that her assailant would punish her for trying to expose him.

Once back in the car, he drove to a motel, forced her inside, and raped her. Then he calmly watched an erotic movie on TV. He lay in bed for awhile, silent. She worried that he was planning how to murder her. She suggested that he handcuff her to the pipes in the bathroom and leave without her.

He didn't take her up on that suggestion. Instead, after several hours in the motel room, he dragged Elizabeth back into the car, gagged her, tied her hands, and headed back toward town. Predawn, the roads were deserted. As they crossed a bridge several miles from the supermarket where the man first abducted her, she could only hope he was driving back to his truck and would let her go. But 10 minutes into their drive, her assailant pulled a sudden U-turn and headed back toward the bridge they'd just crossed. Then he stopped the car, looked into Elizabeth's eyes, and told her to get out.

Once she gained solid footing, she felt relieved, believing that her nightmare had ended and that her captor would soon free her. But he had a different plan. He pointed to the bridge. "He wanted me to jump off. That's when I fainted."

Elizabeth woke up when she hit the icy water 40 feet below. Her assailant had thrown her limp body off the bridge and left her to die. Upon landing there was no pain – just the shock of freezing water, which jolted her awake. Maybe the air pockets in her heavy wool coat had broken her fall. Or, perhaps because she'd fainted, her muscles were relaxed enough to absorb the shock.

Rather than panic, Elizabeth felt an immediate burst of hope. Now she had a chance to get out of this alive. She was an accomplished swimmer, though she'd never tried to swim with her arms tied together. Using only her legs, she rolled onto her back and began to kick toward shore, nearly 100 yards away. After several minutes, her heavy winter coat began to weigh her down. "I was exhausted and worried that I would get hypothermia." Each time she began to sink beneath the surface, she kicked faster and harder. Miraculously she reached the shore.

The river bank was steep, and the mud was thick. Inch by inch, Elizabeth scaled the slick bank of mud and crawled to a nearby road. After being ignored by several passing cars, she successfully flagged down a UPS truck. The driver took her to the nearest convenience store, called the police, and bought her a cup of hot tea.

Not surprisingly, Elizabeth suffered with symptoms of posttraumatic stress disorder. Like many trauma survivors, she felt haunted by memories of her ordeal and lived day in and day out with an overwhelming sense of terror. Even though she knew that her abductor had been arrested, she felt so frightened that she could not stay alone in her house for more than 15 minutes at a time. She moved in with a close friend. When she felt ready to return to work, friends picked her up in the morning and then drove her home at the end of the day. Fortunately, her boss allowed her a flexible schedule; some days she could work, some days she simply couldn't handle it. For months, she recalls, she felt like a helpless infant.

Elizabeth believes that her background in spiritual practices strengthened and helped to protect her during the horrific ordeal. Spirituality also played an enormous role in her recovery. When she regained enough emotional equilibrium to reach out, she sought out spiritual leaders and healers. She meditated, chanted Sanskrit mantras, took various herbal and homeopathic supplements, and studied breathing and movement therapy. Her goal was to reach a higher spiritual plane and, in the process, rise above her trauma. In her pursuit of inner peace, she was relentless.

Several years later, Elizabeth completed additional professional training and left her government job to open a therapy practice focusing on holistic health and well-being. She also forged a loving personal relationship, got married, and became a mother. Despite having lived with debilitating stress, which plagued her for years, Elizabeth believes that her abduction served as a platform for her personal development, forcing her to evaluate her life and gradually change it for the better. She credits her ability to move forward with her life after the abduction to numerous resilience factors, most importantly her dedication to spirituality. She calls it the core and unifying thread that explains her ability to survive, to heal herself and, ultimately, to transcend her trauma. For her, the journey and the path to healing led to a radical change in her world view. Before her ordeal, even though she wasn't a stranger to crisis, she had lived with the belief that "it wouldn't happen to me." Now she had to grapple with the truth: life is fragile and can be taken from us in an instant.

> I believe that the only way to find closure is within yourself. It's not about what's happening outside. I could never go back to feeling that it wouldn't happen to me – it did. Studying spiritual philosophy and practicing meditation and chanting helped me experience the spiritual field, or field of awareness, and the interconnectedness of all that is. I am more completely present in my current reality and yet I feel a deep knowing that I am part of something much greater.
>
> When something bad happens, instead of asking how I can fix it or make sure it doesn't happen again, I recognize that suffering and pain can be a part of life. However, I am not stuck in the experience of pain. The experience of pain dissolves and I can feel completely alive in the face of all that is. This helps me to have faith that every experience, no matter how traumatic, can bring me closer to the essential, to the awakened awareness. This doesn't rule out any reaction of anger that I was raped, however those moments are only part of the journey to the experience of the essential self.

Elizabeth now feels that she was an "unconscious" person at the time of her abduction. "I think he woke me up. I was so asleep and didn't even know it," she says. When her abductor was in prison, she had her meditation community send him spiritual literature, "hoping his time in jail would be like in a monastery. He would be able to grow that way." Many years later, she recalls, "I went out into the woods with a friend, and I felt his spiritual presence and I turned around and faced his presence and I just thanked him for being a teacher along the path. And then I felt his presence leave."

Elizabeth believes that for survivors of trauma, there is a bridge between victimhood and returning to the world. She feels that she crossed that bridge by turning to spirituality and by deepening her connection with a larger view of reality and with a power greater than ourselves. Duke University trauma researcher Kathryn O'Connor notes that "a spiritual approach can be helpful in restoring hope, and acquiring a more balanced view about justice and injustice, safety and danger, good and evil … In posttraumatic stress disorder, the acceptance of a spiritual power may lead to a spiritual awakening" (Connor et al., 2003). This is what Elizabeth discovered. But it was not easy. It took years and it took courage for her to embark on what Joseph Campbell, the great scholar of mythology, has called the "hero's journey." Rather than obsess about revenge and hide in the shadows of fear, she gradually chose to confront the "dark night of the soul," what Carl Jung referred to as "the shadow." For Elizabeth the end result was a spiritual awakening.

God comes first

Like Elizabeth, many of the resilient people whom we interviewed found strength in their spiritual beliefs and practices. This was particularly true among former Vietnam POWs. In fact, in *Honor Bound*, the classic account of American prisoners in Vietnam, Stuart Rochester and Frederick Kiley made the following observation, "There is virtually no personal account in the Vietnam POW literature that does not contain some reference to a transforming spiritual episode" (1998, p. 413).

Major Dick Bolstad is an example of a soldier whose religious faith never wavered, not even during his darkest hour. Today, 45 years after his ordeal as a prisoner of war, Major Bolstad still describes Catholic faith as the very foundation of his life.

Dick grew up in a poor family on the south side of Minneapolis. His father worked as a carpenter who spent most of his waking hours laboring to support his wife and their six children. Even though Dick's father did not have time for church, he insisted that the children attend every Sunday.

For Dick, a defining moment in his life came in the sixth grade when he attended a two-week religious summer program at the Saint Albert's School. On the last day of the program, his teacher announced that the student who had the best attendance was to receive an award, a portrait of Saint Anthony that hung on the wall of her classroom. Dick was the only student who had not missed a single class.

> So she gave me that picture. Saint Anthony, he's the saint who helps you find things. If you lose something or if you lose your mind, you know, he's kind of there for the hopeless cases. Ever since then, I have Saint Anthony to help me.

Dick enlisted in the US Marine Corps Reserves when he was 19 years old. Two years later, during the Korean War, he was called to active duty. As a member of the 1st Marine Division, Bolstad landed at Inchon, Korea where he fought as an infantryman, was wounded, and received a Purple Heart. Years later he was serving as an Air Force pilot when his plane was shot down and he was imprisoned by the North Vietnamese. Major Bolstad prayed to Saint Anthony to help him find courage, hope and endurance.

> Just give me strength to withstand whatever they were doing to me ... During any beating, any time I was being hurt, I'd offer the pain to God ... And I always prayed that I could hold my head high when I returned home ... I prayed that I would have the strength to do what was honorable ... And of course I prayed for other people ... I prayed to Saint Anthony and asked him to pray to Jesus for me, to intercede for me, to ask Jesus to grant my request. Saint Anthony, he's got a little more pull than I do.

In prison, Major Bolstad never felt alone. During his intolerable torture and deprivation, he believed that he was joined by St. Anthony and by Jesus Christ, who suffered and died on the cross, and who now helped Dick bear his own cross.

When Major Bolstad was released from prison, he and his fellow POWs were flown to Clark Air Force Base in the Philippines. Shortly after arriving on base, Dick and the other healthy prisoners were immediately taken to the mess hall. To a group of POWs who had been starved for years, this was a dream come true. But Major Bolstad had other plans.

> My first thought, when we got to Clark, was to get hold of a priest and have him hear my confession before anything else.

When he found a Catholic chaplain and asked him to hear his confession, Major Bolstad was told that he had to wait for morning Mass.

> And I said, "No father, now."
> And he said, "Maybe we could do it a little later."
> I said, "No, now."
> So he set up a room and heard my first confession.
> And then I was fine ... I figured I was squared away with God.

When asked to rank the 10 most important factors that helped him survive in prison, Dick Bolstad placed religion at the top of the list.

> Oh, yeah. There's no doubt about it. I'm not a religious fanatic. I'm just a normal person but I believe in my faith. I practice my faith ... The top ten ... I put my family up there and I put my country up there ... but (my religious faith) is at the top ... There's nothing that's gonna knock that off.

Like Bolstad, former POW Colonel Robbie Risner found that prayer was an important mechanism to connect with loved ones. In his book *The Passing of the Night*, Risner talks about prayer.

> I was praying a lot, for it was one of the few ways I could occupy the day. I would pray not only for my family but also for each one of the prisoners that I knew of. Then I would go through all of my relatives and friends as well as our government leaders. Mentioning names in prayer gave me a feeling of closeness to them that was very meaningful. (2004, p. 87)

Risner also used prayer as an essential tool for surviving torture sessions. Usually he asked God for "the ability to stand it," but when the pain became truly unbearable, he prayed for relief.

> I said, "Lord, I have been in long enough. I am half-sick, miserable and cold and hungry. I am asking you to get me out of these stocks, to provide me more clothes, another blanket and some food." (2004, p. 89)

And when his North Vietnamese guards subjected him to the rope trick (as described in Chapter 1), in which both arms are tied behind the back and then gradually lifted higher and higher until one or both shoulders are pulled out of their sockets, or when his guards wrapped a rope around his throat and tied it to his ankles (bound behind him so that if he relaxed his arched back too much, he would choke), Risner turned to the Bible.

> When the pain started really ripping me I began desperately to pray. I began
> quoting a scripture verse from the Bible over and over: "My grace is sufficient.
> My grace is sufficient." I thought that meant God would give me grace to bear
> whatever I had to bear without giving in. (2004, p. 94)

Another fellow Vietnam POW, Larry Stark, believes that God is always present,
that he understands our "situation," and that he will work as a partner to lighten our
load, if only we recognize his presence.

> I think that one has to recognize that along the way the Lord is there and He
> knows your situation. All you have to do is acknowledge His presence. So no
> matter what, I can handle it. We can handle this thing together. And if you
> do that, then you don't have that great big burden. You don't have to do it all
> yourself … without some religion, it [the imprisonment] would have been a lot
> more difficult and maybe not bearable.

Even during a grueling forced march through the mountains of North Vietnam
when he wondered whether he had the stamina to endure, Stark found signs that God
was by his side.

> We're going up this mountain, and I could see up above the clouds. In fact,
> we walked right up through the lower level to where we were actually looking
> down on the cloud layer. And again I said, "Hey, this is a way for the Lord to say
> hello. Now this is fantastic beauty."

And in *Honor Bound*, ex-POW John McCain recalls,

> To guard against such despair, in our most dire moments, POWs would
> make supreme efforts to grasp our faith tightly, to profess it alone in the dark,
> and hasten its revival. Once I was thrown into another cell after a long and
> difficult interrogation. I discovered scratched into one of the cell's walls the
> creed, "I believe in God, the Father Almighty."

Ritual and ceremony are central elements in most religious and spiritual practices.
Even under circumstances where formal ceremonies are forbidden, people of faith
somehow find a way to worship together. For example, as we mentioned in previous chapters, the North Vietnamese centralized their prison system by housing
large numbers of American POWs in one facility, nicknamed the Hanoi Hilton. In
1970 the North Vietnamese brought many more prisoners to Hanoi from outlying
locations.

Soon dozens of prisoners, against prison rules, held a formal religious service.
Men from all over the prison heard the singing and joined in.

"We agreed that we were going to have a church service and told the Vietnamese,
and they said no," recalled fellow prisoner Bud Day. But on February 12, 1970, the
prisoners went ahead anyway, holding a service and singing songs. "The Vietnamese
broke in and seized the people who were standing against the wall doing the service,"
Day said. "They marched them out of the room at gunpoint. So I stood up and started

singing 'The Star-Spangled Banner,' 'God Bless America,' 'My Country 'Tis of Thee' and every song we could think of."[1]

Even though the organizers of what was later called the "church riot" knew that the North Vietnamese would punish them severely, they proceeded anyway, because they believed that this collective expression of spiritual faith would improve morale. After the service, North Vietnamese guards shackled the organizers for 38 days.

Bob Shumaker, one of the most respected senior officers at the Hanoi Hilton, believes in God but does not see himself as devout. However, as a seasoned prisoner, he offered the following advice when a new POW arrived in the cell next to him:

> The first thing you need around here, old buddy, is faith. I'm not a preacher. I'm not gonna try to convert you. I'm just gonna tell you the truth. If you can't tap into a source of strength and power greater than yourself, you're probably not gonna last.

Some of the POWs we interviewed told us that although they embraced religion and prayed frequently during their imprisonment, they had not considered themselves to be religious before the time of their capture. Being subjected to horrific conditions, where suffering was all around them and death never far away, motivated them to focus on God and to pray far more than they had at any other time in their lives. This so-called "foxhole religion" has been questioned by some religious figures, but for many POWs and other trauma survivors religion and spirituality, whether longstanding or newfound, played an essential role in their survival.

What if you are not religious?

Among the former POWs we interviewed, there were a few who did not call upon religion or their belief in God to stay strong and to survive. Al Carpenter is a former Navy fighter pilot who withstood nearly six and a half years of isolation, torture, and extreme deprivation in a North Vietnamese prison. Other POWs describe him as one of the "real tough guys." When we asked if religion or spirituality played a role in his experience as a POW, he replied,

> Not at all. Well, it was a factor, but it didn't influence me in the long term. I was not a religious person. I had had a normal Protestant upbringing, went to church a couple of times a year. When I ended up in prison, I thought I would never have a better opportunity to seriously explore what truly might be important about it and how it might work in my life. I made a vow that I would pursue it for at least one year no matter how irritated, bored, whatever I might get with it. And I sought out those with different religious backgrounds whom I could get to.

For example, Carpenter tried to learn as much as possible about Catholicism from another prisoner who was devoutly religious.

---

[1] See, for example, http://advanceindiana.blogspot.com/2008/08/mccains-church-riot-in-hanoi-hilton.html accessed 8/21/09; Zuckman (2008).

> I worked on prayer, not to get me out of this situation, but I asked for what I thought was reasonable, to help me cope with my situation and understand better. I really seriously tried. I tried hard and I worked at it all the time. And you know what I concluded? The benefit people get from prayer … is the ability to open up … open up and get a look inside of themselves through verbalization. And I can do the same thing talking to a tree or the wall or whatever. I do not think that a supreme being answered my prayers, giving me comfort. The comfort came from within … and I stopped swearing during this period. I said if you are gonna do this, go whole hog. And that was the toughest thing. That was almost unbearable to not express myself in my old sailor's language. But I did it. I did it for a year. That was tough. But the conclusion I came to was that I can handle things myself. I am very independent.

Even though religion did not prove to enhance Carpenter's resilience, he understands that religion and spirituality can help many people when they face adversity.

Special Forces instructors also turn to God for strength

Given the dangers inherent in their job, it is not surprising that many Special Forces instructors in this book also talked about spirituality or religion as a source of strength and as an aid for controlling fear. Like the former POWs we interviewed, most believed in God, felt that they had a personal relationship with God, and tended to be idealistic and ethical. In fact, over 50% of Special Forces missions are humanitarian in nature.

Mark Hickey has been a member of the Special Forces for most of his adult life. He is a medic who is viewed by his peers as a man of great integrity, strength, and endurance. However, at 5 feet 4 inches tall, he does not derive his stature from his height.

> I'm not the typical picture. I'm not the poster boy for Special Forces, a six-foot-four-inch barrel-chested freedom fighter. I don't see myself physically as anything special. I think the only thing I do have going for me is my relationship with God … I see my brain as just basically a computer. It's going to spit out data but first the data has to be put into it. Who puts that data into it? Well, it's my soul … I see determination, I see courage coming from somewhere outside the brain.

Master Sergeant Hickey has enormous strength. He never quits. As he puts it, "It's the Bible that drives me. The Bible says, 'Do all things unto the glory of God.' I'm going to do my best, not just for me, but for God as well. He is the one I really want to impress."

When we asked Sergeant Hickey what role his belief in God and religion played in his success as a Special Forces soldier and instructor, he said,

> For me it is the reason. It is *the* reason … I believe in an afterlife so if I die I've got someplace to go. It's just the next step. That lets me do some of the things I do because I don't fear death. I may fear a particular way of dying. I don't want to be eaten by a shark, but the thought of death doesn't really scare me because I have faith that there's something else, my faith in God, that there's something else out there.

Cliff Welch, another Special Forces instructor, has similar beliefs:

> The way I look at it, I'm not afraid of dying. And if I do die, I'm gonna be in a
> better place. So, bring it on. You know, I really don't care. And a lot of people say,
> 'It's not a smart man's way of doing things.' But, to me, faith's a big deal. I mean,
> if you don't have faith, you don't have anything. People say there is no God.
> Some of them say religion is just for weak-minded people. That's crap. You gotta
> have faith in something, or you're just a hollow, empty person. And that's pretty
> much the way I've lived my whole life, even from my earliest recollection of
> going to church on Sunday. Always, church has been there.

Faith and recovery

For some survivors, faith assumes a central role in their lives only after their trauma,
when they are trying to recover from their ordeal. Tim Pollock is a young Iraq veteran who was severely injured – according to a *USA Today* interview, an insurgent
"blew off half his skull during a reconnaissance operation in 2004." After returning
home to Ohio and retiring from the Army, Pollock suffered from seizures and other
disabilities stemming from his injury. He struggled with agitation, anxiety, and other
symptoms of PTSD; he "drank hard, bought a gun and considered suicide."

For Pollock, the way back was through studying for the ministry. He found
a renewed sense of purpose by getting involved with Point Man International
Ministries, a nonprofit whose mission is to connect the suffering veteran with other
veterans who are already further along in the transition home. Supported by religious
congregations around the country, Point Man coordinates more than 250 veteran-led
"Outpost" groups worldwide, as well as "Home Front" groups that are led by mothers, wives, and friends to provide support for the families of active service members
and veterans. Pollock visits wounded soldiers in hospitals and coaches veterans living
with PTSD. "I'll always have post-traumatic stress," he observes, "but I'm learning
through God how to control that."

There are, of course, many religion-based programs for trauma survivors of all
faiths who are not necessarily military veterans. Torah and the Twelve Steps, Inc., for
example, focuses on the transformational change needed to overcome addictions,
a common problem in survivors of trauma. As the organization's website explains,
"Drugs and alcohol *mimic* the essential need for a relationship with the Creator
through a 'pseudospiritual' sense of connection and transcendence, and a false sense
of 'good' that in actuality leads to greater dissatisfaction, emptiness, despair and eventually death." Although the program is open to people of all faiths, it offers spiritual support through specific Jewish teachings and their applications to 12 steps of
recovery; interactive classes, with the study of basic Kabalistic thought, and classical
texts on ethics to increase personal character development; and training in leadership
skills and methods to increase learning capacity. Another organization, The American
Association of Christian Counselors, coordinates a nationwide network of resources
for those seeking help in recovering from trauma.

Many survivors who are not affiliated with any formal religion engage in a
variety of spiritual practices to deal with trauma and other life challenges. Some

practices grow out of the Judeo-Christian tradition while many do not. Examples include yoga, t'ai chi ch'uan, qigong, aikido, tantric rituals, sufi mysticism, sadhana, and Native American healing traditions. Research testing the effectiveness of these approaches for trauma survivors is expanding rapidly. In one scientific study conducted by Boston University researcher Bessel van der Kolk and published in a 2006 issue of the *Annals of the New York Academy of Sciences*, patients with PTSD participated in either hatha yoga sessions or group therapy sessions. The patients who practiced hatha yoga showed significantly greater reduction in PTSD symptoms compared to those who received group therapy. Yoga was also associated with improved heart-rate variability, which has been related to emotion self-regulation. Additional recent evidence suggests that yoga may increase levels of gamma-aminobutyric acid (GABA), which is the brain's primary inhibitory neurotransmitter. Drugs that increase GABA availability decrease anxiety and tend to have a relaxing effect (Streeter *et al.*, 2010).

Faith, guilt, and forgiveness

Guilt and forgiveness are complicated topics, particularly in the context of stress, trauma and resilience. Guilt can haunt or even cripple survivors for years, and to forgive a specific person, organization or society that has intentionally caused great harm may be next to impossible for many of us. However, when left unattended, guilt and the inability to forgive can sap us of our personal resources.

For returning war veterans, spiritually based programs often address the guilt that many veterans carry, consciously or unconsciously. For example, Point Man Ministries president Dana Morgan tells veterans that "everybody else can forgive you, and now it's your turn to forgive yourself because God already has."

For someone who is a victim of crime or abuse, forgiving the offender may be an even greater challenge than self-forgiveness. In a *New York Times* article, Elizabeth Kadetsky (2009) describes having been mugged in the hallway of her apartment building by a man wearing a ski mask. "In a dream several months later, the man with the mask was sitting in my hallway waiting for me to come home, holding the mask in his hand. At first when I saw him, I was scared, but when I saw his face I also saw that he was human. He told me he was struggling with guilt over having hurt someone. I tried to imagine if I could forgive him."

The question, "can I forgive?" is a central one. In a 2009 study of more than 100 adults, Nathaniel M. Lambert and colleagues at Florida State University assigned participants either to pray for a specific person, pray about any topic, or think positive thoughts about a specific person every day for four weeks. Those who prayed for the specific person were found to be more forgiving, and showed an increase in selfless concern, compared to the participants in the other conditions. In the process of forgiving, it may be that we develop greater empathy for the other person and his or her perspective, as Elizabeth Kadetsky did in her dream about her attacker. Forgiveness involves letting go of the desire for revenge – a desire that can be counterproductive and can keep us "stuck" in a "victim" frame of mind.

As one survivor said, "if you believe that God loves everyone no matter what, and if you believe that God can forgive anything no matter what – then you must believe that God loves and can forgive your attacker. Even if *you're* not ready to forgive, knowing that God forgives can help you to gain a measure of closure."

Faith as it relates to physical and mental health

The relationship between religious and spiritual faith and resilience that Dick Bolstad, Bob Shumaker, Mark Hickey, and Elizabeth Ebaugh so eloquently describe is supported by scientific research. Recent meta-analyses (summaries of all available well-designed and well-conducted research studies that have been published in the scientific literature on a particular topic) have concluded that practicing religion is associated with physical and emotional well-being among healthy individuals and with better coping among people who are suffering with medical illnesses. For example, a group of researchers led by Michael E. McCullough at the National Institute for Healthcare Research recently analyzed 42 separate published studies that involved a total of 126,000 people and found that those who actively practiced a religious faith lived slightly longer than those who did not (McCullough *et al.*, 2000). There is also reasonable scientific evidence to show that religious faith is associated with lower blood pressure, less hypertension, and possibly better immune function. In addition, studies involving patients with rheumatoid arthritis, severe burns, and organ transplants have found that those who consider themselves to be religious tend to see themselves as healthier, require fewer days in the hospital, and report fewer medical complications than those who do not describe themselves as religious (Powell *et al.*, 2003).

Numerous studies have also shown that higher levels of religiousness are related to lower levels of depression. This has been found in elderly people living in the United States and Europe, medically ill older patients, elderly patients recovering from hip surgery, bereaved adults, and college students. In a study of 838 patients over the age of 50 who were admitted to the hospital for medical illnesses, a group of researchers from Duke Medical School found fewer symptoms of depression in those who described themselves as religious (Koenig *et al.*, 2004). A similar relationship has been reported in adolescents: those who are religious are less likely to express suicidal thoughts and behaviors than those who are not.

There is an important caveat: religious coping is not always associated with well-being or resilience. Some researchers have distinguished between positive and negative patterns of religious coping (Pargament *et al.*, 1998). Individuals who see God as punitive and judgmental may feel that they "deserve" their troubles, and that their fate is controlled by an unsympathetic all-powerful being, leaving them with a limited sense of control.

Although it seems clear that religion is associated with positive physical and mental health as well as resilience, it not known exactly why. It appears likely, however, that regular attendance at religious services may foster a number of resilience factors including optimism, altruism, and a search for meaning and purpose. In addition, as a member of a religious congregation, parishioners routinely interact with positive and resilient role models who encourage them to adopt meaningful social roles where they can give to others through acts of generosity. Religious faith may also protect against destructive habits such as drug and alcohol abuse. By parsing spirituality/religion and focusing on discrete components, like prayer and meditation, or attendance at religious services, science is beginning to uncover which elements of faith and spirituality are most closely related to psychological well-being and resilience. For example, the relationship between resilience and religion may partly be explained by the social quality of religious attendance. The word "religion" comes from the Latin "religare" meaning "to bind." People who regularly attend religious services may have access to a deeper and broader form of social support than is often available in a secular setting. It is not uncommon for a religious congregation to provide food, financial help, and emotional and moral support to fellow members who are under duress and facing crises.

However, the support that practitioners receive may come from their belief in God as well as from fellow human beings. Most formal religions focus on the practitioner's relationship with God, often described as a supreme being who provides guidance, strength, and protection. For some people, their relationship with God bolsters their own feelings of inner strength and self-efficacy and helps them to follow the advice of the Italian renaissance poet and philosopher Dante Alighieri, "Be bold and the mighty shall protect you." Believing that God is at their side, they have the confidence to tackle challenges that otherwise would seem too daunting. In 2006, mental health researchers Roger D. Fallot and Jennifer P. Heckman (2006) found that survivors who used religious coping strategies at the time of traumatic experiences reported lower subsequent levels of distress than those who did not.

Faith strengthens a challenged family

Among the resilient people we interviewed are Ron and Barb Garrett, parents of a son with Down syndrome. When Bryan was born, Ron and Barb were excited and hoping the new baby would be a girl. Barb had chosen the name Heidi.

Bryan's birth, then, came as a shock. Ron and Barb had never had any particular reason to learn about Down syndrome, or even to give it much thought. There had been no prior indication that their baby would be born with any congenital problems. Suddenly, they had to dramatically revise their ideas about parenting and "redefine normal." Because Bryan, like most Down syndrome babies, was born with poor muscle tone and had difficulty swallowing, Barb recalls, "everything that I would normally do, I had to relearn – how to hold him, how to feed him." When Bryan was only six weeks old, he began speech/feeding therapy, occupational therapy, and physical therapy. After Bryan came home from the hospital, Barb remembers staying home from work for the first three months and crying every day, mourning for the normal child she did not have. Some friends seemed to distance themselves, apparently feeling awkward at the idea of a child with such a disability. Barb read a book with the message, "someday you will be happy again," but she did not believe it. When Bryan was an infant, Barb was invited to have lunch with a group of other women who were mothers of Down syndrome children. While this helped her to feel less alone, she relied more on her faith for strength than on other people. Particularly helpful was the phrase, "God gives good gifts," spoken by a missionary whose child had died.

Barb and her husband are evangelical Christians; as Ron explains it, our faith gives us strength for everything, including being parents to Bryan." The Garretts never asked, "Why us?" However, Barb struggled with the question of whether or not Bryan's having Down syndrome was God's doing. As the years passed, she came to believe that God allowed Bryan to have Down syndrome, but that the condition is only temporary. "Because once he's in heaven, he will be whole," she explained.

When Bryan was small, the Garretts sometimes watched *Life Goes On*, a television show starring a teenager with Down syndrome. They found it informative, but also frightening as it foreshadowed problems that might arise in the future. Life with Bryan continued to present challenges. As he grew older, physically stronger and more active, his mental and emotional development lagged far behind. In adolescence his behaviors still resembled those of a much younger child with high energy, near-continuous talking, attention seeking, and the tendency to cause messes around the house.

Over the course of many hours of practice with the "Hooked on Phonics" technique, Bryan learned to read, which made an enormous difference in his education. As a competitor in the Special Olympics, the international program that empowers people with intellectual disabilities to compete in athletic events, Bryan excelled and won numerous medals. Just before his 18th birthday, Bryan graduated from his local public high school, which uses a combined mainstreaming/special education program. He subsequently enrolled in a special needs program called STRIVE, which focuses on practical life skills.

Still, parenting Bryan involves major challenges. For example, Bryan has a knack for disappearing – he has been reported missing from school on numerous occasions, sometimes requiring police cruisers, school administrators, and teachers to comb the neighborhood looking for him; and he once wandered away from his parents in a crowded airport. Barb and Ron continually pray, "Lord, help us keep track of him!"

Bryan has a special talent for making friends with strangers. Barb says he is the friendliest person she has ever known. While she considers herself to be somewhat shy, she has learned to socialize more effectively by watching how Bryan relates to others. In fact, Bryan has become a role model for Barb. Barb, however, does not imitate all of Bryan's social behaviors. For example, several years ago at a large "meet and greet" party, Barb spotted Bryan across the room standing behind a bald-headed man. Without warning, Bryan began to rub the man's head. Fortunately the gentleman did not seem to mind, although Barb was mortified.

Bryan has touched many lives and inspired many people, even influencing the careers of a few who have decided to go into Special Education after getting to know him. Ron and Barb believe that God has a special role for Bryan to play in promoting friendship and cheering people up when they most need it. He is a blessing, and has brought joy to their lives. Still, they look toward eternity in the belief that "this is just temporary – someday Bryan will be in heaven and we will enjoy him without anything holding him back."

Prayer, meditation, and mindfulness

Most varieties of religion or spirituality incorporate some form of prayer, meditation, or mindfulness. These practices have been used for thousands of years to quiet and discipline the mind.

Prayer is, in the simplest terms, talking to God, to a higher power, to the universe. Author Robert Longman Jr. (2002–2009) describes it this way:

> Prayer is, at its heart, the communication that is the fabric of the human being's (and human species') relationship with its Father. When a Jew, Muslim, or Christian prays to God, the very act itself assumes these to be true at the very least:
> - that there's One beyond each and all of us, beyond all that is around us;
> - that this One cares enough to bother with you;
> - that this One cares enough to want your response;
> - that this One cares enough to respond to you;
> - that this One is effective enough for that response to make a difference.

In his book *Letters to Malcolm: Chiefly on Prayer*, the Christian writer C. S. Lewis (1963, 1964) refers to sincerity as the essence of prayer: "The prayer preceding all prayers is, 'May it be the real I who speaks. May it be the real Thou that I speak to.'"

The popular writer Deepak Chopra (2009) broadens this definition further: "Why not consider prayer to be an action in consciousness? It may be too hard for someone in the Judeo-Christian tradition to let go of a personal (and usually masculine) God in favor of something as impersonal as one's own awareness, but I think this is where the focus should lie."

The possible connection of prayer with life satisfaction has been explored by Brandon Whittington and Steven Scher (2010) at Eastern Illinois University in a study of 430 individuals affiliated with a wide range of faiths, including atheism. Although the findings were correlational, like most studies cited in this chapter, and therefore do not prove that prayer *causes* any particular outcome, the results are nevertheless interesting. Using a scale that categorizes prayer into six different types (Laird *et al.*, 2004), participants reported which types of prayer they engaged in. They were also given a battery of assessments related to dimensions of subjective well being, including spiritual support (Ai *et al.*, 2005), optimism (Scheier *et al.*, 1994), meaning in life (Steger *et al.*, 2006), life satisfaction (Diener *et al.*, 1985), and self-esteem (Rosenberg, 1965). Using a regression analysis, the researchers found that three kinds of prayer were associated with positive outcomes. Specifically,

> prayers of *thanksgiving* were significant predictors of subjective well being, of self-esteem, and of optimism. Prayers of *reception* [involving an attitude of

openness and surrender] … [had] significant effects on self-esteem, optimism, and meaning of life. Finally, prayers of *adoration* had positive effects on both optimism and meaning of life. (Whittingham & Scher, 2010, p. 64)

The researchers theorize that "the prayer types which had positive effects on well-being are distinguished by their egoless nature. … This may connect prayer in the Abrahamic faiths [Judaism, Christianity, and Islam] to other religious practices such as Buddhist meditation" (pp. 66–67).

This raises the question: are prayer and meditation different? Most would say yes, though some would also say that one can pray while meditating and vice versa.

Meditation takes a variety of forms. Some are based on mindfulness, which teaches the practitioner to live consciously "in the moment" and to be "fully present" for what is happening right now. With practice, one who meditates learns to become a "participant-observer" who watches the mind as it automatically and repetitively follows the familiar path of old conditioned responses. One monk explained that, while meditating, we can observe our mind going off on a tangent, and gently bring it back as you would correct a child who has wandered from a path. The book *The Power of Now* by German philosopher Eckhardt Tolle (1999) underscores this point.

Cultivating present awareness requires long practice. As the Bhagavad Gita warns, "The mind is restless, turbulent, powerful, violent" and that trying to control it "is like trying to control the wind." Learning to use the mind, as opposed to having the mind use you, is one of life's most challenging tasks. However, many meditative traditions teach that such efforts can increase personal freedom, which grows out of an enlarged capacity to modify thoughts and feelings, as well as change behaviors. Learning to meditate, observe the mind and body, and direct attention to the present moment allows us to "face whatever comes to us calmly and courageously, knowing we have the flexibility to weather any storm gracefully," writes Eknath Easwaran, one of the world's great meditation teachers.

Scientists have begun to investigate neurobiological factors associated with prayer, meditation and mindfulness. We will discuss some of this research in Chapter 9 on Brain Fitness.

Practical suggestions: bringing spirituality into your life

There is no one best way to explore the spiritual dimensions of your life or to build a spiritual practice. You may have been raised in a particular religious tradition in which you feel comfortable and find strength and renewal. Or your religious experiences may have been more limited, less positive, or even negative. You may be like Elizabeth before she was abducted, a seeker of spiritual enlightenment. Or you may have no particular interest in formalized religious or spiritual practices.

Whatever your individual circumstances may be, for those who are interested there are many ways to explore the spiritual dimension of your life and how it might serve as a source of strength. Here are some approaches that may be useful for interested readers.

- Set aside a time for prayer or meditation as part of your daily routine. This is often first thing in the morning, last thing at night, or both.
- Make a regular habit of reading scriptures, sacred texts, or other writings pertaining to your chosen faith or practice.
- Designate a physical location for your daily spiritual practice. This may be a room or smaller space in your home or a location in nature. It might even be in your car.
- Practice a physically active form of spirituality such as walking prayer, yoga, martial arts, or liturgical dance.
- Practice a creative form of spirituality such as chanting, singing or playing sacred music, painting or drawing with the goal of expressing sacred ideals, or writing spiritually inspired poetry.
- Become part of a group that worships or practices together, such as a congregation, a prayer circle, a scriptural study group, or a meditation center. This may be a physical group that meets in person at a designated location, or an online community.

Finally, we would like to share a moving prayer for survivors with PTSD written by Patience Mason, wife of a veteran who returned from Vietnam with PTSD:

> *Higher Power, I know it's not within the harmony of the universe that I be healed from the trauma of remembering without pain.*
> *Help me through the pain.*
> *Surround me with the golden light of healing, fill me with the white light of peace and love.*
> *Help me to bear the pain as I go through the memories.*
> *Help me to cry.*
> *Help me to remember.*
> *Help me to love myself no matter what happened to me or what I did to survive.*
> *Help me to release and let go of my survival skills, the things such as anger and numbness that helped keep me alive, as I become aware of how ineffective they can be in getting me what I want today.*
> *Fill me with light and love until I am green and growing again in the harmony of the universe, if it be Thy will,*
>
> AMEN. (Mason, 1993)

Perhaps more than any of the other resilience factors described in this book, religion and spirituality are deeply personal matters about which people tend to have strong feelings. As a potential source of strength and resilience, religion, spirituality, mindfulness and meditation are available to billions of people across the planet.

References

Ai, A. L., Tice, T. N., Peterson, C., & Huang, B. (2005). Prayers, spiritual support, and positive attitudes in coping with the September 11 national crisis. *Journal of Personality*, **73**, 763–791.

Chopra, D. (2009). Day of prayer: What is it meant to be?" *Huffington Post*, May 7. Accessed 8/21/09 at http://www.huffingtonpost.com/deepak-chopra/what-is-prayer-meant-to-b_b_199109.html.

Connor, K. M., Davidson, J. R. T., & Lee, Li-Ching (2003). Spirituality, resilience, and anger in survivors of violent trauma: A community survey. *Journal of Traumatic Stress*, **16**(5), 487–494.

Diener, E., Emmons, R. A., Larsen, R. J., & Griffin, S. (1985). The satisfaction with life scale. *Journal of Personality Assessment*, **49**, 71–75.

Fallot, R. D., & Heckman, J. P. (2006). Religious/spiritual coping among women trauma survivors with mental health and substance use disorders. *The Journal of Behavioral Health Services and Research*, **32**(2), 215–226.

Graber, A. (2009). *The journey home: Preparing for life's ultimate adventure.* Birmingham, AL: LogoLife Press, p. 19.

Kadetsky, E. (2009). The art of defying death. *New York Times*, October 14. Accessed 10/21/10 at http://opinionator.blogs.nytimes.com/2009/10/14/the-art-of-defying-death/?scp=1&sq=Kadetsky%20The%20art%20of%20defying%20death&st=cse.

Koenig, H. G., George, L. K., & Titus, P. (2004). Religion, spirituality and health in medically ill hospitalized older patients. *Journal of the American Geriatrics Association*, **52**, 554–562.

Laird, S. P., Snyder, C. R., Rapoff, M. A., & Green, S. (2004). Measuring private prayer: Development, validation, and clinical application of the multidimensional prayer inventory. *The International Journal for the Psychology of Religion*, **14**, 251–272.

Lambert, N. M., Fincham, F. D., Stillman, T. F., Graham, S. M., & Beach, S. R. H. (2009). Motivating change in relationships: Can prayer increase forgiveness? *Psychological Science*, **21**(1), 126–132.

Lewis, C. S. (1963, 1964). *Letters to Malcolm: Chiefly on prayer.* New York, NY: Harcourt Brace Jovanovich, Inc.

Longman, R., Jr. (2002–2009). Prayer. Accessed 8/21/09 at http://www.spirithome.com/prayer.html#whatis.

Mason, P. H. C. (1993). *An explanation of PTSD for 12 steppers: When I get sober I feel crazy.* High Springs, FL: Patience Press. http://www.patiencepress.com

McCullough, M. E., Hoyt, W. E., Larson, D. B., Koenig, H. G., & Thoresen, C. (2000). Religious involvement and mortality: A meta-analytic review. *Health Psychology*, **19**(3), 211–222.

Newport, F. (2007). Americans more likely to believe in God than the devil, heaven more than hell: Belief in the devil has increased since 2000.Gallup News Service, June 13. Accessed at http://www.gallup.com/poll/27877/americans-more-likely-believe-god-than-devil-heaven-more-than-hell.aspx.

Pargament, K. I., Smith, B. W., Koenig, H. G., & Perez, L. (1998). Patterns of positive and negative religious coping with major life stressors. *Journal for the Scientific Study of Religion*, **37**(4), 710–724.

Point Man International Ministries mission statement. Accessed 1/26/10 at http://www.pmim.org/.

Powell, L. H., Shahabi, L., & Thoresen, C. E. (2003). Religion and spirituality: Linkages to physical health. *American Psychologist*, **58**(1), 36–52.

Risner, R. (2004). *The passing of the night: My seven years as a prisoner of the North Vietnamese.* Old Saybrook, CT: Konecky & Konecky.

Rochester, S., & Kiley, F. (1998). *Honor Bound: The History of American Prisoners of War in Southeast Asia, 1961–1973.* Washington, DC: Historical Office, Office of the Secretary of Defense.

Rosenberg, M. (1965). *Society and the adolescent self-image.* Princeton, NJ: Princeton University Press.

Scheier, M. F., Carver, C. S., & Bridges, M. W. (1994). Distinguishing optimism from neuroticism (and trait anxiety, self-mastery, and self-esteem): A reevaluation of the Life Orientation Test. *Journal of Personality and Social Psychology*, **67**, 1063–1078.

Steger, M. F., Frazier, P., Oishi, S., & Kaler, M. (2006). The meaning in life questionnaire: Assessing the presence of and search for meaning in life. *Journal of Counseling Psychology*, **53**, 80–93.

Streeter, C. C., Whitfield, T. H., Owen, L., Rein, T., Karri, S. K., Yakhkind, A., *et al.* (2010). Effects of yoga versus walking on mood, anxiety, and brain GABA levels: A randomized controlled MRS study. *Journal of Alternative & Complementary Medicine*, **16**(11), 1145–1152.

Tolle, E. (1999). *The Power of Now: A Guide to Spiritual Enlightenment*. Novato, CA: New World Library.

Torah and the Twelve Steps, Inc. Accessed 1/26/20 at http://www.torahtwelvesteps.org/our_philosophy.html.

van der Kolk, B. (2006). Clinical implications of neuroscience research in PTSD. *Annals of the New York Academy of Sciences*, **1071**, 1–17.

Whittington, B. L., & Scher, S. J. (2010). Prayer and subjective well-being: An examination of six different types of prayer. *The International Journal for the Psychology of Religion*, **20**, 59–68.

Zuckman, J. (2008). McCain and the POW church riot: GOP presidential candidate talks about the faith that sustained him during captivity. *Chicago Tribune*, August 15, p. 1.

6 Social support: learning the Tap Code

In order to thrive in this world, people need other people. We all benefit by knowing that someone cares about our welfare and will support us if we fall. Even better is having an entire network of family and close friends who will come to our aid at a moment's notice. It is also important for us to give of ourselves to help others. Forming relationships may not seem important when times are good, when we tend to take our friends and family for granted. However, close relationships build strength and help to protect us during times of stress and danger. Far from signifying weakness, interdependence with others can provide a foundation for resilience.

Former POW Admiral Robert Shumaker appreciates the importance of social networks. Like nearly all of the resilient people we interviewed, both military and civilian, he knew how to capitalize on a basic biological reality: humans are designed to bond with one another. During his eight years in North Vietnamese prisons, Shumaker used his wits and creativity to help develop an ingenious method of communication, known as the Tap Code, which provided a critical lifeline that allowed scores of prisoners to connect with one another.

Alone in his dark, sweltering, rat-infested cell at Hoa Lo (the Hanoi Hilton), Shumaker wondered whether he would ever see another American again. Every day, he spent hours lying on the soggy floor, peering through a crack at the bottom of his cell door, hoping and praying to see a fellow prisoner. Three months into solitary, a tall, white, emaciated American, escorted by a North Vietnamese guard, walked past Bob's cell on his way to the latrine. Shumaker was elated, but how would he make contact with this prisoner? Bob spent the next several days devising a scheme to communicate with the new arrival. The latrine seemed the only possible place to communicate. The guards rarely entered it themselves; the putrid smell of rat and human urine and feces was overwhelming.

> Once a day the guards would let me out of my cell and take me to this "shower area" where I emptied my [human] waste bucket. I noticed the other American was getting the same treatment. I'd see him come out of this "shower area," which was maybe 100 feet away – I had good eyesight then – and I took a chance. There was a spot of ink on this wooden table in my area and I put water on it and it turned back into ink. On toilet paper I wrote, "Welcome to the Hanoi Hilton." And I told him to "scratch his balls when he walked out [of the shower area]." And he walks out scratching away. So it was a happy day for me when I made contact. And the name "Hanoi Hilton" stuck.

Soon, other Americans began to arrive. When three new prisoners were added to Shumaker's cell, the four talked nonstop for several days, acutely aware that the North Vietnamese would probably soon separate them to prevent an organized resistance.

> We started talking about how we could organize to fight to keep our sanity and maximize survival; and I said, "What we need is some method by which we can communicate."

As the group was brainstorming about communication, one of Shumaker's cell mates, Air Force Captain Smitty Harris, recalled a conversation that he had over-heard years earlier during Jungle Survival School. A former Korean POW had described how American prisoners communicated by tapping on water pipes and then placing their ears on the pipe to listen for tapping responses coming from another building. It consisted of five rows and five columns of letters from the alphabet; the prisoners in Korea called it the AFLQV Code (from reading down the first column).

Shumaker was smart and immediately recognized the importance of Harris' story. Bob, who earned the name "Martini Mixer" for his crucial role in communication among prisoners, had been valedictorian of his high school class, stood 8th in his class of 686 midshipmen at the Naval Academy, held a masters degree in aeronautical engin-eering, and had been selected for the NASA astronaut program. Right away he under-stood that what he later called the "Tap Code" could prove to be a lifesaver for hundreds of American POWs. This is what it looked like:

	1	2	3	4	5
1	A	B	C	D	E
2	F	G	H	I	J
3	L	M	N	O	P
4	Q	R	S	T	U
5	V	W	X	Y	Z

(To understand how the code works, readers will find it helpful to know that the sender taps to indicate the row first, then the column. For example, to send the letter "H," which is in the second row and third column, one would tap twice, then pause slightly, then tap three times. In order to form a symmetrical grid, the letter "K" is omitted from the matrix; "K" is represented by "CC.")

When the four group members were separated into different cells, each one spread the code to other prisoners, and then whenever one of them was transferred from the Hanoi Hilton to a different prison, he would teach the code to a whole new group of prison mates. By tapping with their knuckles and listening with their water cups against the wall, POWs relayed messages to each other. Within months of its adoption, the Tap Code formed the backbone of the prisoners' communication network and resistance efforts at Hoa Lo and beyond.

Here's how Captain Steve Long learned about the Tap Code.

> On one side of me, I had two Navy pilots, and on the other side was an Air Force back seater, a navigator. The first night I was there, the Air Force navigator spoke toward the ceiling so that I could hear over in the next cell.
>
> He said, "Do you know the tap code?" I said no. He says, "It's a 25-square matrix, the left side is A F L Q V. We'll tap in the morning." So I had the rest of the night to figure that out. Of course, brevity was a necessity because we needed to speed up communication, so we went by initials. I was S.L. And the S is the fourth row down, third column over and the L is in the third row down, first column. So I tapped that on the wall, and everybody would know that SL was in camp. That worked real good until Svede Larsen showed up.

Sometimes, instead of tapping on the wall, prisoners used other noises to send messages. If someone was in solitary and didn't share a common wall with another prisoner, he would use coughs or sweeps of a broom to signal numbers. All the prisoners knew that a sniff was 1, a cough 2, clearing the throat 3, a hack 4, and a spit 5.

> Coughing, sweeping with a broom, one, two, three … The one we used that was probably the most ingenious – and we held it as closely as possible so the Vietnamese didn't learn about it – was the voice tap where a cough and a sniff would be a one and a two. Like B is in the first row of the second column and we'd go (sniff, cough) and that's a 1–2 which is a B. A throat clear would be a three and a hack would be a four and a spit would be a five. We shortened everything, like "interrogation" was shortened to "quiz" which was shortened to "Q." When they came to my room and told me that I was going to an interrogation, I wanted to tell the others, so I'd go hack, throat clear (S), throat clear, sniff (L), hack, sniff (Q), and that's SLQ, or "Steve Long Quiz."

Captain Charlie Plumb describes his first exposure to the tap code shortly after being tortured and imprisoned by the North Vietnamese. Pacing back and forth, Plumb heard a chirping noise coming from the corner of his cell and at first thought it was a cricket. But as he listened more carefully, he noticed a distinct rhythm and then saw a piece of wire moving back and forth through a hole at the base of his prison cell wall. On the other end of the wire was Shumaker.

> We were in adjoining cells that were separated by about six feet. Charlie was by himself, and he had a lot of boils. I had stolen some wire – and it was kind of stiff wire, but it wasn't as stiff as a coat hanger – I would hide this wire in the cement wall of my cell. But there was the problem of getting the wire into Charlie's cell, which was about six feet away. Each cell had concrete walls but they also had little drain holes.
>
> Anyway, he was walking up and down the cell, pacing back and forth, and he heard this little cricket and the cricket was chirping and he thought, "Gee, that's a rhythmical chirp." And then he looked down and here was a wire in his cell with toilet paper on the end of it.
>
> He was afraid to pick it up for awhile. And then finally he got the courage up and he took the note and the wire disappeared and he read the note and it said, "Memorize this code and eat this note." And he gulps it down. And then

every day, I'd slip the wire in. Now, the tap code calls for tapping on the wall. Well, we couldn't do that with a wire, so he would put tension on his end and I would put tension on mine. And then I would go: tug – tug, tug, tug, so this became an extension of the tap code.

Plumb (1992) would later describe his feelings when he realized that the chirping cricket was actually a communiqué:

Can you imagine what might be going through your mind in an experience like this? Wow! What an opportunity. Somebody wants to network. Somebody wants to team up with me. Somebody wants to communicate!

Other ingenious forms of "tapping" emerged, depending on the demands of the particular situation. For example, Jerry Denton, who later served as a United States senator from Alabama, blinked the word t-o-r-t-u-r-e while being videotaped by a Japanese film crew.

Shumaker understood that the Tap Code was an essential tool not only for passing on information and organizing resistance but also for preserving sanity. In times of stress and trauma, few things are more painful or more destructive to a person's mental and physical well-being than isolation. Prisoners used the Tap Code to create a vital social network. Supportive communication was especially important whenever a prisoner returned from being interrogated and tortured. Using the Tap Code allowed the prisoner to unburden himself when beset by worry, guilt, or despair about having "given in" and divulged information, and provided a way for prisoners to sympathize and reassure one another. Telling his comrades what he had revealed during the interrogation also helped other prisoners keep their stories straight.

Steve Long believes that the Tap Code saved his life. During the Vietnam War, American and North Vietnamese combat and supply missions spilled over into Laos, even though Laos was not officially involved in the war. Because neither the United States nor Vietnam publicly acknowledged these Laos-based missions, when soldiers were killed or captured in Laos, both sides kept the information a secret. Prisoners captured in Laos were kept separated from other prisoners, held incognito and always listed as missing in action (MIA). For Steve Long and the others caught in Laos, this was a living nightmare. How could anyone back home, especially his family, even know that he was still alive?

We were treated differently. We weren't given privileges. There was no media, there were no letters home, there was nothing for us. We realized that we needed to communicate with them [the "regular" prisoners] so that if one of them got released they could get our names out. We took it upon ourselves, as our self-appointed mission, to get our names as widely spread out as possible. So we communicated extensively, probably more than a lot of the other prisoners, because we felt the need for our own safety, for our own lives.

Long's hunch proved to be correct. When the Vietnam War ended in 1975, the Paris Peace Talks called for an exchange of prisoners between the United States and

North Vietnam. Waves of relief and joy spread throughout the prisons of North Vietnam, but for Steve Long the exhilaration was short-lived.

> When a North Vietnamese soldier came to our cell, he asked, "What do you think?" We thought, "This is great. We're going home." He said, "No. The Vietnam War is over. The Vietnam prisoners go home. When the Laotian War is over, the Laotian prisoners go home." And that was depressing. It took the wind right out of your sails. We would not be released.

One week after the peace accords were signed, the first cohort of American prisoners was released. They immediately met with intelligence de-briefers, who asked for the names of all known American POWs.

> And, of course, our names, at least the four of us who had been up there for a long time and who had communicated extensively, were some of the first names that they mentioned. Well, the intelligence community gave that to the State Department, and the State Department went back to Paris and said, "Hey, look, Vietnamese, we know that Long, Stischer, Bedinger and Brace are in North Vietnam and if you do not release them, then we will resume bombing North Vietnam with B-52s." The Vietnamese had had enough of that. That's why they decided to end the war anyway, because the B-52s were bombing them. So the Vietnamese came up with not only our four names but with six more as well. So it did pay off that we communicated as much as we did.

Strong ties save lives

It is not surprising that Vietnam POWs found ways to bond with each other despite solitary confinement because the military places great emphasis on fostering and sustaining strong personal relationships. Soldiers belong to units: squads, platoons, companies, battalions, and divisions. No one operates in isolation. Problems are addressed and solved by groups rather than individuals. This esprit de corps is conveyed symbolically from the first day of training, when men's heads are shaved, and men and women are issued military fatigues. The specific preferences of the individual give way to the needs of the group.

As we saw in Chapter 4 on moral compass, the POWs in the Hanoi Hilton looked up to Admiral James Stockdale as the senior ranking officer in the prison, and he developed the "BACK-US" principle of resistance to their North Vietnamese captors. Stockdale insisted that after returning from a torture session, prisoners never be left alone to ruminate about their perceived fragility and failure. As soon as prisoners returned from being interrogated, they were to be greeted with supportive messages that fellow prisoners whispered or tapped on the walls of their cell.

Humans, like other animals, are biologically "wired" for survival. When confronted with stressful and dangerous situations, one naturally focuses on one's own welfare. It is normal to protect and fight for resources. However, Stockdale, like so many of the literary and philosophical writers he admired, believed that resilience, courage, and hardiness involved far more than personal strength, acquisition, and the instinct for survival. True resilience and courage were measured by acts of generosity, compassion, and altruism. As he wrote in *A Vietnam Experience*:

> When you are alone and afraid and feel that your culture is slipping away,
> even though you are hanging onto your memories … hanging on with your
> fingernails as best you can, and in spite of your efforts, still see the bottom
> of the barrel coming up to meet you, and realize how thin and fragmented
> our veneer of culture is, you suddenly know the truth that we all can become
> animals when cast adrift and tormented for a mere matter of months. It is then
> that you start having some very warm thoughts about the only life-preserver
> within reach – that human mind, that human heart next door. … [when people
> ask] "What kept you going? What was your highest value?" My answer is: "The
> man next door." (1984, p. 110)

If there was one unifying value, one guiding principle behind Stockdale's heroic brand of stoic leadership, this was it, "You are your brother's keeper." This was the "US" in BACK-US, unity before self. This was Stockdale's "life preserver."

The power of strong connections among soldiers is valued at the highest levels of command. These bonds motivate military men and women more powerfully than do abstractions like patriotism, says General Hugh Shelton, who commanded US Special Operations before becoming chairman of the Joint Chiefs of Staff:

> When you find a high-speed unit in today's Armed Forces, you find that its
> members are more concerned about the individual on the left and right than
> they are about themselves. Everybody is there to accomplish the mission of the
> team. The organizational and social structure recognizes team performance, not
> what one individual carries out. We know that's why people fight – we like to say
> people fight for the flag or they fight for the nation, but they really fight for the
> one on the left and right – their buddies.

The Special Forces provides a strong example of how units foster close ties. For the 12-man team of soldiers the label "band of brothers" has real meaning. A number of factors are considered essential for optimal unit cohesion and functioning. These include trust, healthy competition, reciprocal support and altruism.

After his retirement from the military, when General Shelton gave a talk to corporate managers at Anheuser Busch, he suggested fostering team spirit similar to the kind he had learned and practiced as CEO of the Armed Forces. "This is one team, one fight," he told them. "If we are going to get better, it's all about working together. A rising tide lifts all boats."

Most of the Special Forces instructors we interviewed told us about former team members stationed all over the country who they knew they could count on for the rest of their lives. Even members who have never met one another, total strangers, will welcome fellow SF members into their home and treat them like family. Gordon Smith feels that he has a "family" of team members scattered all over the world who will be there to help him and his entire family at any time, no matter what.

One need not be a Special Forces soldier, however, to experience this kind of mutual support and helpfulness. Freemasons, for example, pledge to help fellow masons and their families if a need arises. The Boy and Girl Scout organizations, although primarily designed for youth, value and encourage service and helpfulness among scoutmasters and other adults as well. And many, if not most, religious denominations see providing help and social support as part of their mission. These are just a few examples of groups that foster a sense of common cause and community.

Reach out for support

Elizabeth Ebaugh, the social worker who was kidnapped and raped, believes that genuine support from friends and professionals was essential during her arduous recovery. Early on, during the first few months after her ordeal, helpers were everywhere.

> One reason I did so well, from that moment throughout my entire healing process, was that I had the best of the best. The police officers were incredibly sensitive, incredibly careful about every word, everything they did. They were so beautifully heartfelt. Plus the UPS driver who drove me to the hospital was like an angel. He couldn't do enough for me. When I got to the hospital, the doctors and nurses were totally on my side.
>
> I really think that [the days and weeks after the trauma] is a crucial time in terms of being able to come through it. To know that you're back into your world and your world is going to rally around you is a huge healing force. At that time, this was the worst crime to happen in this area. I had people calling me 24 hours a day, all my friends, this whole community – coming to see me; getting letters from people I didn't know; people were praying for me. I had to turn the phone off. There was no way I could feel like I was alone and isolated and not cared for. My story was on the front page of the newspaper for at least two weeks.

A colleague of ours, Alice, described similar feelings shortly after her husband died:

> I feel terribly sad and hurt over the loss of my husband, but I don't feel depressed. I feel so much support from people all around me, family and friends, neighbors, and even strangers who have no particular reason to be kind to me. Like the woman at the credit card company when I had to call and tell them to close my husband's account, she was very caring. People at church are praying for me. People where I work who hardly know me have sent cards. My mother and sister are calling me all the time. I just feel very lifted up.

After a trauma, it is not uncommon for the survivor to be showered with an outpouring of help and kindness. But once the initial flurry of attention dies down, the real tests of love and friendship begin. Well-wishers typically return to their normal daily routine shortly after a trauma, and sometimes survivors, themselves, may react to even the most well-meaning approaches with coldness or even hostility. For example, Elizabeth remembers feeling distrustful, angry, and filled with rage; feelings that are commonly seen in posttraumatic stress reactions. She no longer felt that she could fully trust anyone. When she met the man who eventually became her husband, forging a relationship was not easy.

He got the brunt of a lot of my rage. I needed to be in control, and he comes from a background where he wasn't very trusted, so here I was not trusting him. But it wasn't him I didn't trust, it was the world. He hung in there and really was the solidity in my life. … My husband and I complement each other. We are both healers. At times when other couples would have broken apart, we meditated together and asked for help in those really dark moments.

Without caring professionals, steadfast friends, and a loving husband and family, Elizabeth believes that she would still be drowning in the psychological aftermath of her horrific ordeal, alone, helpless, and trapped in the haunting memory of her attack. "We can't do anything without support … The act of leaning in for support opens you," she says. However, she also observes that "supporters need to know not to coddle – there's a difference between supporting and enabling. At some point, we all need somebody to say, it's time to get on with it."

Our friend Victor Daniels found the same was true after he lost his wife of 42 years to cancer. Victor was a cardiac patient with two stents in his heart when his wife was diagnosed with incurable sinus cancer which was rooted too deeply in her brain to be operable. After three years of treatment, she was admitted to a hospice, where she died a few weeks later. Victor and his wife had no children, and his family members were too busy with their own lives to spend much time with him. Several of his friends and neighbors had also lost their spouses, and most seemed to be trapped in grief for years after being widowed. He did not want to follow their example.

On a visit to his primary care doctor, Victor described feeling listless and having trouble getting out of bed in the morning. She recommended that he attend a weekly bereavement support group sponsored by the cancer center at the local hospital. Victor took her advice and began attending the group, where he met a number of other people who were working toward finding a "new normal" and establishing positive directions for their lives after losing a loved one. With their encouragement, Victor began to look ahead focusing on how he wanted to spend the rest of his life, rather than dwelling on what he had lost. He made a list of goals he wanted to accomplish in his "new life." Step one was to resume working part time at a local golf course, which he did. This gave structure to his days and provided social contact with people who were actively engaged in enjoying life. Victor's energy and outlook gradually improved, and with the support of friends and coworkers he continued to achieve his goals. Before long, social networking really paid off: Victor fell in love and remarried. His new wife was a widow whom he had met in the support group.

The act of reaching out for support means taking the initiative to seek assistance from others. It does not mean passively waiting and hoping for someone to rescue us. And when we do seek support, we are opened; our world expands; we find a new and deeper way to relate to those who care about us.

Social support protects against physical and mental illness

The strategies used by resilient soldiers and civilians to create health-promoting social bonds and to foster social support have been studied by researchers for many years;

it is now well known that social isolation and low levels of social support are associated with high levels of stress, depression and PTSD. For example, in a study of 2490 Vietnam veterans, researchers found that those with low social support were more than two and a half times more likely to suffer from PTSD than were veterans with high social support (King *et al.*, 1998). Similarly, when patients with cancer (Manne *et al.*, 1999), cardiac illness (Holahan *et al.*, 1995), rheumatoid arthritis (Revenson *et al.*, 1991) or multiple sclerosis (Mohr *et al.*, 2004) have high levels of social support, they are significantly less likely to be clinically depressed.

Isolation can also affect our physical health. For example, well-designed studies have shown that a small social network or inadequate emotional support is associated with a threefold increase in subsequent cardiac events among patients who have already had a heart attack, and a two- to threefold increase in future coronary artery disease among healthy patients (Rozanski *et al.*, 1999). In fact, the effect of social support on life expectancy may be as strong as the effects of obesity, cigarette smoking, hypertension, or level of physical activity (Sapolsky, 2004).

On the other hand, strong social support is associated with a decreased chance of developing depression, an increased likelihood of recovering from depression, and improved psychological outcomes after severe traumas such as childhood sexual abuse. Strong social support is also associated with fewer negative effects of numerous medical disorders. For example, Alan Rozanski and colleagues (1999) reported that close supportive relationships were instrumental in reducing the rate of high-risk behaviors such as cigarette smoking, excessive alcohol intake, or eating too much fatty food. Charles Holahan and colleagues (1995) found that rich social networks appear to enhance mental and physical health by fostering effective coping strategies; reducing the degree to which dangers are seen as being insurmountable; and increasing feelings of self-worth.

Overall, high-quality positive social support is associated with resilience to stress, and positive physical and mental health. It may even help to protect against developing symptoms of PTSD.

Is it better to give than to receive?

Up to this point in the chapter, we have focused on the value of receiving social support from others. However, giving social support is also valuable; perhaps equally so. Dale Carnegie, author of the classic book *How to Win Friends and Influence People*, gave good advice: "You can make more friends in two months by becoming interested in other people than you can in two years by trying to get other people interested in you" (2009 [1937], p. 56). To make a friend, be a friend.

At least one study suggests that giving social support may be more beneficial for physical health, than receiving it. Stephanie Brown and colleagues (2003) studied older adults over a five-year period, beginning with a questionnaire about the amount of social support each participant received and how much they gave. At the end of five years, there was no relationship between mortality and receiving social support from others. However, mortality was significantly reduced for individuals who reported giving emotional support to a spouse, and for individuals who provided instrumental support (e.g. material goods, services or financial support) to friends, neighbors and relatives. As described in Chapter 4 on moral compass and altruism, Carolyn Schwartz and colleagues (2003) have also identified how helping others can be beneficial to the helper.

In his novel *Charlotte's Web*, the famous twentieth-century author E. B. White expressed the benefits of providing support in these words, spoken by Charlotte the spider: "By helping you, perhaps I was trying to lift up my life a trifle. Heaven knows anyone's life can stand a little of that" (1952, p. 164).

Social neuroscience provides clues to the biology of relationships

In recent years, researchers have developed a new field called social neuroscience that investigates how different brain regions, neurotransmitters and hormones help to bind people together during times of need – parents with their children, husbands with their wives, friends with friends.

Social neuroscientists have found that the hormone oxytocin plays an important role in social communication, affiliation, sexual behavior and anxiety reduction. Oxytocin has also been shown to improve one's ability to recognize a familiar face, to correctly classify a facial expression as either positive or negative, and to correctly infer the mental state of another person (Heinrichs *et al.*, 2009; Lee *et al.*, 2009). It has been suggested that these actions of oxytocin may enhance prosocial behavior by promoting social recognition, trust and social approach (Heinrichs *et al.*, 2009). It is also known that during states of fear or stress, oxytocin reduces anxiety by dampening the cortisol system (HPA axis) and inhibiting the amygdala and related sympathetic nervous system activation.

Some of the most important research on oxytocin and vasopressin has investigated how these hormones affect the social behavior of two species of rodents, the prairie vole and the mountain vole. Prairie voles tend to be monogamous and form attachments with their mates for life. It has been estimated that only 3% of mammals are monogamous. (Humans, obviously, are not on this list.) Mountain voles, on the other hand, typically have many partners.

Oxytocin and vasopressin bind to specific chemical receptors and in so doing set off a cascasde of chemical reactions. Thomas Insel and colleagues at the National Institute of Mental Health have found that the pattern and distribution of oxytocin and vasopressin receptors differ in the brains of prairie voles and mountain voles (Insel & Shapiro, 1992). Prairie vole brains have more oxytocin and vasopressin receptors in several areas of the brain, including the nucleus accumbens and the amygdala. As we noted in Chapter 1, these brain regions are involved in social, emotional, survival, and sexual behaviors. Remarkably, when researchers elevated the number of vasopressin receptors in these brain regions, the previously non-monogamous mountain voles created pair bonds. (Imagine the possibilities for curbing unfaithful behavior in a human mate with a simple additive to his or her morning coffee!)

To further understand the effects of oxytocin on behavior, scientists have employed "knockout" techniques where mice were bred to be identical except for oxytocin genes (Hammock & Young, 2006; Winslow & Insel, 2002). Mice with and without the oxytocin gene were then run through a host of learning and memory tests. No differences in learning and memory were observed between the normal mice and the knockout mice except for social memory. Oxytocin knockout mice showed deficits in social memory, including failure to recognize mice with whom they had shared a cage. On the other hand, injection of oxytocin appears to facilitate affiliative behaviors such as increased touching and grooming. Similar deficits in social memory occur in knockout rats and mice lacking vasopressin receptors (Bielsky & Young, 2004).

This research may have implications for human behavior because human relationships rely heavily on social interactions, including the ability to recognize other individuals, remember their personal qualities, develop trust and form friendships. In studies with human subjects, oxytocin has been shown to increase trust (Kosfeld *et al.*, 2005) and to decrease stress.

Oxytocin not only fosters trust but may also protect against potentially harmful chemicals (e.g. cortisol) that are released during stress. For example, researchers led by Markus Heinrichs of the University of Zürich (2003) studied healthy young men in an experiment that focused on how they handled stress. Some of the men were told to come to the experiment alone, while others were asked to bring a close friend. The subjects were randomized into two groups: one group received a dose of oxytocin (via nasal spray) and the other a dose of placebo. The subjects then participated in two stress tests. Those who had brought a friend were allowed to ask the friend for support before and during the stress tests. The first test involved a mock job interview before a panel of strangers, which most people find highly stressful. In the second stress test, participants were asked to solve an arithmetic problem in their heads. During this test, subjects were constantly pushed by the panel to think faster. Salivary cortisol, as a hormone marker of stress, was measured at several points during the experiment.

The lowest levels of cortisol were found in men who brought a friend to the test and received oxytocin. The next lowest levels were observed in those who brought a friend but received a placebo instead of oxytocin. Men who came to the experiment alone and who received placebo had the highest levels of cortisol. The researchers concluded, "the combination of oxytocin and social support exhibited the lowest cortisol concentrations as well as increased calmness and decreased anxiety during stress" (Heinrichs *et al.*, 2003, p. 1389).

In summary, research has found that oxytocin is released during social situations where it appears to facilitate interpretation of social signals, enhance recognition, increase feelings of affiliation, and promote social approach. Oxytocin's actions in reducing amygdala activation and arousal may help to explain why positive support from others can reduce stress (Heinrichs *et al.*, 2009; Lee *et al.*, 2009).

Researchers have just begun to examine what happens to oxytocin and vasopressin when people do not have the benefit of a strong social network or a "tap code" – when they are isolated, separated from others or friendless. A study by University of Wisconsin researcher Alison Wismer Fries and colleagues (2005) found lower base-line levels of vasopressin and oxytocin in 4-year-old children raised in deprived social settings with deficient care-giving (orphanages in Russia and Romania) compared to levels of children who received more nurturing. This was true even though the orphans had been adopted by US families, in some cases up to 3 years before the experiment took place.

Building ties that bind

Clinicians and researchers, including the authors of this book, have not always fully appreciated the importance of social support. In the past, we focused most of our attention on trying to improve one-on-one psychotherapy techniques and searching for medications to reduce painful symptoms. We didn't spend much time thinking about the social networks of our patients. But that has changed. Our recent work with patients, our interviews with highly resilient individuals, our reading of the scientific literature, and our discussions with expert social scientists have convinced us that supportive social networks have the power to protect us and strengthen us.

So, how can you assess your own social network and how can you strengthen that network? Social scientists have developed a number of ways to measure social networks. These methods assess the extent and/or the quality of a person's network; they typically include questions like "whom could you count on to help you if you had just been fired from your job or expelled from school?" and "whom do you feel would help you if a family member very close to you died?" (Sarason *et al.*, 1983). They may also ask the extent to which you agree with various statements such as: "I am carefully listened to and understood by family members or friends," "Among my friends or relatives, there is someone who makes me feel better when I am feeling down," "I have problems that I can't discuss with family or friends," and "Among my friends or relatives, there is someone I go to when I need good advice" (D. W. King *et al.*, 2003; L. A. King *et al.*, 2006). We recommend that you ask similar questions and statements to evaluate your own social networks.

The resilient people we interviewed invest effort in giving and receiving social support. Ron and Barb Garrett, the parents of a Down syndrome son whom we described in Chapter 5, go out of their way to help neighbors with everyday needs; former Vietnam POWs stay in touch with one another through an active website as well as local and annual meetings. In this way they remain connected and take care of one another; Tim Cooper calls upon his extensive national network of fellow Special Forces members for help with problems no matter how large or small. Many groups have been formed in recent years to provide social support for veterans of the Iraq and Afghanistan wars. For example, women veterans have formed Service Women's Action Network (SWAN), whose mission is not only to connect female veterans with each other but also to press the Pentagon to improve its treatment of women in the military.

As General Hugh Shelton noted, the resilience enhancing effects of a strong, supportive and trustworthy social network are by no means restricted to the military. We all can find strength by reaching out and connecting with friends, colleagues, mentors and family. This is particularly true during times of high stress, fear, and loss.

There are myriad ways to broaden and strengthen the extent and strength of your relationships. Gaining and giving social support is a process, not an event; it doesn't happen overnight. Nevertheless, even if you feel friendless or isolated, it is important to start somewhere. No matter how small or weak your current network may be, you can take steps to increase its size and strength. For example, you might make a habit of smiling and saying "hello" to the neighbor at the elevator or the coworker who sits near you, or you might pick up the phone and call a family member who is lonely, or take the time to have coffee with a classmate who has just done poorly on a test.

For some of us who are shy or lacking in self-confidence, striking up a one-on-one conversation may seem difficult. In that case, try to attend social gatherings of any kind – join a hiking group or a book club or enroll in a continuing education class; take part in religious services or help out at a community event. Another step might involve joining a committee within an organization. As a committee member, you may be assigned specific tasks and goals, which will allow you to interact in a productive way with other group members.

A third way to build one's social network is to join a support group. Support groups of many kinds can provide the crucial social support that helps us recover after a trauma, or to endure an ongoing ordeal such as living with cancer or HIV/AIDS, or raising a child with special needs. Members of support groups are likely to understand the challenges that others in the group are facing, and they can learn how other members are coping with problems similar to their own. The range of support groups available is almost limitless and we encourage readers to seek a group that meets their specific needs. If you can't find one that works for you, start one!

Effective social support typically involves genuine communication that reaches beyond the superficial. In a study of the conversations between college undergraduates, Mattthias Mehl and colleagues (2010) at the University of Arizona found that conversations of a substantive nature, as opposed to trivial or "small talk" conversations, were correlated with greater happiness. As the authors note, the findings are purely correlational – they don't show whether in-depth conversations cause happiness, nor do they indicate whether or not being a happy person causes one to have more in-depth conversations. Further research on this topic may explore such cause–effect relationships.

In summary, those who know how to build strong positive social networks reap many benefits. Strong positive relationships are associated with better physical health, protection against depression and stress disorders such as PTSD, enhanced emotional well-being, and longer life. In our experience, most resilient individuals take advantage of the profound strengthening effects of positive social networks. In fact, Special Forces soldiers often deny having exceptional personal strength, sturdiness, or resilience. Instead, they believe that they acquire their strength and courage from their squad, from their buddies, from their "family" of fellow soldiers. The same is true for civilians. Elizabeth Ebaugh believes that family, friends, and caring professionals provided a "container" for her healing and in that container she found strength and courage to endure, and eventually to flourish. But, for most of us, our support network, even if it is extensive and strong, will not automatically reach out to embrace us when we are most in need. Rather, we would be wise to follow the example of the resilient individuals in this book by taking action, reaching out and "leaning into" those who care about us most. Very few resilient individuals go it alone – and neither should you.

References

Bielsky, I. F., & Young, L. J. (2004). Oxytocin, vasopressin, and social recognition in mammals. *Peptides*, **25**(9), 1565–1574.

Brown, S. L., Nesse, R. M., Vinokur, A. D., & Smith, D. M. (2003). Providing social support may be more beneficial than receiving it: Results from a prospective study of mortality. *Psychological Science*, **14**, 320–327.

Carnegie, D. (2009, original 1937). *How to win friends and influence people*. Reissue edition. New York, NY: Simon & Schuster.

Hammock, E. A. D., & Young, L. J. (2006). Oxytocin, vasopressin and pair bonding: implications for autism. *Philosophical Transactions of the Royal Society of London, Series B, Biological Sciences*, **361**(1476), 2187–2198.

Heinrichs, M., Baumgartner, T., Kirschbaum, C., & Ehlert, U. (2003). Social support and oxytocin interact to suppress cortisol and subjective responses to psychosocial stress. *Biological Psychiatry*, **54**, 1389–1398.

Heinrichs, M., von Dawans, B., & Domes, G. (2009). Oxytocin, vasopressin, and human social behavior. *Frontiers in Neuroendocrinology*, **30**(4), 548–557.

Holahan, C. J., Moos, R. H., Holahan, C. K., & Brennan, P. L. (1995). Social support, coping, and depressive symptoms in a late-middle-aged sample of patients reporting cardiac illness. *Health Psychology*, **14**(2), 152–163.

Insel, T. R., & Shapiro, L. E. (1992). Oxytocin receptor distribution reflects social organization in monogamous and polygamous voles. *Proceedings of the National Academy of Science*, **89**(13), 5981–5985.

King, D. W., King, L. A., & Vogt, D. S. (2003). *Manual for the Deployment Risk and Resilience Inventory (DRRI): A collection of scales for studying deployment-related experiences in military veterans*. Boston, MA: National Center for PTSD.

King, L. A., King, D. W., Vogt, D. S., Knight, J. A., & Samper, R. (2006). Deployment Risk and Resilience Inventory: A collection of measures for studying deployment-related experiences of military personnel and veterans. *Military Psychology*, **18**(2), 89–120.

King, L. A., King, D. W., Fairbank, J. A., Keane, T. M., & Adams, G. A. (1998). Resilience-recovery factors in post-traumatic stress disorder among female and male Vietnam veterans: Hardiness, postwar social support, and additional stressful life events. *Journal of Personality and Social Psychology*, **74**, 420–434.

Kosfeld, M., Heinrichs, M., Fischbacher, U., & Fehr, E. (2005). Oxytocin increases trust in humans. *Nature*, **435**, 673–676.

Lee, H. J., Macbeth, A. H., Pagani, J. H., & Young, W. S. (2009). Oxytocin: The great facilitator of life. *Progress in Neurobiology*, **88**(2), 127–151.

Manne, S. L., Pape, S. J., Taylor, K. L., & Dougherty, J. (1999). Spouse support, coping, and mood among individuals with cancer. *Annals of Behavioral Medicine*, **21**, 111–121.

Mehl, M. R., Vazire, S., Holleran, S. E., & Clark, C. S. (2010). Eavesdropping on happiness: Well-being is related to having less small talk and more substantive conversations. *Psychological Science*, **21**(4), 539–541.

Mohr, D. C., Classen, C., & Barrera, M. Jr. (2004). The relationship between social support, depression and treatment for people with multiple sclerosis. *Psychological Medicine*, **34**, 533–541.

Plumb, J. Charles (1992). *Overcoming adversity*. Audio cassette. Calabasas, CA: Author.

Revenson, T. A., Schiaffino, K. M., Majerovitz, S. D., & Gibofsky. A. (1991). Social support as a double-edged sword: the relation of positive and problematic support to depression among rheumatoid arthritis patients. *Social Science and Medicine*, **33**, 807–813.

Rozanski, A., Blumenthal, J. A., & Kaplan, J. (1999). Impact of pscychlogical factors on the pathogenesis of cardiovascular disease and implications for therapy. *Circulation*, **99**, 2192–2217.

Sapolsky, R. M. (2004). *Why zebras don't get ulcers: An updated guide to stress, stress related diseases, and coping* (3rd ed.). New York, NY: Henry Holt & Co.

Sarason, I. G., Levine, H. M., Basham, R. B., & Sarason, B. R. (1983). Assessing social support: The Social Support Questionnaire. *Journal of Personality and Social Psychology*, **44**(1), 127–139.

Schwartz, C., Meisenhelder, J. B., Ma, Y., & Reed, G. (2003). Altruistic social interest behaviors are associated with better mental health. *Psychosomatic Medicine*, **65**, 778–785.

Stockdale, J. B. (1984). *A Vietnam Experience: Ten Years of Reflections*. Stanford, CA: Hoover Institution, Stanford University.

White, E. B. (1952). *Charlotte's Web*. New York, NY: Harper & Row, p. 164.

Winslow, J., & Insel, T. (2002). The social deficits of the oxytocin knockout mouse. *Neuropeptides*, **36**(2), 221–229.

Wismer Fries, A. B., Ziegler, T. E., Kurian, J. R., Jacoris, S., & Pollak, S. D. (2005). Early experience in humans is associated with changes in neuropeptides critical for regulating social behavior. *Proceedings of the National Academy of Science*, **102**, 17 237–17 240.

Chapter 7

Role models: providing the road map

One of the first psychologists to study resilience, Emmy Werner, followed the lives of children who were raised in impoverished homes with an alcoholic, abusive, or mentally ill parent. Werner observed that resilient children – the ones who grew up to be productive, emotionally healthy adults – had at least one person in their lives who truly supported them and served as an admired role model (Werner, 1993; Werner & Smith, 1992). Our research has found a similar pattern: all of the resilient individuals we interviewed have role models whose beliefs, attitudes and behaviors inspire them.

Francine Cournos, a Professor of Clinical Psychiatry at the Columbia University School of Medicine, looked to her parents as role models of strength. As a young girl, Francine lived through the deaths of her mother and father, rejection by her extended family and placement in the foster care system. Yet the memory of her parents continued to inspire her.

> I had a really good connection with my mother that I internalized – of someone who had my best interest at heart – a very good role model for how to handle adverse situations. She was very stoic and never revealed vulnerabilities. She never talked about being ill. Any adverse event I had, I always tried to be like her. Even during my episode of major depression, I was smiling, and people were shocked. My mother was like that. She worked until the day she died. She was a role model for how you function no matter what. I learned from my mother that survival is the most important thing. You must survive first. I admired her ability to get up and go to work no matter how she felt. Toward the end she was very sick; she had metastatic cancer; she couldn't breathe and had pleural effusions removed from her lungs. But she just didn't succumb. I viewed my mother as having tremendous physical toughness, and, by comparison, psychological pain was nothing. That was my view of it. So I felt that if she didn't give herself any excuses, I certainly didn't have any excuses. I was healthy.

Dr. Cournos barely knew her father, as he died when she was only three. Most of what she knows of him has come from newspaper clippings, court testimony, and conversations with relatives. As a young man, Alexander Cournos had been a member of the Industrial Workers of the World, known as the "Wobblies," a labor group whose goal was to organize all the world's workers into "one big union." In 1917, he was imprisoned because of his political activism and spent the next six years in prison. He was described as a man with "great strength of character and unbelievable moral stamina, courageous beyond description and uncompromising and unshakeable when it came to matters of his conviction and integrity." In her memoir, *City of One*, Cournos (1999) describes how her father's memory has been a guiding light for her own life:

> I held onto the positive image: I now knew that my father believed deeply in a cause, that he had a fighting spirit. Over the years I would feel him watching over me whenever I needed to defend my own beliefs, and I tried to live up to what I imagined he would have expected of me.

In addition to parents (living or deceased), role models can include relatives, teachers, coaches, or clergy. They may be older or one's own age: friends, siblings, colleagues at work or military buddies. Role models can even be children – and not necessarily our own children.

Dorinne Naughton, who worked with us for years as a good friend and dedicated administrative officer, was initially shocked when she learned that she had cancer and needed chemotherapy. Within the previous 12 months her fiancé, mother, and father had all died of cancer, and now it was her turn to face a potentially lethal form of the disease. Five days a week for over a month, Dorinne went to the Oncology division of the National Institute of Health for radiation treatment.

> Every day I saw a little boy there in the waiting room. His name was David and he was five years old with a great attitude. He and I would play checkers or tic-tac-toe while we were waiting. Seeing that little boy made me realize that I was pretty lucky to go through 50 years without ever being sick. He had a brain tumor and had been through surgery, but he was the happiest little kid, not scared a bit. He used to bounce in and say hello to me. He once said, "I'm going to teach you tic-tac-toe so you can beat all of your friends and you'll win all of the time."

Role models may also be people we have never met. Barb Garrett, the mother of a son with Down syndrome whom we described in Chapter 5 on religion, cites Joni Eareckson Tada as one of her "heroes." Paralyzed from the neck down as a result of a water sports accident when she was a teenager, Joni has dedicated her life to a ministry for the disabled and suffering. From the time Barb was in high school, she has admired Joni's spirit and found inspiration in her radio program, writings, and other creative expressions. Joni is an artist who paints by holding the paintbrush between her teeth. She is also a talented singer; Barb says she listens to Joni's songs to dispel feelings of self-pity. In one song, Joni expresses how she would like to peel potatoes, change a baby's diaper, and do various other mundane tasks that people who are not paralyzed take for granted. Barb says, "Listening to that, and knowing she can't move – no matter what I'm facing, I know it can't be that bad!"

Role models may be famous athletes, political leaders, historical figures, or even fictional characters from literature. Deborah Gruen, the Yale University graduate and Paralympic swimmer born with spina bifida whose story we told in Chapter 2 on optimism, sees Franklin Delano Roosevelt as one of her role models:

> Franklin Roosevelt really exemplifies what it's like to be a person with a disability in an able-bodied world. I mean, you don't understand how hard this

guy had to work just to walk. When he gave speeches and he was standing up, he grabbed the podium so hard to keep himself steady. He hid the fact that he had a disability, but at the same time it was always with him. And I think having polio really changed him. I feel like that's me, too.

Deborah may not realize it, but she herself serves as a role model for some of her teammates and classmates. Deborah's parents tell the story of their daughter's first college interview:

> The first time you go to a college visit with this kid, you wonder, how is this ever going to work? How is this kid going to swim on a varsity Division 1 team? So four-and-a-half-foot Deb walks into the coach's office and says, "This is what I want to do here at your college on your swim team."
>
> [The coach] probably thinks, "I'll just gladhand these people for 20 minutes and get them out the door."
>
> But then Deborah gets into it with him. "I swim 25 to 35 miles per week, that's 1,500 miles per year, and I have been doing that for the past four years, which makes 6,000 miles."
>
> Eventually he says, "So you don't need your own lane? And you don't need special coaching?"
>
> And she says, "No, I don't need my own lane and I don't need special coaching." And then she gets right to the point and asks him, "So can I swim here on this team?"
>
> And you can see him begin to shake.
>
> But then … he starts to get it, and all of a sudden you can see the little gears going around and around and the light bulb goes off and he realizes that this kid really can be important to his team.
>
> And he says, "You know I can't help you get into the school."
>
> And she says, "I'm not asking you to help me get into this school." So she shows him her GPA and her SAT scores.
>
> And he says, "Oh, yeah. No problem."
>
> But why would they want her on their team? She is not going to score points for them in their championship. They want her there because some of the other kids are whiners and complainers. And that's just not going to happen with Deb. When this kid walks on the pool deck, she'll be the first one there and the last one to leave. An hour later the coach is recruiting her! What was I worrying about?

The expectation that Deborah would model positive attitudes and "can-do" behavior to her teammates was fulfilled during her years at Yale. She was the 2010 recipient of the Amanda Walton Award, which is given to an outstanding athlete who has "excelled on the field of play and who has shown spirit and courage in transcending unforeseen challenges," as well as the David Everett Chantler Award, given to the graduating senior who "best exemplifies qualities of courage, strength of character and high moral purpose."

In some families, resilient role models span multiple generations. Hardy grandfathers and grandmothers beget hardy sons and daughters, who, in turn, raise their own resilient children. Tim Cooper, a Special Forces (SF) soldier, who works as an instructor teaching other less experienced soldiers, comes from one of these families.

> I had family, relatives who were in the military. It's all about serving your country. I had a grandfather who was a paratrooper in World War II; my father was Special Forces in Vietnam. He passed away. And my uncle, he was Special Forces. He … would occasionally come home on the weekends and run me up to the Green River, teach me how to do camouflage and stuff like that … and he was the one who guided me into my initial unit.

While parents or grandparents often serve as primary role models for children who later become competent and sturdy adults, sometimes other adults, from unexpected places, can serve as mentors.

Lew Meyer, whom we mentioned in Chapter 2 as being influenced by Norman Vincent Peale's *The Power of Positive Thinking*, was working as a civilian fire protection specialist for the US government in South Vietnam when his field unit was overrun by North Vietnamese Regulars during the Tet Offensive of 1968. After a three-day siege, his unit surrendered, and he spent the next five years in prison.

Meyer remembers two adults who guided him through his difficult childhood years. First was his truant officer, Ed Rowe, whose job was to catch Meyer and bring him back to school after he climbed out the classroom window, which he and his best friend Dave had a habit of doing whenever the teacher left the room. Officer Rowe pursued and reprimanded them. However, he also looked out for them; he was the one who got them summer jobs with the forestry service and started Lew's firefighting career.

Once, when Lew and Dave had no sponsor for their neighborhood baseball team, they stole baseball gear from a well-equipped rival team.

> Our baseball team all of a sudden showed up with catching paraphernalia and bats and balls. … Officer Rowe, instead of catching us, talked to us and told us if we could find the guys who did it and tell them to return it, then he would get us a sponsor. … So we went through the fence and under the bleachers and into the lockers and returned the stuff. Then the police sponsored our team, and we went to our games in police cars and everything. The local patrols would stop to watch us while we were playing. I think that's how he started turning us around.

Lew Meyer's second role model was Captain Herman Shawver, the strict but patient local fire captain. Shawver took a liking to Lew, caring enough about him to intentionally break firehouse rules by allowing the young boy to hang around the station. Lew stuck close to the Captain, watching how he ran the firehouse, how he inspired his men, how he sized up a fire and then, without hesitation, marched into the flames. In the end, Lew followed in Captain Shawver's footsteps and became a firefighter and fire chief himself.

As he grew older, Meyer continued to look for sturdy adult role models. During his late teens, while playing on a military football team, Meyer turned to his coach.

His coach expected a great deal of Lew and never let him take the easy path, despite the fact that he was the smallest player on the squad. During one game against a particularly rugged team, Meyer remembers being called to the sideline for a quick breather. Beaten up and bruised, he turned to his coach and said, "Coach, they're killing me in there."

Lew never forgot his coach's reply: "I know it. Now get back in there."

Role models don't necessarily have to be older and wiser. Sometimes our peers can guide and inspire us. Air Force pilot Steve Long was 25 years old when, on a flight out of Thailand, he was shot down over Laos. Throughout his ordeal, he drew inspiration from his fellow POWs.

> The routine is they beat you and torture you until they get the information that they want, until they think they've got all the information they're going to get out of you. … And they do that until they eventually feel like they've got the information and then if you live through that, they'll give you medical treatment.
>
> But the role models we had were just fantastic. People referred to us as heroes, and I don't think any of us consider ourselves as a hero. But those guys are my heroes, the ones who got us through these ordeals. You'd hear stories, sometimes you'd hear some guy being beaten down the cell block from you and just resisting. And you felt really bad for him, but it pumped you up to know that you were just proud to be serving in the same military with a guy like that. There was always somebody there to set a standard.

At the top of Steve Long's list was Ernie Brace, a civilian pilot whose plane was shot down over Laos in 1965. He spent the next three years in the jungle on the side of a mountain, strapped inside a bamboo cage.

> Talk about solitary confinement! Three-and-a-half years in a bamboo cage! He escaped three times and was beaten horribly. The last time he escaped, they buried him in a hole for a week. He lost all control of his body from his chest down. When they pulled him out, he couldn't walk. He was paralyzed. So he got around dragging his body by his elbows. And I guess out in the jungle, he got to the point where he could sit up. They brought him into Hanoi and put him in one of the cells next to John McCain. But Ernie was able to crawl over to the corner and by holding on to two walls, he could stand up. And eventually, he regained the ability to walk. … And you know what, Ernie was one of those guys who never complained.

Jerry White, co-founder and CEO of Landmine Survivors Network, which shared the Nobel Peace Prize in 1997, honoring the work of the International Campaign to Ban Landmines, never served in the military. Still, one of his role models was a wounded Israeli soldier. As an 18-year-old foreign exchange student to Israel from the United States, Jerry lost his foot when he stepped on a landmine while hiking in the Golan Heights. He was taken to a hospital in Tel Aviv where initially he became depressed and discouraged.

> The guy in the next bed wanted to die after losing both legs. I needed to distance myself from that. Then an Israeli soldier came for a peer visit. He walked up to

my bed and said, "I stepped on a landmine, too. Can you tell which leg I lost?" He had a perfect gait. I said I couldn't tell and he said, "That's the point. The battle isn't down there." He pointed to his legs. "It's up here." He pointed to his heart. When he found out that I still had my knee, which meant that I wasn't that bad off, he said, "What you have is a nose cold. You'll get over it."

He tapped into my spirit. Could I engage or not? I got the message very clearly. This was peer support with a kick in the pants. The soldier was saying "I've been through it, and if I can do it, you can too. Get on with it."

He wasn't the typical peer supporter, but better, a role model. No pity. Don't enable and fuel people's victimhood with pity and condescending sympathy. He modeled for me, and today I am a good peer role model. It's not about the thing, it's about you. You can make of this what you want. It's your choice.

Role models need not be perfect. Everyone has their own unique strengths and weaknesses, and we believe that searching for the perfect role model is futile. Years after his amputation, while co-directing Landmine Survivors Network, Jerry White became a friend of Diana, Princess of Wales, and learned to emulate the strengths he saw in her. Princess Diana used her high-profile position to bring attention to landmine survivors and to advocate for an international treaty banning landmines. On a trip to Bosnia with Diana, Jerry began to appreciate the complexity of her personality.

In working with Diana, I learned you could be all of these things: You can be catty and competitive and crazy at times and insecure, but also have a true gift of compassion. … Isn't that great, you can be all of these things? What's more interesting than a range of personality traits with virtues and vices and real gifts, where you try to play to your best self? In that last year of her life, she was coming into her own, blossoming and calling her own shots. She understood that every survivor we meet has a date, the date of their trauma. She said to me, "I'm July 29, 1981," and then burst out laughing. That was the day she got married. Her gift was compassion and dignity in the face of raw suffering. Her gift was the way she could touch people. One of the classiest peer supporters I've ever seen. She cared enough to show up and she listened. "Relax," she said. "Play to your best self. Don't give in to the demons but feed the angels."

Jerry White believes that both of his parents also served as influential role models while he struggled to adapt to the loss of his leg. Jerry's father owned his own business while his mother stayed at home to raise the children. His parents believed in education and in striving to reach one's potential. But they also believed in social justice and reaching out to others while climbing the ladder of life.

My father was a role model because he never changed, but was always kind and good. He made sure things were taken care of, phone calls covered. No fanfare, but solid and good and generous. He was the old-fashioned kind of father. My mother gave me the kick in the pants, the fire of social justice. She said I had an obligation to serve, to fight for justice and to get it right.

White considers himself lucky because he was given a sturdy foundation to deal with adversity. He had two strong parents who helped to shape his response to trauma.

Like his father, Jerry remained solid, good and generous even during the most trying times. And like his mother, he refused to let the fire of social justice die out. In fact, his tragedy became fuel for a life devoted to helping others.

The negative role model: what not to imitate

Although we generally think of role models as providing positive examples to admire and emulate, in some cases a particular person may stand out in the opposite way – embodying traits we emphatically do *not* want to have. We can think of such a person as a negative role model.

Laurie Harkness, Clinical Professor of Psychiatry at the Yale University School of medicine and a national leader in psychiatric rehabilitation at the Connecticut Veterans Hospital, was in her early 50s when she was diagnosed with leukemia. In the course of undergoing treatment, she encountered a number of other cancer patients, one of whom seemed to be "giving up," resigning himself to the idea that he would never get better. Laurie clearly remembers the moment she thought, "I will *not* be like that." Throughout her treatment and recovery, whenever she felt discouraged, she would remember this "negative role model" and use that memory as a motivation to fight the disease and strive for a positive outlook. And that's exactly what she did. Despite feeling weak and nauseated for weeks at a time, Laurie never gave up. If anything she picked up the pace. Since receiving her diagnosis eight years ago, she has worked tirelessly to develop vocational and housing opportunities for individuals and families who struggle with homelessness or are at risk of homelessness. She has partnered with community agencies to successfully procure over $50 million dollars of Federal, State, private and foundation grants to develop over 500 new units of permanent housing for homeless Veterans.

During our work with various clients, we have often encountered people who were mistreated in childhood by one or both parents. Such individuals are often fiercely determined to live a life different from that of their abuser. Rather than imitate the negative behavior, they make a great effort to learn new, more positive behaviors. Like Laurie Harkness, they use the example of the abuser as a guidepost for what *not* to do and what *not* to become. This becomes a mission that they carry out as they develop relationships and raise their own families.

Everybody needs resilient role models, especially children

Abundant research shows that parents, as well as coaches and non-parent adult mentors, play vital roles in a young person's ability to handle trauma and overcome adversity. Parents often ask, "How can I be a strong role model for my child or teenager?" One answer is to practice the resilient behaviors that we outline in this book, and to give your child ample opportunities to do the same.

Children who are resilient and well-adjusted typically receive support and encouragement from committed mentors and resilient role models. As we mentioned at the beginning of this chapter, psychologist Emmy Werner found that even children who have suffered neglect or abuse can do well if they have someone in their life who truly cares about them and gives unconditional support and encouragement.

Ideally, mentors help to foster resilience through their words and actions. They teach and they demonstrate. Good mentors inspire, motivate, provide consistent and reliable support, and foster self-esteem. By emulating and imitating their mentors, children and adolescents learn right from wrong, how to handle challenging situations, and when and how to control their impulses, delay gratification and soothe themselves. They learn about moral and ethical integrity and about courage. They begin to take responsibility for their actions and their lives. Children have much to learn from mature and loving mentors and role models.

Research has shown that teens with dedicated mentors have more positive attitudes toward school, better grades and attendance, greater maturity and better mental health with less depression and anxiety. They also are less likely to begin drinking alcohol and using illegal drugs. This is particularly true of kids with mentors who are part of their natural social environment – that is, relatives, neighbors, teachers, and coaches. These kinds of mentors tend to be more effective than volunteers who come from outside the child's natural social network. Especially effective are non-parental relatives, such as grandparents or uncles and aunts, who know and understand the child's story and his or her personal, family and cultural history (Southwick *et al.*, 2006).

Volunteer mentors from outside the child's natural social network tend to be less effective than those from within because they often invest limited time and energy and because they tend to have only a superficial understanding of family and cultural issues. This does not mean, however, that volunteer mentors cannot be helpful. Big Brothers and Big Sisters, for example, have experienced impressive success over the years, but their success generally involves situations where the mentor–mentee relationship lasts for at least one year. In fact, the longer the mentor–mentee relationship, the greater the likelihood of success.

Of course, modeling continues to be an important form of learning well into adulthood and even old age. We are never too old to learn from the example of others.

How role modeling works

Imitation is a powerful form of learning and plays an important role in shaping human behavior. Throughout our lives, each of us learns by imitating the attitudes, values, skills, and patterns of thought and behavior of those around us, yet we are often unaware that we are doing so. How does role modeling actually work?

Role modeling depends, in part, on *observational learning*: learning that takes place not by being taught, but merely by watching what someone else is doing. According to a Buddhist proverb, "A child learns more from his mother's back than from her face." Thus, without intending to teach her child, the mother is providing opportunities for observational learning all day long simply by being within sight of the child.

Someone traveling in a foreign country for the first time may be unfamiliar with subtleties of the local culture, such as the particular way in which people wait for an available table in a restaurant, summon a taxi, or line up to use a public restroom. Rather than asking a native how to go about these behaviors, they might simply observe the natives and "do as the Romans do." In this case, they have employed observational learning.

Albert Bandura, one of the most influential psychologists of the twentieth century, believes that modeling often involves more than simple mimicry, imitation or observational learning (Bandura, 1977, 1986). Instead, it involves learning rules of behavior that then serve as guides for future action. By developing such rules, the learner is able to incorporate thoughts, values, behaviors and emotional reactions that resemble those of the role model but that fit the particular personality and circumstances of the learner.

Suppose, for example, that you enjoy golf and you want to improve your putting stroke. With modeling in mind, you might first watch your role model/instructor putt the ball from different angles and distances; you would then carefully analyze his/her putting technique and subdivide it into natural segments; finally, you would transform each individual segment into a rule designed to guide that specific aspect of the putting stroke. Such rules are essential because no two putting situations are identical and the rules allow you to apply what you have learned from your role model.

As you watch your instructor putt the ball on numerous greens, you notice that he never takes his eye off the ball. Like a hawk, he zeros in on the ball and stares at it during short putts, long putts, uphill putts and downhill putts. You the learner can now transform your observations into a rule that applies to all of your own future putts no matter what the conditions or circumstances. Your rule: whenever I putt, I will continuously keep my eye on the ball.

Suppose you have a lifelong friend who always seems to handle stressful situations with relative ease. You admire this resilient friend and wonder how she does it. So you intentionally begin to observe and study her behavior. When her mother dies, you notice that she reaches out to friends and family, and actively solicits their support. A year later, she is laid off from work; she immediately calls former employers and fellow employees and asks if they can assist in her job search. On another occasion, she falls ill with pneumonia. Rather than staying at home alone, she moves in with her sister until she has recovered. Watching how your friend handles these different stressful situations, you notice a pattern: during periods of high stress, she actively reaches out to others and seeks their assistance. You can now turn this pattern into a rule that you can adopt for yourself during a wide variety of your own stressful situations. The rule: to enhance your resilience during stressful situations, you must actively reach out to your family, friends and colleagues for their advice, assistance and emotional support. By formulating this rule, you have constructed a guiding principle that can enhance your resilience to stress and that you can apply to a myriad of challenging situations.

Is there a neuroscience to learning from role models?

The ability to imitate appears to be inborn. Even in the first days of life, infants can imitate rudimentary facial expressions (Meltzoff & Moore, 1989). This ability to imitate persists throughout life and plays an essential role in acquiring behaviors, skills, mannerisms, social bonds, empathy, morality, cultural traditions, perhaps even language.

In exploring how imitation works, researchers have performed neuroscience experiments of various kinds. As early as 1975 – before brain imaging methods such as MRI or PET scans became standard research tools – Seymour M. Berger and Suzanne W. Hadley at the University of Massachusetts, Amherst examined movements of the arm, hand, and mouth by attaching electrodes to the arms, palms, forehead and lips of research participants. These electrodes allowed the researchers to measure muscle activity while the participants watched a video of someone stuttering and a separate video of two men arm wrestling. The highest level of muscle activity in the lips was recorded as participants watched the stuttering video, while the highest muscle activity in their arms was recorded while they watched the arm wrestling video. That is, while observing muscle activity in another person, participants experienced muscle activity in their own analogous muscles.

Further advances in neuroscience continued to illuminate not only the muscle activity but also possible brain mechanisms that underlie imitation. In the mid-1990s, researchers from the University of Parma in Italy discovered "mirror neurons" in monkeys in areas of the brain that control movement. Later research with humans has implicated a far broader network of neurons involved in processing movement, perception, emotions and language. Researchers found that when humans observe the behavior of another person, the same brain regions that are activated in the other person's brain while he or she performs the behavior become activated in the observer's brain. Thus, it appears that some of the same brain regions that fire when we catch a football also fire when we watch someone else catch a football. Perhaps we are able to understand and, in a sense, vicariously experience the movements and actions of others because we have our own neuronal template for similar movements and actions.

Even hearing or reading about a behavior may activate areas of the brain responsible for carrying out the behaviour (Aziz-Zadeh *et al.*, 2004). In an experiment at the University of California, Los Angeles, Lisa Aziz-Zadeh and colleagues (2006) used fMRI (functional magnetic resonance imaging) to observe specific areas of the brain known to control movement of the hand when participants read sentences such as "Grasp the banana." They compared this to the brain activity when the same participants watched video clips of someone grasping an apple. The brain areas associated with hand movement became activated under both conditions. Similarly, reading sentences such as "Bite the peach" or watching a video clip of someone biting an apple, activated areas of the brain known to control movement of the lips and mouth.

In addition to simulating movement and action, some evidence suggests that mirror neurons may also help us to understand the emotions of another person and to empathize with others. In his book *Mirroring People: The New Science of How We Connect With Others* (2008), Marco Iacoboni at the University of California, Los Angeles hypothesizes that when we observe the facial expression of another person, our own analogous facial muscle mirror neurons become activated. These cortical mirror neurons then send signals to the emotion center of the brain, helping us to experience the same emotion that we are observing in the other person.

A 2003 fMRI study by a team of European researchers led by Bruno Wicker provides another example of this connection between observation and emotion. The research team found that the same areas of the brain became activated when participants either experienced feelings of disgust themselves or observed another person experiencing feelings of disgust. Perhaps, to understand the feelings of others, we must literally activate the analogous brain regions in ourselves.

This research suggests that mirror neurons may play a role in facilitating social interactions by promoting shared understanding and perhaps even empathy.

Much remains to be learned about this fascinating and relatively new area of research.

How can I use role models to become more resilient?

Imitation and modeling can be used as a tool to increase resilience. During his POW experience, Rod Knutson preserved his integrity in enduring torture sessions by modeling the moral strength and discipline of his father; while struggling to find his identity as a young man, Lew Meyer looked to and modeled the maturity and leadership of Fire Captain Herman Shawver; during his 49 months in a North Vietnamese prison, Steve Long turned to his peers to find inspiration and to model techniques for resisting the enemy. And after losing his leg to a land mine, Jerry White emulated the no-nonsense "kick in the pants" approach of an Israeli amputee in order to "get on with it."

You can also do this in your own life. Earlier in this chapter, we described how one might imitate the social behaviors of a resilient friend. In further studying this resilient friend, you notice that during times of high stress, she not only solicits assistance from others, she also makes every effort to maintain adequate nutrition, sleep and exercise. Now you have two potential rules to enhance resilience during times of high stress. First, actively reach out to your family, friends and colleagues for their advice, assistance and emotional support. Second, make every effort to eat nutritious food, stay hydrated and get ample sleep and exercise.

Over the years, researchers have conducted experiments to determine the most effective and efficient ways to learn from role models. We have summarized the following principles based on our understanding of these findings. When trying to model behavior, begin by carefully studying the behavior. Then:

1. Break it into simple segments: if you want to use modeling to learn a complex skill, it helps to subdivide the complex skill into simple segments and then focus on one segment at a time. If, on the other hand, you try to model the entire complex skill (e.g. putting, becoming more resilient) without breaking it into segments, you will likely be bombarded with too much information, will make many errors, and will have great difficulty mastering that skill.

2. Observe the skill in a variety of settings: breaking a complex skill into simpler segments will require time and concentration. You will need to observe the skill numerous times and in a variety of different settings.

3. Practice: you will find it helpful to practice in between observations. You may do this by imagining that you possess a particular attitude, personality style, or behavior that resembles that of your role model, or by actually enacting the desired attitude, style or behavior in your own life. Both forms of practice appear to be effective, although real life enactment is eventually required for successful imitation.

4. Obtain feedback: whenever possible, obtain constructive feedback. An expert, or someone with a trained eye, can point out similarities to and differences between your behavior and the behavior that you are attempting to model. This expert can then recommend steps to correct deviations from the model.

Obviously, most people are less scientific in the way they use modeling and benefit from it. It's entirely possible to learn from role models without even being aware of it.

As we have seen from a number of the examples in this chapter, most people typically have more than one role model. This makes good sense, because it is rare, if not impossible, for any of us to be strong in every area of life. We are all human with our own strengths and weaknesses. Thich Nhat Hahn, one of the world's great Buddhist teachers, suggests that each of us try to internalize the best qualities of family members who came before us, even those who we have never met. If our mother is depressed but courageous, then imitate her courage. If our father is dedicated but punitive, then imitate his dedication. As the landmine survivor Jerry White might say, "Search for resilient role models, imitate their best qualities and then play to your best self." When successful, the end result is a resilient tapestry constructed from the characteristics of multiple hardy role models.

References

Aziz-Zadeh, L., Iacoboni, M., Zaidel, E., Wilson, S., & Mazziotta, J. (2004). Left hemisphere motor facilitation in response to manual action sounds. *The European Journal of Neuroscience*, **19**(9), 2609–2612.

Aziz-Zadeh, L., Wilson, S. M., Rizzolatti, G., & Iacoboni, M. (2006). Congruent embodied representations for visually presented actions and linguistic phrases describing action. *Current Biology*, **16**, 1818–1823.

Bandura, A. (1977). *Social learning theory*. Englewood Cliffs, NJ: Prentice-Hall.

Bandura, A. (1986). *Social foundations of thought and action: A social-cognitvie theory*. Englewood Cliffs, NJ: Prentice-Hall.

Berger, S. M., & Hadley, S. W. (1975). Some effects of a model's performance on an observer's electromyographic activity. *The American Journal of Psychology*, **88**(2), 263–276.

Cournos, F. (1999). *City of One: A Memoir*. New York, NY: W.W. Norton.

Iacoboni, M. (2008). *Mirroring People: The New Science of How We Connect With Others*. New York, NY: Farrar, Straus and Giroux.

Meltzoff, A. N., & Moore, M. K. (1989). Imitation in newborn infants: Exploring the range of gestures imitated and the underlying mechanisms. *Developmental Psychology*, **25**, 954–962.

Southwick, S. M., Morgan, C. A., Vythilingam, M., & Charney, D. S. (2006). Mentors enhance resilience in at-risk children and adolescents. *Psychoanalytic Inquiry*, **26**(4), 577–584.

Werner, E. E. (1993). Risk, resilience, and recovery: Perspectives from the Kauai Longitudinal Study. *Development and Psychopathology*, **5**, 503–515.

Werner, E. E., & Smith, R.S. (1992). *Overcoming the odds: High risk children from birth to adulthood.* Ithaca, NY and London: Cornell University Press.

Wicker, B., Keysers, C., Plailly, J., Royet, J. P., Gallese, V., & Rizzolatti, G. (2003). Both of us disgusted in My insula: The common neural basis of seeing and feeling disgust. *Neuron*, **40**(3), 655–664.

Chapter 8

Training: physical fitness and strengthening

It is no secret that physical training is good for our health. Scientific studies have repeatedly shown that becoming physically fit enhances general health and can help to prevent or reduce the debilitating effects of high blood pressure, cardiovascular disease, stroke, diabetes, arthritis, and a variety of other chronic medical disorders.

Physical training and mastering physical challenges can also improve mood, cognition and emotional resilience. Many of the resilient individuals we interviewed have a regular habit of exercise and believe that staying fit has helped them, both during their traumatic ordeals and during their recovery. In fact, some of them credit physical exercise with saving their lives.

Surviving with the Air Force 5BX and the "daily dozen"

Korean War veteran Lew Meyer, whom we have mentioned earlier in the book, was a civilian firefighter working for the military in South Vietnam when his post in Hue was overrun by North Vietnamese soldiers during the Tet offensive in 1968. After three days of fighting, Meyer and 12 others were captured and force-marched through the jungle for an arduous five months, ultimately reaching Skid Row Prison, 60 km northwest of Hanoi. There Lew was imprisoned in a dark 8-by-4 foot cell, where he remained alone for the next 22 months. By the time of his release on March 27, 1973, he had spent more than five years as a POW; only then did he find out that he had been listed as Missing In Action (MIA) the entire time.

Meyer exercised in prison whenever possible, even when he felt tired or weak. Sometimes he jogged in tiny circles around his cell and sometimes he did isometric exercises, but at other times it was as many sets as possible of the Air Force 5BX, Army "daily dozen" or "JFKs" (exercises recommended by President John F. Kennedy's Council on Physical Fitness). These widely known calisthenic routines contain a variety of exercises such as sit-ups, pushups, squat jumps, and jumping jacks. Meyer's cell was so small that his fingernails would strike the wall leaving scratch marks when he did jumping jacks.

Lew continued to exercise even while shackled in leg locks that were embedded in the concrete floor of his tiny cell.

> In the morning I asked them to take my legs out of the locks. I wanted to do my JFKs, my exercises. But they didn't listen. So I started doing sit-ups. Then they pushed me back, yanked my leg locks off, removed them from the cell, and never put the leg locks on me again because the locks helped me do more sit-ups.

When transferred to a larger cell with roommates, Meyer increased the intensity of his workout routine and included his cellmates in practicing the Air Force 5BX and the Army daily dozen. They started with one repetition of each exercise and then progressed to two, three and four repetitions. Devotion was matched with creativity: the routine often included "weight lifting," using the smallest prisoner as a weight.

When we interviewed Lew, we asked how many pushups he could do at the height of his prison training. He responded, "One arm or two arms?" Anyone who has ever tried to do one-arm pushups knows how difficult they are and how much strength and balance is required. Most people, even if they can do numerous two-arm push-ups, can't do even one of the one-arm variety. Meyer could do 64.

One year into his captivity, Lew Meyer acquired a cellmate named Jim Thompson, a Green Beret who had been held in primitive camps in the mountains of South Vietnam and Laos for five years, where he was starved, brutally tortured and subjected to years of solitary confinement. When Thompson was finally transferred to the Skid Row prison in North Vietnam, he was gravely malnourished, weighing less than 100 pounds. Mike O'Connor, a fellow POW, couldn't believe what he saw when Thompson first arrived.

> He was standing right next to me. This guy is dead, I thought. As part of some cruel joke, I thought, they had stuck a corpse up against the door. Then I realized he was moving. He looked like something out of Auschwitz. ... I didn't know how he stood up, how he breathed, how he did anything. His features were so distorted ... I could literally see his entire skeleton and the balls of his joints around his knees and elbows. ... His stomach was completely wrapped under his rib cage. ... It took him half an hour to stand. ... Talk about a gutsy guy. (Philpott, 2002, p. 159)

On their first morning together, Lew began the day with his customary exercise routine. When he got to push-ups, Thompson tried to join him but was so weak that his arms gave way and his face struck the concrete floor. He couldn't do a single push-up.

Meyer then changed his routine and began to coach Thompson back to health. Each morning, the two began their day with exercise. At first Thompson could tolerate only deep breathing exercises and gradually some bending and stretching. Every day, Lew would patiently coach his roommate, and within six months, Thompson successfully completed the daily dozen. That was just the beginning.

With time, Thompson's health improved enough that the two men devised an escape plan. Success would depend on preparation and on their ability to navigate the dense surrounding jungle. For over a year, they planned and trained for the extreme physical demands that lay ahead. Gradually their exercise routine became more and more challenging. For aerobic conditioning, they stacked their beds on top of one another and ran laps around their tiny cell, initially in their rubber-tire Ho Chi Minh sandals, and eventually barefoot to build up calluses. At the height of their training, Meyer ran for 24 hours without stopping until he noticed blood in his urine. Remarkably, Thompson ran for 15 hours.

Like Lew Meyer, fellow prisoner Rod Knutson believes that rigorous exercise fosters physical and psychological resilience.

> I worked hard to stay in shape. In 1969, when I lived in a cell with seven guys, we had – I forget what we called it – an Iron Man Contest or something. It involved sit-ups and pushups, and they had to be regulation style pushups, regulation style sit-ups. A guy by the name of Cole Black won the pushup contest at 501 pushups. I won the sit-up contest at 1615. I was in bad shape after I did that, because I wore all the hide off my tailbone and I got boils. Every single morning we would practice for one more pushup. By the time we finally had the contest, it was all we had in us, period. And we even did it on a terrible diet.
>
> Most of us did keep an exercise regimen. And it depended on the cell block you lived in, because sometimes you couldn't exercise. I lived in one cell block without floorspace. All there was were the two pallets. And so if you wanted to walk, it was two paces to the end of your pallet, a turn, and then two paces back to the other end of your pallet. But there was always room to do sit-ups or pushups or deep-knee bends, or something like that.
>
> Another thing. We had a guy who loved to walk on his hands, so he would teach us to walk on our hands. I frequently did handstand pushups or walked on my hands. When I got to the States, to a hospital in Oakland, the morning coffee show was to watch me come out of my room walking on my hands, walk down to the coffee urn and get a cup of coffee, and then come back.

For each of these POWs, rigorous exercise in prison was not just a hobby or a way to pass the time, it was a necessity. It helped them feel better and sleep better. It gave structure and purpose to their days and became a routine that enhanced confidence. It saved lives: Meyer described knowing four or five prisoners who didn't make any effort to preserve their physical well-being. In his words, they said "they were planning to take a pill" to restore themselves to health when they got back to the States. Instead, he said, "all of them ended up dying within a few years after release."

American POWs, having been through boot camp and many other advanced military training exercises, were already accustomed to physical challenges. They understood the value of making the effort to stay fit, even under adverse conditions. A retired sergeant, Bruce Norwood, describes the rigorous physical training in the military Ranger Indoctrination Program.

> You'd get up at four, go on a twelve-mile run, come back and eat breakfast, do two hours on a very hard obstacle course. … It is a very organized type of training with continuous and constant feedback, both positive and negative. They first teach you to crawl, then walk, and finally run. It's a great way to teach a new skill set. If you do something wrong you're held accountable and told to correct it, or you might have to drop and give them fifty push-ups.

Exercise makes civilians tougher too

For civilians in far less stressful circumstances, physical exercise can be a valuable vehicle for improving physical and mental hardiness and self-esteem (Gould, 2000). A 2009 article by the Mayo Clinic notes that regular physical activity:

- improves mood
- combats chronic diseases
- helps manage weight
- boosts energy level
- promotes better sleep
- improves sex life
- can be fun!

Deborah Gruen, the young woman who was born with spina bifida, began team swimming when she was six years old because her sister swam and it looked like fun. Deborah immediately took to the water.

> I've always been really comfortable in the water; I had a disability that impaired my walking but I always found that water leveled the playing field a little bit. I could keep up with everyone else. I really liked that and plus I didn't need to use any sort of helping device, any sort of device to help me swim. I could just do it on my own ... I could master the full turns, I could play on kickboards, I could swim across the pool; I could keep up with other kids during games.

The lifeguards at the neighborhood swimming club taught Deborah how to swim and she learned rapidly. When her sister, Michele, joined a local swim club, Deborah again followed her:

> I joined too and the coaches treated me like I wasn't anyone different. I didn't kick as well as everyone else and I was slower than kids in my own age group. But, every once in a while in a swim meet, I do beat able-bodied kids, and if you've never swum before I'll totally blow you away; it's not even close.

As a member of the US Paralympic team, Deborah practiced 8 times a week, swimming an average of 26 miles. By pushing herself far beyond her own initial expectations and the expectations of others, Deborah has discovered an inner reservoir of power that carries over into other areas of her life. Becoming familiar with and tapping into this inner reservoir has dramatically enhanced Deborah's self-esteem.

Swimming has also helped Deborah understand the fortifying effects of support from others, including coaches and teammates.

> We're all on the same boat. It's January and it's like zero degrees outside, the pool is cold, it's dark, and your coach is there and he doesn't want to be there either and I'm going, "Oh this is really bad." But then you come together and realize we have two hours, we're clearly not going home, and you just get in and you do it. That's when it really helps, when you have support from other people. When you have to go it alone, that's when it becomes really difficult.

Finally, like many people, Deborah sees swimming as a good prescription for reducing stress.

I don't worry because I have a disability. I worry about whether my term paper is going to be late, is my paper good enough? I swim it out. Swimming is so good for that. Really gets your mind off it. That's why I love sports. I think everybody should learn to compete. It just takes out all the stress.

Training boosts recovery after trauma

General Hugh Shelton, the former Ranger, Green Beret and Chairman of the Joint Chiefs of Staff whom we have mentioned earlier in the book, has been a physical fitness advocate ever since he joined the United States Army as a young man. Shelton looks like a general. He is 6'5" with close cropped silver gray hair. He is thoughtful and articulate and speaks with a soft Southern accent. General Shelton is passionate about the military, about its mission to promote stability and peace throughout the world, about its focus on high ethical and moral standards and about the unwavering dedication and superior quality of its members. He is goal-oriented and shares his vision with exquisite clarity.

After retirement from the military, General Shelton chose a new career and became a highly successful business leader. As before, he continued to push himself physically, running an average of four miles each day and doing his own home repairs and heavy yard work. On a Saturday morning in March of 2002, Shelton had an accident of the kind that could happen to anyone. A ladder on which he was standing while trimming trees in his yard was struck by a branch. As he fell toward the ground, Shelton saw that he was about to be impaled by the chain-link fence that bordered the house, so he instinctively pulled his feet together, as he had so many times while parachuting, and twisted his body to avoid it. However, the fence caught his feet, forcing his head to strike the ground first.

Although he felt no pain, he initially could not breathe and, for a moment, thought he would die. He could not move his head, his arms, or his legs. As he lay motionless, knowing that he was seriously injured, he thought about the dangerous jumps he had survived during his days as an Army Ranger paratrooper. Some jumps had been at night from 20,000 feet with an oxygen mask and no light to see what lay below. What an irony, he thought, if after surviving a career of 246 life-threatening assignments in the military, he were to perish from a 10-foot fall in the back yard of his North Carolina home.

Forty minutes later, a neighbor finally heard his cries for help and alerted his wife, who called an ambulance. He was rushed to a local hospital, where doctors braced his neck and scanned his spinal cord. The results were not good. According to one doctor, the general would never walk again and might never regain the use of his hands. Shelton later learned that he suffered from "central cord syndrome," where several cervical vertebrae compressed against the spinal cord, causing paralysis.

When Maj. Gen. Hal Timboe, Commander of Walter Reed Army Medical Center, learned what had happened, he immediately sent two surgeons from the prestigious Walter Reed Army Medical Center to examine Shelton. His prognosis improved: the military surgeons told him they needed to get him to Walter Reed immediately and that time was critical. His best chance for recovery would be to elevate his blood pressure to a level that would put him at risk for a heart attack or stroke, but it would get a much needed blood supply to the damaged area of the spinal cord. Several weeks later they performed surgery to decompress the spinal cord.

Fortunately, Shelton did not appreciate the severity of his injury and refused to give up. Until he was discharged from Walter Reed after nearly three months, he didn't know that the medical staff believed he would remain a quadriplegic for life, and that on the day he was admitted to the hospital, his surgeon gave him a very low chance of ever walking again.

> At the time, I didn't realize how bad it was. It helped not knowing the extent
> of trauma. It wasn't until the 83rd day at Walter Reed, the day before I walked
> out, that an assistant neurosurgeon came to my bed around five in the morning
> and said, "General, I'm out of here today and you'll be walking out tomorrow.
> I gotta tell you, we never thought we'd see the day you'd walk." That's when the
> hair on the back of my neck stood up. That's when I realized how bad it had
> been. That's when it came back to me: during the second week of my stay, the
> OT and PT people came in and started talking about long-term rehab hospitals
> in New York and Texas. I kept thinking, "What's wrong with Walter Reed?" I
> never realized I wasn't expected to recover.

Shelton says that he owes much of his recovery to a physical therapist, Lieutenant Zack Solomon, who believed that Shelton would walk again one day. Solomon was a soldier's soldier: disciplined, determined, positive. Solomon worked with Shelton twice a day in the hospital gym and swimming pool. And even though physical therapy was tiresome and painful, neither of them backed down. In fact, Shelton often volunteered to do more. The two were a team and with Solomon by his side, Shelton gradually, over the course of months, began to walk. Solomon's loyal determination exemplifies the military ethic to "never leave one of your own behind."

These days General Shelton gives speeches all across the country, continues to support his alma mater, North Carolina State University, and serves as a board member for numerous corporations. He not only walks without assistance, he exercises on a regular basis and keeps physically fit. He remains mentally and physically tough.

Physical exercise improves physical and mental health

It may seem obvious that physical exercise improves physical health, but do we know specifically how? A 2009 article in *Scientific American* (Ballantyne, 2009) summarized findings by a US Department of Health and Human Services committee on physical activity chaired by William Haskell of Stanford University. A committee member, Jonathan Meyers of the Palo Alto Veterans Affairs Health System in California, explains that

> … when a person exercises, the heart muscle contracts forcefully and
> frequently, increasing blood flow through the arteries. This leads to subtle
> changes in the autonomic nervous system, which controls the contraction
> and relaxation of these vessels. This fine-tuning leads to a lower resting heart

rate (fewer beats to pump blood through the body), lower blood pressure and a more variable heart rate, all factors that lower the risk of developing cardiovascular disease.

In their 2008 report, *Physical Activity Guidelines for Americans*, the committee found strong evidence that physical activity in adults lowers risk of:

- early death
- stroke
- Type II diabetes
- high blood pressure
- adverse lipid profile
- metabolic syndrome
- colon and breast cancer

Further, the committee found that 3–6 months after starting an exercise program, formerly sedentary people had experienced a drop in levels of C-reactive protein (a marker for inflammation often used to assess risk of cardiovascular disease) of 30% on average – as much as would occur if given a statin drug. There was moderate evidence for lower risk of hip fracture, reduced bone density, and lung and endometrial cancer.

Aerobic exercise can also be helpful in reducing symptoms of depression. In a study of 156 middle-aged men diagnosed with major depression, James A. Blumenthal and colleagues (1999) found that 16 weeks of aerobic exercise was as effective in lowering symptoms of depression as 16 weeks of treatment with the antidepressant drug Zoloft. Although over 60% of participants in both groups had a good response, there were differences. Those who took Zoloft tended to responded faster, while those who exercised responded more gradually but were less likely to relapse and experience a return of their depressive symptoms. Many other studies find that exercise is substantially effective in reducing symptoms of mild to moderate depression (Barbour *et al.*, 2007). For patients who receive psychotherapy, exercise may be a valuable adjunct. Aerobic exercise even appears to lessen mild symptoms of depression and sadness in normal people who do not suffer from major depression.

In addition, aerobic exercise has been shown to decrease anxiety. This is true for normal healthy individuals as well as for people diagnosed with generalized anxiety disorder and panic disorder. Exercise may be particularly helpful for people with "anxiety sensitivity," which refers to misinterpreting and catastrophizing the physical sensations that generally accompany anxiety, such as perspiration, rapid heart rate, and rapid breathing. People with anxiety sensitivity often imagine that these symptoms are actually being caused by a serious life-threatening illness such as heart failure. Researchers believe that during vigorous aerobic exercise, the "anxiety-sensitive" person is forced to tolerate many of the same symptoms (that is, rapid heart rate, sweating, and rapid breathing) that frighten him or her during periods of anxiety. Over time, the "anxiety-sensitive" individual who continues to exercise vigorously can learn that these symptoms of arousal are typically not dangerous, and the fear that these symptoms trigger gradually decreases in intensity (Salmon, 2001).

Abundant scientific evidence shows that physical exercise also can improve brain function and cognition, which includes thinking and memory (Cotman & Berchtold, 2002). Researchers from the University of Urbana-Champaign recently reviewed findings from 111 animal and human studies and concluded that aerobic exercise can improve attention, planning, decision making, inhibition and memory. These positive effects of exercise may be related to a number of recent findings: exercise training has been shown to increase the size of the hippocampus and serum levels of BDNF, and increase brain volume (prefrontal cortex) in older adults (Erickson *et al.*, 2011). In fact, exercise in midlife is associated with decreased rates of developing dementia and Alzheimer's disease (Andel *et al.*, 2005). Among patients already diagnosed with dementia, and even among normal elderly individuals, exercise may slow age-related memory decline.

Exercise may even enhance your sex life. In 2009, Benson Hoffman and his colleagues at Duke University Medical Center reported on 200 depressed adults, aged 40 years or older, who were sedentary and generally overweight. They divided the participants into three groups, assigning one group to exercise by walking, running, or biking, 30 minutes a day, 3 days a week, to 70%–85% of their heart rate reserve. The other two groups received either an antidepressant (Zoloft in its generic form) or a placebo pill. After four months, the participants took the Arizona Sexual Experiences Questionnaire (ASEX). The test results indicated that the group that exercised reported better sex than the placebo group, and marginally better sex than the Zoloft group.

Exercise, resilience and the brain

A number of different neurobiological mechanisms may help to explain the antidepressive, anti-anxiety, and stress-protective effects of aerobic exercise. First, exercise has been shown to increase concentrations of chemicals that are known to improve mood (e.g. endorphins) and lessen depression (e.g. serotonin and dopamine).

Second, regular exercise helps to protect against the hormonal effects of chronic stress. During stress, the hypothalamic–pituitary–adrenal (HPA) axis releases high levels of the stress hormone cortisol, which over time can damage neurons in the hippocampus. The good news is that this response may be dampened in exercise-trained individuals. Dampening of the HPA axis would most likely mean lower cortisol production, less brain exposure to cortisol, and therefore less damage to neurons in the hippocampus.

A third potential neurobiological mechanism involves neurogenesis, the making of new brain cells by "turning on" relevant genes. Aerobic exercise enhances the growth of neurons in the brain by increasing production of neurotrophic (growth) factors such as BDNF. ("Neuro" means "brain" and "troph" means "nourish.") BDNF is a protein that is known to promote the growth and repair of brain cells. BDNF and other growth factors play an important role in cell survival, formation of connections between neurons based on how these neurons are used, the repair of damaged nerve cells, and learning (Duman *et al.*, 2001; Krishnan & Nestler, 2008). Stress, especially when chronic, is known to reduce the production of these neurotrophic factors.

Aerobic exercise may even protect against the effects of future stress and depression. Carl Cotman and Nicole Berchtold at the University of California, Irvine (2002) assessed level of depression in 19,000 adults at the beginning of their study and again eight years later. They found that regular exercise over the eight-year period predicted freedom from depression. Not all studies, however, have found such a protective effect for physical activity. Assessing the capacity for aerobic exercise to prevent stress-induced anxiety, depression, and cognitive decline is an important and exciting area for future research in both animals and humans.

How can you use exercise to increase your resilience?

For most of human history, people have spent their waking hours engaged in the physical demands of daily life. The human body evolved for living as gatherers, scavengers, toolmakers, hunters, and artisans. Like our hunter-gatherer ancestors, modern humans are living with a genome, body, and brain that evolved with physical activity at its core and that is designed to respond rapidly to relatively short bursts of physical stress. However, over the past few centuries, with the advent of the industrial revolution and advances in technology, we have adopted a dangerously sedentary lifestyle, rarely engaging in physically demanding work and often sitting for long hours in front of a computer or television set. Writing in *The Lancet*, German researchers Rainer Hambrecht and Stephan Gielen (2005) reported that modern humans, per kilogram, use only about one-third of the energy expended by our Paleolithic ancestors. In fact, in 2009, Steven Blair of University of South Carolina's Arnold School of Public Health reported that the Aerobics Center Longitudinal Study found that 25–35% of American adults were living very sedentary lives (i.e. worked at sedentary jobs, had no regular physical exercise program, and were inactive around the house) (American Psychological Association, 2009). This kind of sedentary lifestyle has many drawbacks, and in the context of this book, we can say that it does not serve to boost resilience.

While many Americans do exercise with some regularity, building resilience typically goes beyond "routine maintenance" exercise; to become more resilient, we need to challenge ourselves. One strategy relevant to physical training is known as "stress inoculation" (Lyons & Parker, 2007), which involves continually pushing the healthy limits of strength and endurance. In order to maximize the growth-enhancing effects of stress inoculation, one must first learn to accurately assess the upper and lower limits of optimal stress exposure. As we've said, stress that is too mild leads to no growth – merely maintenance – or even decline. However, too much stress (i.e. stress that is unmanageable or overwhelming) can also lead to weakening or sometimes even to physical and/or emotional breakdown.

Like most world-class athletes, champion cyclist Lance Armstrong adheres to a training program that is rigorous, methodical and based on good science. In their book *The Lance Armstrong Performance Program*, Armstrong, Chris Carmichael, and Peter Joffe Nye (2000) describe a stress inoculation physical training program that recommends exercising within precise upper and lower target heart rates, not too low and not too high. Heart rate is a good measure of physiological stress for those who are training to increase cardiovascular fitness and resilience. Armstrong explains,

> I use my heart rate ceilings for my training rides. They keep me in my upper aerobic capacity to avoid crossing my lactate threshold, which is when the body can no longer process oxygen quickly enough to remove waste products associated with energy production. The object is to end my training ride having ridden almost entirely aerobically. ... (pp. 81–82)

In his book *Toughness Training for Life*, Jim Loehr, co-founder of the Human Performance Institute, agrees: "Stress that toughens falls between maintenance stress and excessive stress ... distinguishing between insufficient stress and maintenance stress and also between adaptive stress and excessive stress – it's a vital toughening skill" (1993, p. 48). In another book, *The Power of Full Engagement*, Loehr goes on to say:

> Growth and change won't occur unless you push past your comfort zone, but pushing too hard increases the likelihood that you will give up. Far better to experience success at each step of a progressive process. Building confidence fuels the persistence to pursue more challenging changes. (Loehr & Schwartz, 2003, p. 179)

The *US Army Combat Stress Control Handbook* describes a similar program for building physical fitness:

> To achieve greater tolerance or acclimatization to a physical stressor, a progressively greater exposure is required. The exposure should be sufficient to produce more than the routine stress reflexes. Well-known examples of acclimatization are heat acclimatization, cardiovascular (aerobic) fitness, and muscle strength ... you can become aerobically fit only by exerting yourself to progressively greater degrees of physical effort. ... In other words, you must stress the system. After doing that for several days, the same effort raises the heart rate and sweating only a little. You become less short of breath and the effort seems much easier. To become more aerobically fit, you have to increase the work stressor even more until the body again shows the stress of increased heart rate, shortness of breath, and sweating. ... The issue for master fitness trainers is how to keep the physical work stressors and stress in the positive range, which increases strength and fitness. They must control the stressors and stress so they are not extreme – too little or too much. (Department of the Army, 2003, pp. 29–31)

Cliff Welch, a Special Forces instructor, describes it this way, "If you do things in incremental steps, you know, harder and harder, the person will get better. They'll get stronger and they'll get harder. And that starts from day one of basic training, and it never really ends the whole time you're in the service."

Of course, most people reading this book are not aspiring to become world-class athletes or SF soldiers. But how much exercise is enough to enhance resilience? And what type of exercise is best for your physical health? How about for your mental health? Is it best to exercise alone or with others? Should you consider hiring a trainer so that you can learn proper exercise techniques? What about cross-training?

These are complex questions that we will not cover in this book. However, bookstores and libraries are filled with excellent books that outline sensible and scientifically sound exercise programs geared toward maintaining good health. At the most basic level, panels of experts agree that most adults should exercise for at least 30 minutes at a moderate level of intensity nearly every day of the week.

A note of caution is also in order: this material is not intended to take the place of medical advice. Before beginning any exercise program, it is always wise to check with your doctor, who can assess any conditions you may have that would limit the amount and types of exercise that are appropriate for you.

Physical resilience requires recovery

Exercise physiologists emphasize that we do not build strength, agility, and coordination only by exercising. Instead, we need to alternate periods of exercise with periods of rest. This is true both in the context of an individual workout and in the longer view of a weekly fitness routine, where you will give your body more challenges on some days than others. Without the opportunity to recover, the body becomes exhausted and worn down.

Recovery includes proper nutrition; the old adage "you are what you eat" applies. The USDA Dietary Guidelines (2005) recommend a diet composed predominantly of a variety of fruits, vegetables, and whole grains. Modest amounts of lean meat, legumes, and low-fat dairy products are included, while fats and sugars are to be eaten sparingly. In terms of caloric intake, USDA recommendations range from 1600 to 2400 calories a day for women and 2000–3000 calories a day for men. Younger adults generally need more calories than older adults because our metabolism tends to slow down with age. Still, the more physically active you are, the more calories you need to maintain your weight. Thus, if you are under 30 and get plenty of exercise, your appropriate calorie consumption will be higher than that of someone who is over 40 and/or who leads a more sedentary life. A healthy diet also involves limiting intake of alcohol – for some people, avoiding it altogether – and avoiding tobacco, as well as other substances of abuse.

Sleep is another key component of recovery and is essential to good health and well being. For most adults, this means about 8 hours of sleep every night. Among other benefits, adequate sleep is necessary for optimum coordination and reaction time, according to Harvard Medical School physiologist Martin C. Moore-Ede, whose 1993 book *The Twenty-Four-Hour Society* remains a classic. In his 1998 book *Power Sleep*, Cornell University psychologist James B. Maas points out that many of us go through years of our lives at less than peak performance because we are chronically mildly sleep deprived. And *The Lance Armstrong Performance Program* (Armstrong *et al.*, 2000) affirms that while training, most athletes need 8–10 hours of sleep per night.

Moreover, it has become increasingly clear that the benefits of sleep go far beyond just feeling alert and rested. In 2000, researchers in Australia and New Zealand reported that "16 to 60 percent of road accidents involve sleep deprivation," and that "people who drive after being awake for 17 to 19 hours performed worse than those with a blood alcohol level of .05 percent … the legal limit in many European countries" (CNN, 2000). At the 2009 annual meeting of the Associated Professional Sleep Societies, researchers presented evidence of the association between inadequate sleep and weight gain. Also in 2009, the American Heart Association reported a study headed by Lisa Rafalson of the University at Buffalo that linked inadequate sleep (less than 6 hours per night) to the onset of Type II diabetes (American Heart Association 2009).

Of course, we recognize that getting a healthy amount of sleep is easier said than done, given our busy schedules and the rapid pace of our society. This is particularly true for the many people who suffer from insomnia, sleep apnea, or other sleep disorders. Although diagnosing and treating sleep disorders is beyond the scope of this book, there are many good resources for sleep hygiene. What we wish to emphasize in this chapter is that good sleep hygiene enhances recovery, physical and emotional health, and resilience. In fact, Lance Armstrong has included a "dare" to get plenty of sleep on his Livestrong.com wellness website.

There are many neurobiological factors associated with recovery, optimal performance, and resilience. The neurobiology of optimal performance and recovery is highly complex. One important area of investigation involves regulation of the SNS. For example, in 1989, Richard Dienstbier from the University of Nebraska reviewed a series of studies showing that people tend to perform best when their SNS activity is low at baseline, accompanied by a robust increase of norepinephrine and epinephrine during stress, and followed by a relatively rapid return of these neurotransmitters to baseline levels once the stress is over. We believe that resilient individuals, who perform well under stress, are likely to fit Dienstbier's description: they maintain the SNS within an adaptive window of activation, not so high as to cause incapacitating anxiety and fear, but high enough to appropriately respond to danger.

One of the neurochemicals that helps to modulate the norepinephrine response to stress is Neuropeptide Y. When norepinephrine is released during periods of high stress, neuropeptide Y is released with it. As described briefly in Chapter 1, NPY helps to decrease anxiety and restore calm after stress, in part by inhibiting the further release of norepinephrine. This helps to keep the SNS from "overshooting." Support for the stress-modulating effects of NPY has come from an innovative series of studies conducted by Yale University and National Center for PTSD researcher Charles A. Morgan MD (Morgan *et al.*, 2002, 2004). Morgan, an expert in the neurobiology of resilience, found that Special Operations soldiers with high levels of NPY performed better during extremely stressful training procedures than did soldiers with lower levels of NPY. Some researchers have referred to NPY as a neurobiological resilience factor.

Another neurochemical that has been linked to stress recovery, performance during stress, and resilience is dehydroepiandrosterone (DHEA). DHEA is an adrenal steroid that is released under stress and helps to protects against the potentially damaging effects of cortisol. In his studies with elite Special Operations soldiers, Morgan found that a higher ratio of DHEA to cortisol was associated with better performance during intensive survival training and stressful underwater navigation.

The notion that resilience and recovery go hand in hand has been strongly supported by the eloquent research of Rockefeller University professor Bruce McEwen and Stanford University researcher Robert Sapolsky. Repeated failure to shut off our own stress response can cause damaged to our body and brain. For example, stress that is chronic and inadequately regulated can lead to changes in neurons located in the amygdala, the hippocampus and the prefrontal cortex. These changes may be accompanied by anxiety, memory impairment, increased sensitivity to alcohol and drugs, diminished mental flexibility, and depressed mood (McEwen 2006, 2012; Sapolsky 2004; Sarina *et al.*, 2009).

Building physical fitness habits

While many types and intensities of exercise have medical and psychological benefits, for those of you who wish to use exercise as a means to enhance physical and emotional resilience, and become better prepared to deal with stress, we recommend an exercise regimen that is manageable but at the same time challenging. In 2008, The Department of Health and Human Service recommended at least 2 hours and 30 minutes of moderate intensity aerobic exercise (i.e. walking fast or pushing a lawn mower) or 1 hour and 15 minutes of intense aerobic activity (e.g. jogging or running, swimming laps) as well as 2 days of muscle strengthening activities. In general, even greater health benefits can be achieved for those who exercise more than these basic guidelines. We believe that such a regimen should incorporate the following elements.

1. Learn as much as you can about how physical fitness can improve your health and well-being.

2. Consult your physician before beginning a physical fitness program.

3. Try different forms of physical exercise. Cross-training has many benefits.

4. Develop a set of well-defined goals for your physical exercise regimen and try to stick to those goals. Record the details of your workouts to ensure that you are achieving your goals.

5. Consider working with an experienced trainer or coach as you build your fitness.

6. Reward yourself as your goals are met.

7. Gradually increase the intensity of your cardiovascular and strength training. While continually repeating the same comfortable routine with the same level of intensity each time you workout may help to ward off some medical illnesses, it

will not do as much to enhance your physical resilience. To increase your physical, as well as mental and emotional strength, you need to stress yourself and your body beyond your normal comfort zone but not to the point of damage.

8. After each workout, allow your body to recover adequately before beginning your next workout.

9. Practice healthy eating and sleep habits.

10. Find friends or family members who will support your physical training. Even better, train with a friend or family member who also has the goal to become more resilient.

11. Notice and focus on the positive feelings and greater sense of self-esteem and mental toughness that typically accompany increases in physical resilience.

12. Try to reach the point where being physically fit becomes part of your sense of self, a part of who you are.

There is no easy way to become physically fit and resilient. It takes planning, desire, drive, consistency, perseverance, and the willingness to live with discomfort. But the benefits are many. For Hugh Shelton, being physically resilient prepared him to face and overcome possible paralysis. For Deborah Gruen, it leveled the playing field. For Lew Meyer, it meant living to see another day.

References

American Heart Association (2009). "Short-sleepers" may develop blood sugar abnormality that can lead to diabetes." Press release, March 11. Accessed 12/3/09 at http://americanheart.mediaroom.com/index.php?s=43&item=693.

American Psychological Association (2009, August 10). Sedentary lives can be deadly: Physical inactivity poses greatest health risk to Americans, expert says. *Science Daily*. Retrieved July 20, 2010, from http://www.sciencedaily.com/releases/2009/08/090810024825.htm.

Andel, R., Hughes, T. F., & Crowe, M. (2005). Strategies to reduce the risk of cognitive decline and dementia. *Aging Health*, 1(1), 107–116.

Armstrong, L., & Carmichael, C., with Nye, P. J. (2000). *The Lance Armstrong performance program*. Emmaus, PA: Rodale Press.

Ballantyne, C. (2009). Does exercise really make you healthier? We examine five claims about the benefits of weight lifting and aerobics to see which carry the most…weight. *Scientific American*, Jan. 9. Accessed 12/3/09 at http://www.scientificamerican.com/article.cfm?id=does-exercise-really-make&print=true.

Barbour, K. A., Edenfield, T. M., & Blumenthal, J. A. (2007). Exercise as a treatment for depression and other psychiatric disorders: A review. *Journal of Cardiopulmonary Rehabilitation and Prevention*, 7(6), 359–357.

Blumenthal, J. A., Bayak, M. A., Moore K. A., Craihead W. E., Herman, S., *et al.* (1999). Effects of exercise training on older patients with major depression. *Archives of Internal Medicine*, 159, 2349–2356.

CNN (2000, September 20). Sleep deprivation as bad as alcohol impairment, study suggests. Available online at http://archives.cnn.com/2000/HEALTH/09/20/sleep.deprivation/.

Colcombe, S. J., Erickson, K. I., Scalf, P. E., Kim, J. S. *et al.* (2006). Aerobic exercise increases brain volume in aging humans *Journal of Gerontology A. Biological Science and Medical Science*, 61(11), 1166–1170.

Cotman, C. W., & Berchtold, N. C. (2002). Exercise: A behavioral intervention to enhance brain health and plasticity. *Trends in Neuroscience*, **25**, 295–301.

Department of the Army (2003). *U. S. Army combat stress control handbook.* Guilford, CT: The Lyons Press.

Dienstbier, R. A. (1989). Arousal and physiological toughness: Implications for mental and physical health. *Psychological Review*, **96**, 84–100.

Duman, R. S., Malberg, J., & Nakagawa, S. (2001). Regulation of adult neurogenesis by psychotropic drugs and stress. *Journal of Pharmacology and Experimental Therapeutics*, **299**(2), 401–407.

Erickson K. I., Voss M. W., Prakash, R. S., Basak, C., *et al.* (2011). Exercise training increases size of the hippocampus and improves memory, *Proceedings of the National Academy of Sciences*, USA, **108**(7), 3017–3022.

Gould, D. C. II (2000). *Do sports build Character? A study of the intramural sports program of the United States Air Force Academy.* Master's Thesis. Ft. Leavenworth, KS: Army Command & General Staff College.

Hambrecht, R., & Gielen, S. (2005). Essay: Hunter-gatherer to sedentary lifestyle. *The Lancet*, **366**(Suppl 1:S60–1), 560–561.

Hoffman, B. M., Babyak, M. A., Sherwood, A., Hill, E. E., Patidar, S. M., Doraiswamy, P. M., *et al* . (2009). Effects of aerobic exercise on sexual functioning in depressed adults. *Mental Health and Physical Activity*, **2**(1), 23–28.

Krishnan, V., & Nestler, E. J. (2008). The molecular neurobiology of depression. *Nature*, **455**, 894–902.

Loehr, J. (1993). *Toughness training for life: A revolutionary program for maximizing health, happiness and productivity.* New York, NY: Dutton.

Loehr, J., & Schwartz, T. (2003). *The power of full engagement: Managing enery, not time, is the key to high performance and personal renewal.* New York, NY: Free Press.

Lyons, D. M. & Parker, K. J. (2007). Stress inoculation-induced indications of resilience in monkeys. *Journal of Traumatic Stress*, **20**, 423–433.

Maas, J. B. (1998). *Power sleep: The revolutionary program that prepares your mind for peak performance.* New York, NY: Harper Paperbacks.

Mayo Clinic Staff (2009). Exercise: 7 benefits of regular physical activity. Online article from http://www.mayoclinic.com/health/exercise/HQ01676.

McEwen, B. S. (2006). Protective and damaging effects of stress mediators: central role of the brain. *Dialogues in Clinical Neuroscience.* **8**, 367–381.

McEwen, B. S. (2012). Brain on stress: How the social environment gets under the skin. *Proceedings of the National Academy of Sciences.* Oct 8. [Epub ahead of print]

Moore-Ede, M. D. (1993). *The twenty-four-hour society: Understanding human limits in a world that never stops.* Reading, MA: Addison-Wesley.

Morgan, C. A. III, Wang, S., Southwick, S. M., Rasmusson, A., Hazlett, G., Hauger, R.L., *et al.* (2000). Plasma neuropeptide Y concentrations in humans exposed in military survival training. *Biological Psychiatry*, **47**(10), 902–909.

Morgan, C. A. III, Southwick, S. M., Hazlett, G., Rasmusson, A., Hoyt, G., *et al.* (2004). Relationships among plasma dehydroepiandrosterone sulfate and cortisol levels, symptom of dissociation and objective performance in humans exposed to acute stress. *Archives of General Psychiatry*, **61**, 819–821.

Philpott, T. (2002). *Glory denied: The saga of Vietnam veteran Jim Thompson, America's longest-held prisoner of war.* New York, NY: Plume Books.

Salmon, P. (2001). Effects of physical exercise on anxiety, depression, and sensitivity to stress: A unifying theory. *Clinical Psychology Review*, **21**, 33–62.

Sapolsky, R. M. (2004). *Why zebras don't get ulcers.* New York, New York. Henry Holt and Company.

Sarina, R. M., Ledoux, J. E., Sapolsky, R. M. (2009). The influence of stress hormones on fear circuitry. *Annual Review of Neuroscience*, **32**, 289–313.

United States Department of Agriculture (2005). *Dietary guidelines for Americans 2005: Chapter 2, Adequate nutrients within calorie needs.* Available online at http://www.health.gov/dietaryguidelines/dga2005/document/html/chapter2.htm.

Chapter 9

Brain fitness: challenge your mind and heart

In challenging situations, it helps to be mentally sharp. It helps to focus on the problem, process information quickly, remember what we already know about coping with related challenges, find strategies to solve the problem, make wise decisions, and learn new information. It is also helps to regulate our emotions; to control them rather than being controlled by them. These mental and emotional abilities equip us to face challenges, find solutions, and recover from setbacks – in essence, to be more resilient.

Just as we can train our body to become fit and resilient, so we can train our brain. The brain has extraordinary abilities to learn, to process information, and to remember. In our experience, resilient people tend to be lifelong learners, continually seeking opportunities to become more mentally fit. We never know when we will be called upon to meet a challenge that requires mental sharpness and keen regulation of our emotions.

On the afternoon of January 15, 2009, US Airways pilot Chesley Sullenberger was captain of a routine flight from New York's LaGuardia Airport when, just seconds after takeoff, the plane collided with a large flock of geese, leaving both engines disabled (*New York Times*, 2009). Suddenly the 150,000-pound aircraft was coasting, flying like a glider over one of the most densely populated areas in the nation. Lacking the necessary speed and altitude to return to the airport, Sullenberger quickly weighed alternatives and realized that the best available option was to attempt a water landing on the Hudson River. This would mean the loss of a multi-million-dollar aircraft, but if successful it would save lives. Seconds later, Sullenberger and his copilot Jeffrey Skiles succeeded in making the emergency landing – an extremely difficult maneuver that requires the plane to make contact with the water at a precise angle and precise rate of speed. Not only did the plane narrowly miss hitting the George Washington Bridge and successfully land on the river without crashing, it continued to float long enough for all aboard to evacuate. No lives were lost and there were no serious injuries.

As Sullenberger describes in his book *Highest Duty*,

> What I focused on, extremely quickly, was that this situation was dire. This wasn't just a few small birds hitting the windshield. … I heard the noise of the engines chewing themselves up inside as the rapidly spinning, finely balanced machinery was being ruined, with broken blades coming loose. (Sullenberger, 2009, p. 209)

Sullenberger credits his own training and that of the crew for their successful emergency landing. He reflected, "I did not think I was going to die. Based on my experience, I was confident that I could make an emergency water landing that was survivable. That confidence was stronger than any fear" (p. 237).

As we noted in earlier chapters, the Vietnam pilots we interviewed often reported relying on their training when they were shot down or otherwise disabled. To become a combat pilot, a candidate must acquire a battery of mental skills as well as the emotional stability to respond to emergencies such as enemy fire, aircraft malfunctions, and crashing. You may recall that in Chapter 3, Facing Fear, we related the story of Al Carpenter being shot down; at one point he stated, "Then your training kicks in and you determine what you're going to do next."

Another Vietnam pilot, Steve Long, describes how training saved his life:

> We got into the target area and took a hit. The airplane started coming apart. I saw about two feet of the left wing separate and the rocket pods were falling off. When I realized that the airplane was no longer flyable, it went into a nosedive and I decided to get out. And when I released my seatbelt to go out the door, I hit my head on something and it knocked me out. I was thrown out of the airplane, unconscious. But I guess the fresh air rushing by revived me enough so that I was able to get to my D-ring in time. And about the time that the chute popped open, I slammed into the ground pretty hard.

How many of us would be well-enough trained to pull the D-ring of a parachute while falling through the air after having been briefly knocked unconscious?

The power of the human brain

The capabilities of the human brain are indeed remarkable. In a world full of distractions, many of us tend to rush through our lives, not really focusing on details or even being "fully present" in the moment. However, when we are forced to stop and reflect, we notice the rich details of life around us and are often surprised by elaborate memories of seemingly long "forgotten" events. Many of the POWs we interviewed learned to appreciate the scope and power of the brain during their months or years in solitary confinement, where there were few outside distractions. Prisoners were often astonished with the brain's extraordinary capacity to access previous memories and to remember large volumes of new information. Many of them reconstructed whole chapters of their lives with the precision of diarists, and were able to retrieve distant moments and trivial details with exquisite clarity.

In Chapter 2 on optimisim, we described how Lew Meyer remembered passages from *The Power of Positive Thinking* by Norman Vincent Peale. Paul Galanti recalled, "When I was in solitary my memories would go way back … I started going through algebra and calculus…. I remembered the periodic table and started chemical equations in my head." Bob Shumaker spent 12–14 hours a day building and rearranging his dream house.

> I built a house in my mind. I would buy all the lumber and materials and everything for it. I knew how many bricks were in it; how much it weighed;

the square footage. … So, it kept me busy, but I think even more than that it kept me hopeful, you know, that some day I would actually build this house. … Which I did.

Charlie Plumb (1973) reported that one POW sports enthusiast, Galand Kramer, "memorized the names of over 750 baseball players, and after that the list became tiresome and he memorized it in reverse." Jack Fellowes replayed whole ball games and reproduced team rosters, including "the entire lineup for both teams in the 1946 World Series" (Plumb, 1973, p. 179).

These accomplishments are minor when compared to those of a young Navy apprentice seaman, Douglas Hegdahl. The self-effacing 19-year-old South Dakotan was in the Navy less than 6 months when he was captured in the predawn hours of April 6, 1967. During a night of bombardment, he had gone topside on the guided missile cruiser USS Canberra without authorization and had been knocked overboard by the concussion of the ship's giant guns. After staying afloat for six hours, he was picked up by a fisherman, turned over to the North Vietnamese army and force-marched to Hoa Lo – the Hanoi Hilton.

Most of the POWs were offered early release, but refused because of their Code of Conduct, and the strength of their unity. However, the senior ranking officers selected Hegdahl to accept the offer of early release. Why? Because Hegdahl had been able to memorize the first, middle, and last names of 256 POWs, their capture dates, method of capture, and personal information (dog's name, kid's name, and social security number). He was also able to recite the names of their next of kin, their hometown, and telephone numbers. How did he do it? He memorized all the information to the tune of "Old MacDonald Had a Farm"!

Seaman Hegdahl was released from the Hanoi Hilton on August 5, 1969. The first thing he did was to travel around the US, from west coast to east coast, north to south. He went to each hometown he had memorized, spoke to each prisoner's relatives, and told them that their loved one was alive. In 1970, Hegdahl testified at the Paris Peace Talks, where he confronted the North Vietnamese about the torture and other maltreatment of prisoners he had witnessed.

There are many examples beyond Vietnam, even if most are not quite as remarkable as Hegdahl's. In 1987, Anglican church envoy Terry Waite was kidnapped and held hostage by Shiite fundamentalists in Lebanon for 1763 days (almost 5 years). During his captivity he mentally "wrote" his autobiography, which was published soon after his release with the title *Taken on Trust*.

Another example of the power of memory involves the reconstruction of music by women held captive on the Indonesian island of Sumatra during World War II. As the Japanese invaded the islands of the South Pacific, they rounded up thousands of Dutch, British, and Australian women and children into overcrowded internment camps with deplorable conditions: food was scarce, disease rampant, and discipline harsh. Among the women imprisoned in one of these camps were Norah Chambers, a civil engineer's wife who was a graduate of the Royal College of Music in London; and Margaret Dryburgh, a Presbyterian missionary with musical training. Using scraps of scrounged paper, the women not only composed songs but also reconstructed from memory the orchestration of classical music compositions. As the Australian music critic Neville Cohn recounts in *OzArts Review* (2008), these included the first movement of Beethoven's "Moonlight" Sonata, Chopin's "Raindrop" Prelude, Dvořák's Largo movement from the "New World" Symphony, Grieg's "Morning" from *Peer Gynt*, and Ravel's *Bolero*. Lacking musical instruments, the women in the camp formed a vocal orchestra, singing the various parts. Survivors later related how the activity of singing increased their resilience. When they sang, said one survivor, "we experienced a wonderful surge of optimism and hope – and that was a real comfort." The story of this musical feat inspired the 1997 movie, *Paradise Road*.

To this point, we have been talking about mental feats by people who were imprisoned, but there are also many examples in our everyday world of people who have developed their cognitive capacities to an impressive degree. This is especially true of individuals who have disabilities. Those who are blind or deaf learn braille or signing in addition to learning to read and use language and mathematics.

Recall that in Chapter 2 on optimism we described how Helen Keller had to learn an entire new set of braille symbols before taking her exam in mathematics to graduate from Radcliffe. Leaving the exam aside, simply attending college was a profound accomplishment in itself. Helen could neither see nor hear her professors; very few of the assigned course books had been translated into braille; and nearly all of her time was consumed in preparation for her classes. Keller described her experience:

> In the classroom I am of course practically alone. The professor is as remote as if he were speaking through a telephone. The lectures are spelled out on my hand (by Anne Sullivan) as rapidly as possible, and much of the individuality of the lecture is lost to me in the effort to keep in the race. Words rush through my hand like hounds in pursuit of a hare which they often miss ... I cannot make notes during the lectures, because my hands are busy listening. (Keller, 1903, chapter 20)

Although few of us will ever face circumstances as grueling as those of a POW or of being deaf and blind, we can all challenge our brains and increase our mental fitness. Doing so may help to build resilience and the capacity to cope well under stress.

Brain plasticity: a possible key to brain fitness

One of the most exciting findings of brain research over the past decade has been the observation that we can enhance brain fitness. This means that through a series of brain exercises, we may be able to improve our cognitive abilities. The vast majority of us do not reach our full brain potential.

As we noted in Chapter 1, the brain is far more plastic than scientists had previously believed. Neurons that are actively used tend to make more connections with other cells and transmit their messages more efficiently. This "use-dependent" neuroplasticity has been observed in animals and humans. For example, in a much-heralded study, Edward Taub and colleagues from the University of Konstanz (Elbert *et al.*, 1995) reported that violinists, who constantly shift the fingers of their left hand in precise movements across the strings of the violin, have greater cortical brain space devoted to fingers of the left hand compared to fingers of the right hand, which hold the bow of the violin and engage in relatively fewer precise movements. Moreover, cortical space associated with fingers of the left hand was much greater in the violinists compared to a group of non-musicians, although there were no differences in cortical space dedicated to fingers of the right hand. While violinists who learned to play the violin before the age of 12 had the largest areas of cortical tissue allocated to fingers of the left hand, even violinists who learned to play as adults had similar but less pronounced expansion of cortical brain space. These findings provide strong support for activity-dependent neuroplasticity and brain reorganization where greater activity results in enhanced growth of brain cells and increased allocation of brain space to the processing of that activity.

In a series of experiments on use-dependent cortical reorganization, Alvaro Pascual-Leone and colleagues (2001) found that volunteers who practiced a five-finger exercise on a piano keyboard two hours per day for five days showed a modest expansion of the brain region that controls movement of the fingers. To the surprise of many scientists, another group of volunteers who simply *imagined* practicing these five-finger exercises for an identical period of time also showed an expansion of this same brain region. It is possible that even thinking about movement, like movement itself, can stimulate neurogenesis and reorganization of the cortex.

Musical training also has benefits beyond becoming a better musician. In research presented at the 2009 annual meeting of the Society for Neuroscience, Northwestern University auditory neuroscientist Nina Kraus found that classically trained musicians were better than non-musicians at being able to hear a spoken sentence when masked by background noise (Hamilton, 2009; Parbery-Clark *et al.*, 2009; Song *et al.*, 2009; Strait *et al.*, 2009). Kraus proposes that years of practice in ensembles where the musician must hear his or her own instrument or singing part actually trains the brain to zero in on a desired auditory focus.

Recent published brain-imaging studies have found that training in other skills, including juggling (Scholz *et al.*, 2009) and golf (Bezzola *et al.*, 2011), also results in enlargement of task-relevant brain regions. Researchers at the University of Michigan have offered the following tentative conclusion: "Structurally, training has consistently been associated with volumetric increases in brain structures thought to be critical for performance of the trained task" (Lustig *et al.*, 2009).

Brain plasticity after traumatic injury

For individuals who have suffered a brain injury, brain plasticity is especially good news because the brain can regenerate itself to a degree. And it can compensate: if a particular area of the brain is injured or damaged, other areas may take over some of its functions. Examples of brain plasticity are abundant among civilians and veterans who have suffered traumatic brain injuries resulting from car accidents, falls, explosions and the like.

In January 2006, ABC News correspondent Bob Woodruff was injured in a road-side bomb explosion in Iraq. As described in a *New York Times* story, Woodruff suffered severe brain trauma and spent more than a month in a medically induced coma (Stelter, 2009; Southern Methodist University, 2008).

In a 2008 interview with Alvaro Fernandez, who is co-author of *The SharpBrains Guide to Brain Fitness*, Woodruff's wife Lee described her husband's recovery process.

> … rehab is a long process. Doctors told me that Bob, despite the severity of his injuries, had better chances to recover than other victims, because of the reserve of neurons and connections he had built thanks to an intellectually stimulating and diverse life, including living in China for several years and traveling to dozens of countries, having worked as a lawyer and as a journalist, and his overall curiosity and desire to learn. It seems that more and more research shows how people who are mentally active throughout their lives, either through their jobs, or doing puzzles, sudokus … are, of course up to a point, better prepared to deal with problems such as TBI [traumatic brain injury].
>
> Still, recovery is a long process. Bob had six months of structured cognitive therapy focused on speech and languages areas, because that was the part of his brain that had been most damaged. The therapist identified the main tasks for him to work on in a challenging, yet familiar way, usually asking Bob, for example, to read the *New York Times*, then try to remember what he had read, and write a short essay on his thoughts and impressions. … I am amazed to watch in real time how, even today, how he gets better and better. To give you an example of his motivation to recover: he recently took on Chinese lessons to see if working on that also helped him. (Fernandez, 2008)

Just 13 months after being wounded, Woodruff was able to return to television, hosting an hour-long prime-time documentary, *To Iraq and Back*, which chronicled his recovery and what it means to suffer a traumatic brain injury. He went on to continue his full-time career as a correspondent at ABC News, and also served as anchor for "Focus Earth," a weekly series on Discovery Communications' Planet Green cable network.

"I have wanted to 'get back on the horse again' since my recovery," Woodruff wrote in a July 2009 blog post. "This will be a different horse, probably not as big, not as fast and without running outside the 'wire,' " [meaning that he would stay within military bases] "without going out on the streets or battle zones" as he did in the past.

Mental exercises to enhance brain function: do they work?

All of us would like our brain to work more effectively. Just as Bob Woodruff challenged himself by taking Chinese lessons and writing a summary of a news article he had read, most of us can find ways to challenge our brains. In recent years, scientists have begun to develop "mental exercises" to improve brain function and hopefully to stave off the decline in mental capacity that we often associate with aging. These exercises are of special interest to millions of people approaching old age, for whom developing memory problems, particularly dementia, is of great concern.

Responding to such concerns, a number of commercial products, or "mind games," have been developed that claim to improve cognitive performance (Rochman, 2010). Although we don't yet know how effective they are, these approaches are based on neuroplasticity and the idea that repeated "exercise" of brain systems involved in learning and memory will be beneficial. Nintendo markets a series of Brain Age games with the the the slogan, "Train your brain in minutes a day!" Even though it is described as an entertainment product, Brain Age was developed in collaboration with neuroscientist Ryuta Kawashima, who prompts and guides the user in many of the exercises. In the UK, MindWeavers markets MindFit, as "Based on science, proven in practice, fun to play." Posit Science, based in the US and cofounded by the distinguished University of California neuroscientist Michael Merzenich, claims to be "clinically proven to help people think faster, focus better, and remember more."

The mental exercises in these products include mathematical challenges (e.g. calculations), verbal challenges (e.g. word lists), and spatial challenges (e.g. mazes). They appear to target specific skills such as:

- mnemonic strategies (organization, visualization, association) to enhance memory
- reasoning training (strategies for finding patterns in letter or word series) to enhance decision-making
- speed of processing training (identifying an object on a computer screen at increasingly brief exposures) to promote rapid processing of information.

Some also aim to to build accuracy and strengthen retention. In the case of Posit Science, by 2010 three different programs were available: one focusing on auditory input (processing sounds), a second on visual input, and a third on improving the user's driving skills.

The available evidence on cognitive training clearly suggests that when a person practices mental tasks, performance improves on those tasks. The largest independent trial completed to date, the Advanced Cognitive Training for Independent and Vital Elderly (ACTIVE), was published in 2006. This 10-session multi-institution study, which was led by Sherry Willis at Penn State University, assigned 2832 healthy people with a mean age of 74 to one of four groups: memory training, reasoning training, speed training, and a no contact control group. The five-year follow-up data revealed all three training programs were effective at improving the target of their training. However, the improvements in training were highly specific – for example, people assigned to memory training showed improvement in memory, but did not display improved reasoning or speed of processing (Willis *et al.*, 2006). Of note, at the five-year evaluation the reasoning training group also reported significantly less decline in activities of daily living (e.g. meal preparation, housework, finances) compared to the control group.

More recently, researchers have found preliminary evidence that training in a specific task may generalize to other, similar tasks. In a study conducted by Glenn Smith from the Mayo Clinic and sponsored by Posit Science, 487 adults aged 65 and older (average age 75) (Smith *et al.*, 2009) practiced six computerized exercises designed to enhance the speed and accuracy of auditory information processing (i.e. listening). Training in speed and accuracy of processing auditory information was selected because age-related declines in cognition may be related to reductions in the quality of sensory information (e.g. auditory) flowing to areas of the brain responsible for cognitive functioning. The study, which was called IMPACT (Improvement Memory with Plasticity-Based in Adaptive Cognitive Training), was the first large-scale randomized controlled clinical trial to demonstrate that training in one cognitive skill can improve the performance of other cognitive skills. Although the training focused on enhancing auditory skills, "… [m]any participants also reported significant improvements in everyday cognitive activities such as remembering names or understanding conversations in noisy restaurants" (University of Southern California, 2009).

In 2008, a potentially ground-breaking investigation led by Susanne Jaeggi at the University of Michigan examined fluid intelligence. Fluid intelligence is an important component of general intelligence that relies on abstract thinking and helps us to reason logically, adapt to new situations, deal with complex information and develop strategies to solve problems we have never seen before. It does not depend on knowlege that we have already acquired, such as facts about history or vocabulary. In this study, 70 healthy young participants (average age 26) were trained in a very demanding task of memory which involved keeping track of a continually changing series of visual diagrams. Training sessions lasted approximately 25 minutes each day, with different groups of participants receiving 8, 12, 17, or 19 days of training. Participants' scores on a test of fluid intelligence before the experiment began were compared with scores after the training was completed. The results demonstrated that training in the task improved fluid intelligence and that more training sessions resulted in greater improvement. This finding is important for two primary reasons. First, fluid intelligence is closely related to education and professional success, especially in complex and demanding environments. Second, fluid intelligence was previously thought to be immutable. These results suggest, in contrast, that with appropriate cognitive training this very important form of intelligence can be improved. A critical step will be to demonstrate this effect in individuals across a broad age range.

So, what can we recommend at this point? Making a habit of challenging your intellect can't hurt, and may boost your cognitive fitness and resilience. You are never too old to learn new information and develop new skills. Indeed, a 2004 study by Cathie Hammond at the University of London concluded that lifelong learning was associated with

> … a range of health outcomes; well-being, protection and recovery from mental health difficulties, and the capacity to cope with potentially stress-inducing circumstances; … self-esteem, self-efficacy, a sense of purpose and hope, competences, and social integration. Learning developed these psychosocial qualities through extending boundaries, a process which is quintessential to learning. (Hammond, 2004)

Training the emotional brain

The ability to regulate emotions is an essential life skill that takes years to develop. Children and adolescents typically struggle with their unruly emotions for years. Even in adulthood many of us find it difficult to tame our impulses and contain our feelings. In fact, much of psychotherapy is designed to help clients deal with emotions such as sadness, grief, anxiety, anger, and fear.

Emotions are charged with psychic and physiological energy. If we underreact emotionally, we may allocate too little energy to solve the problem at hand. If we overreact emotionally, we may become flooded with too much energy, which disrupts our ability to process information and make good decisions. By learning to recognize our emotions, and then regulate their intensity, we can channel their energy into productive cognitive and behavioral responses, which has great utility when dealing with stress and adversity.

One effective technique that can help regulate emotions is the practice of mindfulness, which we discussed earlier in Chapter 5 on religion and resilience (Kabat-Zinn, 1990). "Mindfulness means paying attention in a particular way: on purpose, in the present moment, and non-judgementally" (Kabat-Zinn, 1994). The practitioner of mindfulness learns to develop calm and accepting awareness of thoughts, feelings, perceptions and bodily functions. Through this practice, we can learn to tolerate negative emotions better without impulsively acting upon them.

Another approach to emotion regulation during times of high stress involves focusing on the specific task at hand. In Chapter 3 on facing fear, we mentioned the book *In Extremis Leadership: Leading As If Your Life Depended on It* by Col. Thomas Kolditz, head of the Department of Behavioral Sciences and Leadership at the United States Military Academy at West Point. In this book, he writes,

> Don't try to control your emotions … You can learn to sharpen your focus and skills, to turn outward and make sense of the environment, in periods of high risk rather than getting emotional, dysfunctionally excited, and self-absorbed. (2007, pp. 132–133)

As we described earlier in this chapter, pilot Chesley Sullenberger focused most of his attention outwardly on the technical procedures needed to land his plane safely after both engines were disabled. However, even though he appeared calm to others, he later described the emotional reaction that hit him when the engines went silent.

> I felt abnormal, severe vibrations. … I'll never forget those awful, unnatural noises and vibrations. … It was shocking and startling. … I knew that this was the worst aviation challenge I'd ever faced. It was the most sickening, pit-of-your-stomach, falling-through-the-floor feeling I had ever experienced. (Sullenberger, 2009, p. 210)

This is a powerful example of observing one's emotions but not allowing them to interfere. Sullenberger *felt* the emotion, but did not *become* the emotion. He did this by inwardly observing his emotions as well as by focusing on the precise behavioral tasks needed to land his plane safely.

As we mentioned in Chapter 1, both of your authors have tried to apply the principles of resilience in our own lives. For us, athletic competition, particularly competitive kayak racing, has provided a consistent venue for practicing many of these principles. A few years ago, we decided to compete in a 90-mile, 3-day kayak race in the Adirondacks. For a competition of this length, it is vital to train for many months in advance. But one of us didn't start training until about 5 or 6 weeks before the race.

The day before the race, I realized I wasn't in good enough shape to do it justice. I almost called Dennis to tell him that I needed to back out, but I just couldn't do it. Here we were writing a book about resilience and I was about to quit before we had even started. Not good. Not possible. Fortunately, perhaps as a desperate attempt to reframe the upcoming race, I began to think about mindfulness, a discipline that I had been practicing for several years. I remember thinking, "This will be great. I can turn the race into a self-experiment in mindfulness and resilience."

When we got to the race, there were about 500 competitors. The course covered the last 90 miles of an old Native American trade route through the lakes and rivers of the Adirondacks. I was a little nervous at first, but when the starting pistol fired I began to paddle furiously. I immediately forgot all about my mindfulness experiment and within minutes was gasping for air wondering how I would ever make it through the first day. No one else looked like they were breathing that hard. In fact, to me they looked relaxed and comfortable.

About one hour into the race, my neck began to hurt. An almost unbearable pain gripped the right side of my neck from my ear all the way down to my shoulder blade. "You complete idiot," I thought. "You've got 85 miles left and you're already in excruciating pain. What were you thinking? What are you trying to prove? You're not in shape. Now you're gonna have to quit and look like a real jerk."

But then, thankfully, I remembered my intention to turn the race into a self-experiment in mindfulness. For most of the next 85 miles, to my amazement, I thoroughly enjoyed the race, and I paddled faster than I had anticipated. Somehow, for much of the time, I was able to remain in the "present moment" and observe my thoughts and emotions without constantly judging them. I even spent time marveling at the beauty of the Adirondacks and feeling invigorated by nature. It was pouring with rain on the second day, but I didn't care. On the last day as I was churning along, I passed one guy who looked totally exhausted. He asked, "Do you know how many miles we have left?" I told him I didn't know – which was true – and privately thought, "Who cares? I'm just enjoying every minute of this!"

(I should disclose that by the end of the race my shoulders were so inflamed that I could not touch them; I was unable to kayak for 6 weeks afterwards.)

Emotions and brain activity

The neurobiology of emotion regulation is highly complex. Here we briefly discuss emerging neuroscience findings related to two promising approaches to regulating emotions, meditation/mindfulness and real-time neurofeedback. In most but not all studies, mindfulness mediation has been shown to help individuals cope with symptoms of stress, anxiety and depression (Niazi & Niazi, 2010; Newberg, 2011; Bohlmeijer *et al.*, 2010). Mindfulness meditation has also been associated with improved ability to focus attention, increased flexibility of thinking, more rapid speed in processing visual information, and improved verbal memory as well as greater feelings of psychological well-being (Newberg, 2011).

Neurobiological mechanisms associated with meditation/mindfulness are not yet well understood. However, a number of studies have implicated the prefrontal cortex, the anterior cingulate cortex (ACC) and the amygdala, among others, as brain regions involved in the process of meditation. For example, a number of studies have reported an association between mindfulness meditation and increased activation of the prefrontal cortex along with decreased activation of the amygdala (Creswell *et al.*, 2007; Holzel *et al.*, 2011). Modulation of the amygdala by prefrontal cortical systems is thought to play an important role in emotion regulation (Oschner & Gross, 2005). Similarly, recent findings of greater activation and cortical thickness (i.e. increased neuronal cell bodies, etc.) of the ACC among experienced meditators compared to novice meditators suggests that meditation/mindfulness might strengthen ACC function and attention performance (Grant *et al.*, 2010). German researchers Brita Holzel and colleagues speculate that the ACC may help to regulate attention, partly by enhancing cognitive control over distracting memories and external events that complete with the task of maintaining focus during meditation.

In one small study, prolonged meditation has also been associated with increased concentration of gray matter in the right hippocampus (Holzel *et al.*, 2007). Ott and colleagues (Heather) point out that the hippocampus aids in turning down the stress response and that enhanced function of the hippocampus might help to reduce excess arousal and anxiety under stressful circumstances. Of note, it is not yet clear whether differences in specific brain regions among experienced meditators existed before they began to meditate, or whether the practice of meditation actually changed brain structure and function (Urry *et al.*, 2004). Researcher Richard Davidson raises a fascinating question:

> Might meditation strengthen the cortical circuitry that modulates the activity of the limbic system, like a thermostat regulating this furnace of emotions? Might mental training rewire the brain's emotion circuits and alter forever the sense of well-being and contentment? … Just as people now see the value of exercising the body consistently and for the rest of their life, it's similar with emotional skills. … training is seen as important for strength, for physical agility, for athletic ability, for musical ability – for everything except emotions. The Buddhists say these are skills, too, and are trainable like any others. … (Begley, 2007, pp. 230–231)

Davidson believes that repeated practice in techniques of emotion regulation (e.g. cognitive behavioral techniques and meditation) can lead to enduring changes in brain activation, such as increased activation in the left prefrontal cortex (Schwartz & Begley, 2002).

The second promising approach to regulating emotions, real-time neurofeedback, involves training yourself to increase or decrease activity in various brain regions. The advent of real-time functional magnetic resonance imaging (rtfMRI) makes it possible to observe the biology of one's own brain while thinking, feeling, and acting. It appears that people can learn to control brain activation in localized regions, with corresponding changes in their mental operations, by observing information from their own brain while inside an MRI scanner.

Researchers from Wales and the Netherlands have used real-time fMRI to record the activation of the amygdala, the sACC, and other brain areas in response to two different forms of negative stimuli (Johnston *et al.*, 2009). First, the researchers measured fMRI activity while participants were shown a series of standard pictures that have been pre-tested and rated as negative. Next, participants were asked to think of negative imagery or memories from their own personal lives that would activate the same brain areas. As they did this, the participants looked at a "thermometer" representing the amount of activity in the target brain area, so that they could see the results of different strategies, such as imagining terrifying scenes, thinking of people they disliked, and so forth. Their goal was to activate these brain areas as much as they could. This represents another step in understanding how people can learn to regulate the activity of brain areas related to specific emotions.

Other fMRI studies have focused on a brain structure called the anterior insula, located in the fold of the cerebral cortex marking the boundary between the frontal and temporal lobes. The anterior insula is involved in many functions related to emotions, and it appears to play a key role in representing one's own and others' emotional states. For example, in a 2004 experiment led by Tania Singer at University College of London, activations in the insula were associated with the affective (emotional) but not the sensory components of pain.

A 2007 study by a team of European researchers led by Andrea Caria found that healthy participants could voluntarily gain control over right anterior insular activity. Using rtfMRI, participants were provided with continuously updated visual feedback of the level of insula activation. While in the scanner and receiving this feedback, they were instructed to recall memories of personal events with positive or negative emotional significance. Within three feedback sessions of 4 minutes each, participants were able to successfully regulate blood flow in the right anterior insular cortex. These findings are important because for the first time self-regulation of an emotionally relevant region of the brain was demonstrated with rtfMRI. The researchers speculate that these findings may be useful in helping to develop new treatments for anxiety disorders and other problems.

Another brain structure important in the regulation of emotion is the subgenual anterior cingulate cortex (sACC) (Hamilton *et al.*, 2008). Ian Gotlib and colleagues from Stanford University recently demonstrated that healthy (non-depressed) individuals were able to use neurofeedback from real-time fMRI to modulate activity in the sACC. This suggests that people prone to depression might also be able to use rtfMRI neurofeedback to decrease sACC activation and, potentially, decrease symptoms of depression.

Researchers have also explored the possibility of teaching self-regulation to patients with obsessive compulsive disorder (OCD). OCD is a debilitating mental illness which, like PTSD, is classified as an anxiety disorder. Through the use of brain imaging techniques, researchers have found that OCD is characterized by overactivity of the orbital frontal cortex and the striatum, two brain regions that are involved in worry, anxiety, and detecting errors. The OCD patient repeatedly experiences intrusive thoughts and impulses, and feels driven to repeat behaviors like hand-washing, counting, and checking that doors are locked.

In a study at the University of California at Los Angeles, Lewis Baxter, Jeffrey Schwartz and colleagues used cognitive behavioral therapy with OCD patients in combination with Positron Emission Tomography (PET) brain imaging. The goals were to enable the patients to (1) observe and experience the symptom without reacting to it emotionally – something we might describe as mindfulness – and (2) realize that the feeling that "something is amiss" is the result of nothing more than a "wiring defect" in the brain. The study found that by viewing their own PET scans, patients were able to achieve both of these goals. Moreover, PET scans after treatment showed significant decreases in orbital frontal cortical activity in 12 of the 18 patients. "Therapy had altered the metabolism of the OCD circuit," Schwartz said (Begley, 2007, p. 147). Thus, learning to re-label the anxiety-related symptoms as a wiring defect actually appeared to result in changes in regional brain activity. The researchers observed that these changes in brain activity resembled those that are typically observed after successful treatment of OCD with medication (Baxter *et al.*, 1992).

With the advent of these newer laboratory techniques, it may soon be possible to add a whole new dimension to treatment which will allow the patient to correlate his or her thoughts and feelings with actual brain activity. This information should provide a powerful tool for regulating emotions.

Cognitive and emotional training work hand in hand

Even though we have organized this chapter into sections that focus on intellectual training on the one hand and emotional training on the other, in fact the two are closely related when it comes to brain activity. Increasingly, researchers are finding that mental training increases activity in not only the brain's cognitive circuits but also the emotional circuits. Through mental training, it may be possible to increase our capacity to regulate emotions.

Cognitive behavior therapy has been referred to as a form of mental and emotional training. For example, in Chapter 2 on optimism, we mentioned that optimists tend to have a positive explanatory style (i.e. they explain events to themselves in ways that promote hopefulness and satisfaction) whereas pessimists tend to have a negative explanatory style. Cognitive behavior therapy teaches people to recognize their typical explanatory style, test it against reality, and decide whether it is dysfunctional. Patients are then taught to reappraise their understanding and explanation of the situation in which they find themselves.

Sleep is a good example of the interdependence of mental and emotional functioning. Most of us have observed how children often become cranky – less able to regulate their emotions – when they have not had enough sleep. As adults, we too can become irritable and emotionally volatile when we are tired and sleep-deprived. The effects of sleep deprivation can be observed in both behavior and brain function. For example, in a study titled "The human emotional brain without sleep: A prefrontal amygdala disconnect", researchers from Harvard Medical School and the University of California at Berkeley (Yoo *et al.*, 2007) used fMRI to examine participants as they viewed a series of emotionally positive and negative images after they had either slept normally or been kept awake for 35 hours. The sleep-deprived participants had much stronger reactions to the emotionally negative stimuli, leading the researchers to conclude that sleep loss leads to emotionally irrational behavior and overreaction to negative events because it impairs the prefrontal cortex's capacity to regulate emotions (Contie, 2007). U.C. Berkeley researcher Matthew Walker explained, "Sleep appears to restore our emotional brain circuits. … sleep is not a luxury that we can optionally choose to take whenever we like. It is a biological necessity, and without it, there is only so far the band will stretch before it snaps, with both cognitive and emotional consequences" (Science 2.0 News Staff, 2007).

It is also well known that sleepy children do not learn or perform well in school. The same is true of adult workers. In his book *Power Sleep*, Cornell University psychologist James B. Maas (1998) outlines the ways in which inadequate sleep impairs cognitive and emotional performance: mood shifts, increased irritability and loss of sense of humor; anxiety and loss of coping skills; reduced ability to concentrate, remember, handle complex tasks, think logically and critically, and assimilate and analyze new information.

In our own field, sleep deprivation among medical residents is known to have detrimental effects on patient care because it impairs thinking and emotion regulation. In 2006, a landmark study by Charles Czeisler at Harvard found that when "residents worked 5 marathon shifts in a single month, their risk of making a fatigue-related mistake that harmed a patient increased 700 percent, and the risk of making an error that resulted in a patient's death shot up by 300 percent" (Fackelmann, 2006; see also Barger *et al.*, 2006), a powerful argument for the importance of sleep. This research has helped to shape graduate medical education policy: recently, the number of consecutive hours that residents are allowed to work without sleep has been reduced dramatically.

Physical, mental, and emotional conditioning: a win–win effect

In the previous chapter we emphasized the benefits of physical exercise on our health. What is less appreciated, however, is that physical conditioning can also have a positive impact on our capacity to think clearly and to handle emotional stress. Mastering physical challenges can improve confidence and self-esteem, and overcoming physical adversity can help to foster mental toughness.

General Hugh Shelton makes the connection between the physical, cognitive and emotional this way:

> The physical is not separate from the mental. A tremendous amount of mental toughness comes from having endured physical challenges. The best thing I've ever done – the thing that provided me with the confidence to know that no matter what I faced, I could probably overcome it, was Ranger school. ... It was the mental toughness that I developed out of that course, knowing that no matter how adverse the conditions, I could keep going. I had to keep going for the team around me, going for prolonged periods of time, being run ragged to the point of exhaustion, pushing you to the limit, where you didn't think you could do one more repetition of whatever it was, one more pull-up, and then being required to do even more, or suffer the consequences, which usually was additional pushups. The physical piece was important. At the same time, you were developing this mental attitude of "I can do it. I can beat them at their own game."

Training requires discipline

Once the skills have been taught, it takes discipline to maintain and improve upon them. This is true for cognitive training, emotion regulation training and physical training. Rigorous training is never easy. Thoughts and emotions can easily sabotage our best intentions. That's where discipline, drive and consistency come in.

From the time she was in high school, Jeff Gruen's daughter Deborah, whose story we told in Chapter 2 on optimism, has routinely gotten up at 5 a.m. for predawn swimming workouts. Does she enjoy the jarring ring of her alarm clock, or dragging herself out of bed, or walking with the assistance of her two canes through the snow to the school gym, or jumping into the chilly water to swim 150 lengths of the pool before breakfast? "Of course not! There are some days that I just want to stay in bed," she says.

Then why does she do it? Why does she get out of bed and make it to practice on time every day?

> Because the clock never lies. If my lap times are slow, there is a very good reason. Here's an example: your heart rate, you take it and you immediately know if you're not working hard. ... If I didn't study, I know I didn't study. The truth is, I always know because of my conscience, it is always there, it doesn't go away. At the end of the season, if you're not where you hoped, you know why. It's because I didn't get in the water on time and I didn't get to practice on time. You can't get around it. If you added a minute to your time, there is a very good explanation for it. But people are like, "Oh, it's because of the coach." I don't think so. Or, like, "I failed the class because of the teacher." Well, that doesn't go so well when the medical school you applied to is looking at your grades. "Oh, you didn't like your teacher, well that explains everything. That explains why you failed. No problem." I don't think so.

While Deborah certainly has a winning attitude, she has encountered her share of losses. And as Deborah's father realized from observing his daughters, it is not necessary to win to be happy; instead, what matters is knowing that you did your best. Even better is the ability to use every loss or failure to your advantage. In the book *Mental Toughness*, Karl Kuehl and colleagues point out that "... failure is an education. It educates you by telling you that something is not working, that it is time to try something new, time to make an adjustment" (Kuehl *et al.*, 2005, p. 196).

Training requires precision

The most successful training involves what K. Anders Ericsson, author of the *Cambridge Handbook of Expertise and Expert Performance* (Ericsson, 2006) refers to as deliberate practice, or "engaging in a practice activity (typically designed by teachers) with full concentration on improving some aspect of their performance."

The late Russian tennis coach Larisa Preobrazhenskaya was famous for turning out champions from the Spartak Tennis Club in Moscow (Nowak, 2007; *Russia Today*, 2009; Zarakhovich, 2003). In fact, half of the 2007 top ten players in the Women's Tennis Association Tours trained with her. How did she do it? Working with several groups of up to eight children aged 4–16, six times a week, Preobrazhenskaya would "insist (without concession) that her students are bio-mechanically efficient before they are allowed to compete" (Gonzalez, 2007). Typically this technical training would last three years – something that American parents might find frustrating, as they would be unwilling to wait that long to see their children compete and win! But that was not Preobrazhenskaya's way. In 2007, a *New York Times* reporter noted that she slammed her fist for emphasis when she told him, "If you begin playing without technique, it is big mistake. Big, big mistake!" (Coyle, 2007).

But why the need to practice skills precisely, over and over again for years, before engaging in competition? The answer lies in the structure of our nervous system. A fatty material called myelin coats a portion of many neurons and speeds the transmission of these impulses. When we repetitively practice a behavior, we are building myelin. Myelin wraps around and insulates the nerve so that electrical pulses do not diffuse out. When a nerve is stimulated over and over, myelin grows thicker, and the thicker the myelin, the faster the electrical signal travels down the nerve. Increased speed and accuracy of nerve signals means improved control of cognitions and movements. George Bartzokis, a professor of neurology at the University of California, Los Angeles, explained it to a *New York Times* reporter this way: "What do good athletes do when they train? ... They send precise impulses along wires that give the signal to myelinate that wire. They end up, after all the training, with a super-duper wire – lots of bandwidth, high-speed T-1 line. That's what makes them different from the rest of us" (Coyle, 2007).

For any training, whether physical, cognitive or emotional, it is important to be disciplined and systematic in planning and executing your training sessions. If you want to improve your physical, cognitive, and emotional skills you need to strive for perfection. To succeed, you must "target" your practice by pinpointing what you are doing right and what you are doing wrong. Then correct your mistakes. Precision is critical.

Make training as realistic as possible

It is generally best to make training as realistic as possible. This is true for cognitive, emotional and physical training. While books, classroom demonstrations and videos are useful, they cannot substitute for experiential, hands-on learning in realistic settings where the individual repetitively practices skill sets needed to become cognitively, emotionally and physically stronger and more resilient (Castro & Adler, 2011).

Scenario-based training is a form of highly realistic training that has been shown to be very effective. It is based on learning through doing, where trainees are provided with constructive feedback in real time so that they learn to master the information and skills they have been taught. This approach is widely used in training firefighters, police officers, soldiers, pilots, and others who work in high-stress situations where split-second decisions may save a life. Many of us have seen news photos of "disaster drills" in which a large number of actors portray injured victims with artificial wounds and scripted behaviors similar to what would actually happen in an earthquake, bomb attack, or other emergency. Scenario-based training is also familiar to anyone who has taken a course in cardiopulmonary resuscitation (CPR).

An extreme example of scenario-based training is the Army's SERE (Survive, Evade, Resist, Escape) course. As we described in Chapter 1, SERE is designed to teach soldiers survival field craft so that they can maneuver in enemy-controlled areas, escape detection, and return unharmed to friendly forces. This training is as much mental and emotional as it is physical.

Special Forces instructor Cliff Welch describes how SERE simulates the horror and chaos of actual war.

> We try to replicate casualties with moulage kits – fake blood, real blood sometimes – pig blood, things like that. It's better to do it in training if we're having a kid fumbling, you know, all thumbs. Do it in training all you want, so when it comes time for the real deal, he's not all thumbs. He's fluid. He knows what he's doing. His adrenaline's up there, way up there, but he knows what he's doing. And he can pretty much do it without having to think, because it's all almost programmed into him.

Another instructor, Gordon Smith, also describes how SERE mimics the "real deal."

> He might get to the edge of a field, starved, the sun comes up and it's a war torn area, there might be a dead cow there. It's bloated, you can tell it's been dead two or three days, and they might have a guy who went through SERE school, and he'd say, 'When it gets dark again, we're going to just hack off a piece of that because we've got to have some food' …
>
> [I tell them,] 'We're going to give you the instructional knowledge to survive. We're going to teach you how to do it, then we are going to make you

do it. … We're gonna make you do things you have never done before, maybe you've never started a fire using nothing but what is out there in the woods and two matches. And so we're going to give you the knowledge verbally, and we're gonna show you and then we are going to make you do it.' … I say, 'Look here guys, we're going to challenge you out there in the woods … we're going to give you a road kill. And I've got a choice. I've got a bunny rabbit that got hit last night, still nice and fresh, or I've got a maggot-ridden possum. It's been dead for two days. What do you think I am going to give you?' And they're like, 'Yeah, the rabbit.'

But anybody can eat an old bunny rabbit. … 'I'm going to challenge you so that you can find out how far you can go … and I will make you do it under a controlled environment, which this is, a school. Now if you get sick, you get in trouble, we can fix it now, because it's a learning environment. It's not a learning environment once you're out in the real world. … I'm going to teach you how to cook and eat this disgusting animal now. … We want you to be out in the world and be able to see that and say, "Hey, that's a source of food."'

End of conversation.

The SERE course is harsh because it needs to be as realistic as possible in portraying the harsh conditions of actual combat. Former POWs frequently describe this type of training as invaluable when they were called upon to endure the real thing.

Taking responsibility for your own brain fitness: practical applications

Change requires mental and/or physical activity. One cannot become physically stronger simply by wishing for larger muscles. Similarly, one cannot develop or enhance mental skills by allowing the mind to wander randomly from one thought to the next. Instead, change requires focus as well as systematic and disciplined activity. The principles are simple, but the execution demanding. To change in a desired direction, one must identify what needs to be changed, develop a rigorous but realistic training schedule and then follow that schedule. Becoming more resilient may require training in multiple areas, such as mindfulness and meditation, physical strengthening and endurance. It may require adopting new styles of thinking in order to view hardship and failure as opportunities. The process of systematic self-initiated change, while challenging and often difficult, is highly rewarding and can foster a powerful sense of mastery.

In a brief book titled *Keep Your Brain Alive: 83 Neurobic Exercises*, Duke University neurobiologist Lawrence C. Katz (1999) describes simple, everyday ways to build and maintain brain fitness, such as writing or brushing your teeth with your non-dominant hand, or getting dressed with your eyes closed. When you make these small changes in your daily routine, "Suddenly you brain is confronted with a new task that's engaging, challenging, and potentially frustrating" (p. 33). Katz also recommends some more challenging exercises, such as teaching oneself to read braille well enough to use an elevator with your eyes closed. "Learning to make distinctions and associations with your fingers activates a whole new set of pathways linking the cognitive regions of your cortex … to the sensory regions. By the time you're able to 'read' the button for your floor, using just your fingertips, you'll have built quite a bit of new circuitry in your cortex" (p. 76).

As Katz explains, "Neurobics requires you to do two simple things you may have neglected in your lifestyle: Experience the unexpected and enlist the aid of *all* your senses in the course of the day. … By doing so, rarely activated pathways in your brain's associative network are stimulated, increasing your range of mental flexibility" (pp. 31, 32).

By placing ourselves in environments that are conducive to learning, by surrounding ourselves with people who stimulate our personal growth and by systematically practicing specific desired skills, we have the capacity to influence the structure and function of our brain and acquire new skills. For Bruce Norwood, there is no substitute for training. Like other SF soldiers, he has been trained to deal with stress in a staggering array of circumstances. During his career in the SF, Norwood has completed dozens of challenging training courses that include day and night parachute schools, jungle survival school, desert survival school, mountain climbing school, six or seven weapons proficiency courses, hand-to-hand combat courses, two foreign language schools, bodyguard school, lock-picking courses, numerous counter-terrorist courses, multiple driving courses for motorcycles, Jeeps and large trucks, surveillance detection schools, numerous computer courses, horseback riding courses, and more.

When asked how training has affected his life, Sergeant Norwood replied,

> I've tried to explain it to my family. I would have no qualms if they came into my house in the middle of the night, took me out of my bed naked, put a blindfold on me, threw me in an airplane, and flew me anywhere south of Mexico and chucked me out with a parachute and nothing else in the middle of nowhere. In a week I'd be living in a nice place, maybe somebody's house. I'd have a vehicle I could use. I'd be clothed. I'd be eating. And I have total confidence I could do that. Why? Because that's what I've been trained to do.

References

Barger, L. K., Ayas, N.T., Cade, B.E., Cronin, J.W., Rosner, B., Speizer, F.E., *et al.* (2006). Impact of extended-duration shifts on medical errors, adverse events, and attentional failures. *PLoS Medicine*, 3(12):e487.

Baxter, L. R., Schwartz, J. M., Bergman, K. S., Szuba, M. P., *et al.* (1992). Caudate glucose metabolic rate changes with both drug and behavior therapy for obsessive-compulsive disorder. *Archives of General Psychiatry*, **49**(9), 681–689.

Bezzola, L., Merillat, S., Gaser, C., & Jancke, L. (2011). Training-induced neural plasticity in golf novices. *J Neurosci*, **31**(35), 12 444–12 448.

Bohlmeijer, E., Prenger, R., Taal, E., & Cuijpers, P. (2010). The effects of mindfulness-based stress reduction therapy on mental health of adults with a chronic medical disease: A meta-analysis. *Journal of Psychosomatic Research*, **68**(6), 539–544.

Caria, A., Veit, R., Sitaram, R., Lotze, M., Weiskopf, N., Grodd, W., *et al.* (2007). Regulation of anterior insular cortex activity using real-time fMRI. *NeuroImage*, **35**(3), 1238–1246.

Castro, C. A. & Adher, A. B. (2011). Military mental health training: building resilience. In S. Southwick, B. Litz, D. Charney, & M. Friedman (eds)., *Resilience and Mental Health: Challenges across the Life Span.* Cambridge: Cambridge University Press.

Cohn, N. (2008). Concentration camp music. *OzArts Review*, June 3. Available online at http://ozartsreview.hostingsuccess.com/tag/japanese-internment-camp/.

Contie, V. (2007). Lack of sleep disrupts brain's emotional controls. National Institutes of Health, Research Matters, November 5. Retrieved from http://www.sleepeducation.com/Article.aspx?id=637.

Creswell, J. D., Way, B. M., Eisenberger, N. I., & Lieberman, M. D. (2007). Neural correlates of dispositional mindfulness during affect labeling. *Psychosomatic Medicine*, **69**(6), 560–565.

Elbert, T., Pantev, C., Wienbruch, C., Rockstroh, B., & Taub, E. (1995). Increased cortical representation of the fingers of the left hand in string players. *Science*, **270**(5234), 305–307.

Ericsson, K. A. (2006). *The Cambridge handbook of expertise and expert performance.* New York, NY: Cambridge University Press.

Fackelmann, K. (2006). Study: Long hospital shifts, sleep deprivation can kill. *USA TODAY*, 12/11. Available at: http://www.usatoday.com/news/health/2006-12-11-sleep-study_x.htm.

Fernandez, A. (2008). ABC reporter Bob Woodruff's incredible recovery from traumatic brain injury. *Huffington Post*, September 15. Available at: http://www.huffingtonpost.com/alvaro-fernandez/abc-reporter-bob-woodruff_b_125863.html.

Gonzalez, A. C. (2007). Prepvolleyball.com. From http://www.volleyballforums.com/viewtopic.php?t=6033.

Grant, J. A., Courtemanche, J., Duerden, E. G., Duncan, G. H., & Rainville, P. (2010). Cortical thickness and pain sensitivity in zen meditators. *Emotion*, **10**(1), 43–53.

Grossman, P., Niemann, L., Schmidt, S., & Walach, H. (2004). Mindfulness-based stress reduction and health benefits. A meta-analysis. *Journal of Psychosomatic Research*, **57**(1), 35–43.

Hamilton, J. (2009, October 19). Music News: Say what?! Musicians hear better. National Public Radio. Available at: http://www.npr.org/templates/story/story.php?storyId=113938566.

Hamilton, J. P., Glover, G. H., Hsu, J. J., & Gotlib, I. H. (2008). *Down-modulation of subgenual anterior cingulate cortex activity with real-time neurofeedback.* Annual Meeting of the Society of Biological Psychiatry.

Hammond, C. (2004). Impacts of lifelong learning upon emotional resilience, psychological and mental health: Fieldwork evidence. *Oxford Review of Education*, **30**(4).

Holzel, B. K., Carmody, J., Vangel, M., Congleton, C., Yerramsetti, S. M., Gard, T., *et al.* (2011). Mindfulness practice leads to increases in regional brain gray matter density. *Psychiatry Research*, **191**(1), 36–43.

Jaeggi, S. M., Buschkuehl, M., Jonides, J., & Perrig, W. J. (2008). Improving fluid intelligence with training on working memory. *Proceedings of the National Academy of Sciences*, doi: 10.1073/pnas.0801268105.

Johnston, S. J., Boehm, S. G., Healy, D., Goebel, R., & Linden, D. E. J. (2009). Neurofeedback: A promising tool for the self-regulation of emotion networks, *NeuroImage*, **49**, 1066–1072.

Kabat-Zinn, J. (1990). *Full catastrophe living: Using the wisdom of your body and mind to face stress, pain, and illness.* New York, NY: Delacorte.

Kabat-Zinn S. (1994). *Wherever you go, there you are: mindfulness meditation in everyday life.* New York, NY: Hyperion.

Katz, L. C., & Rubin, M. (1999). *Keep your brain alive: 83 neurobic exercises to help prevent memory loss and increase mental fitness.* New York, NY: Workman Publishing.

Keller, H. (1903). *The Story of My Life*, chapter 20. New York, NY: Doubleday.

Kolditz, T. A. (2007). *In extremis leadership: Leading as if your life depended on it.* Hoboken, NJ: John Wiley & Sons.

Kuehl, K., Kuehl, J., & Tefertiller, C. (2005). *Mental toughness: A champion's state of mind*. Chicago, IL: Ivan R. Dee.

Lustig, C., Shah, P., Seidler, R., & Reuter-Lorenz, P. A. (2009). Aging, training, and the brain: A review and future directions. *Neuropsychology Reviews*, **19**(4), 504–522.

Lutz, A., Greischar, L. L., Rawlings, N. B., Ricard, M., & Davidson, R. J. (2004). Long-term meditators self-induce high-amplitude gamma synchrony during mental practice. *Proceedings of the National Academy of Sciences*, **101**(46), 16 369–16 373.

Maas, J. B. (1998). *Power sleep: The revolutionary program that prepares your mind for peak performance*. New York, NY: Harper Paperbacks.

Nash, W. P. (2011). US Marine Corps and Navy combat and operational stress continuum model: A tool for leaders. In E.C. Ritchie (ed.), *Operational behavioral health* (pp. 193–204). Washington, DC: Borden Institute.

Newberg, A. B. (2011). Spirituality and the aging brain. *Generations*, **35**(2), 83–91.

New York Times (2009, June 9). Times Topics: US Airways Flight 1549. *New York Times*. Available at: http://topics. nytimes.com/top/reference/timestopics/ subjects/a/airplane_accidents_and_ incidents/us_airways_flight_1549/index. html?scp=2&sq=Sullenberger&st=cse.

Niazi, A. K., & Niazi, S. K. (2010). Mindfulness-based stress reduction: A non-pharmacological approach for chronic illness. *North American Journal of Medical Sciences*, **3**, 20–23.

Nowak, D. (2007). Mother of Russian Tennis. *The Moscow Times*, November 12. Available at: http://www. themoscowtimes.com/sitemap/ paid/2007/11/article/mother-of-russian-tennis/193046.html.

Ochsner, K. N., & Gross, J. J. (2005). The cognitive control of emotion. *Trends in Cognitive Sciences*, **9**(5), 242–249.

Parbery-Clark, A., Skoe, E., & Kraus, N. (2009, October). *Biological bases for the musician advantage for speech-in-noise*. Poster session presented at the annual meeting of the Society for Neuroscience, Neuroscience 2009, Chicago.

Pascual-Leone, A. (2001). The brain that plays music and is changed by it. *Annals of New York Academy of Sciences*, **930** (June), 315–329.

Plumb, J. Charles (1973). *I'm no hero: A POW story as told to Glen DeWerff*. Calabasas, CA: author.

PositScience (n.d.). Brain training program design. Accessed 10/22/10 at http:// www.positscience.com/science/teams-and-approach/design-approach.

Russia Today (2009). All-Russian tennis final: Recipe for success. June 6. Available at: http://rt.com/Sport/2009–06–06/ All-Russian_tennis_final__recipe_for_ success.html.

Rochman, B. (2010, January 18). Workouts for your brain. *Time* magazine. Accessed 7/2/10 at http://www.positscience.com/ news/workouts-your-brain.

Scholz, J., Klein, M. C., Behrens, T. E., & Johansen-Berg, H. (2009). Training induces changes in white-matter architecture. *Nature Neuroscience*, **12**(11), 1370–1371.

Schwartz, J. M., & Begley, S. (2002). *The mind and the brain: Neuroplasticity and the power of mental force*. New York, NY: Harper.

Science 2.0 News Staff (2007). Sleep deprivation and the brain's emotional "disconnect" [Web log post, October 22]. Retrieved from http://www.science20. com/news_account/sleep_deprivation_ and_the_brains_emotional_disconnect.

Singer, T., Seymour, B., O'Doherty, J., Kaube, H., Dolan, R. J., & Frith, C. D. (2004). Empathy for pain involves the affective but not sensory components of pain. *Science*, **303**(5661), 1157–1162.

Smith, G. E., Housen, P., Yaffe, K., Ruff, R., Kennison, R. F., Mahncke, H. W., *et al.* (2009). A cognitive training program based on principles of brain plasticity: Results from the Improvement in Memory with Plasticity-based Adaptive Cognitive Training (IMPACT) study. *Journal of the American Geriatric Society*, **57**(4), 594–603.

Song, J., Skoe, E., Banai, K. & Kraus, N. (2009, October). *Enhancement of* brainstem encoding of the fundamental frequency in listeners with good speech perception in noise. Poster session presented at the annual meeting of the Society for Neuroscience, Neuroscience 2009, Chicago.

Southern Methodist University (2008). Turner Construction Student Forum: Roadside bomb explosion changed their lives. News and communications, March 5. Available at: http://smu.edu/newsinfo/stories/bob-woodruff-4march2008.asp.

Stetler, B. (2009). TV journalist wounded in Iraq returns to the war. *New York Times*, July 13. Available at: http://www.nytimes.com/2009/07/14/arts/television/14woodruff.html.

Strait, D. L., Kraus, N., & Ashley, R. (2009, October). *Musical experience shapes top-down auditory mechanisms: Evidence from masking and auditory attention performance*. Poster session presented at the annual meeting of the Society for Neuroscience, Neuroscience 2009, Chicago.

Sullenberger, C. B. III, with Zaslow, J. (2009). *Highest duty: My search for what really matters*. New York, NY: HarperCollins.

University of Southern California (2009, February 11). Computer exercises improve memory and attention, study suggests. *ScienceDaily*. Retrieved July 2, 2010, from http://www.sciencedaily.com/releases/2009/02/090211161932.htm.

Urry, H. L., Nitschke, J. B., Dolski, I., Jackson, D. C., Dalton, K. M., Mueller, C. J., *et al.* (2004). Making a life worth living: Neural correlates of well-being. *Psychological Science*, **15**(6), 367–372.

Willis, S. L., Tennstedt, S. L., Marsiske, M., Ball, K., Elias, J., Koepke, K. M., *et al.* (2006). Long-term effects of cognitive training on everyday functional outcomes in older adults. *Journal of the American Medical Association*, **296**(23), 2805–2814.

Woodruff, B. (2009). Why I've gone back to Iraq [Web log post at *The World Newser: World News' Daily Blog*, July 13, 8:40 AM]. Accessed 6/22/10 at http://blogs.abcnews.com/theworldnewser/2009/07/bob-woodruff-why-ive-gone-back-to-iraq.html.

Yoo, S., Gujar, N., Hu, P., Jolesz, F. A., & Walker, M. P. (2007). The human emotional brain without sleep – A prefrontal amygdala disconnect. *Current Biology*, **17**(20), R877–R878.

Zarakhovich, Y. (2003). Tennis, everyone? *Time* magazine, August 24. Available at: http://www.time.com/time/magazine/article/0,9171,901030901–477901–3,00.html#ixzz0YeVMDwUR.

Chapter 10

Cognitive and emotional flexibility

People who are resilient tend to be flexible – flexible in the way they think about challenges and flexible in the way they react emotionally to stress. They are not wedded to a specific style of coping. Instead, they shift from one coping strategy to another depending on the circumstances. Many are able to accept what they cannot change; to learn from failure; to use emotions like grief and anger to fuel compassion and courage; and to search for opportunity and meaning in adversity.

As entrepreneur and motivational speaker Pete Koerner (2010) observes, "Life = change. If you're changing anyway, why not change for the better? Better or worse are your only choices; you can't stay where you are forever."

When life blows up

As a young man, Jerry White attended Brown University, where he majored in Judaic Studies. Jerry was raised in the Catholic Church and was particularly interested in the teachings of Jesus Christ. He wanted to walk in the footsteps of the prophets, so during his junior year at Brown he chose to study in Israel.

When school closed for Passover, Jerry and his friends Fritz and David went camping and hiking in the Golan Heights.

> We wanted to get away from people, off the beaten track. We found a primo camping spot, where we could see the valleys of Syria and Jordan. An old bunker from the Six Day War seemed like the perfect shelter. It was a beautiful sunny day, April 12, 1984. I was walking out ahead of my friends, with a song in my heart. I like being the leader, the one out in front. Then, BOOM! A huge explosion. The whole earth seemed to be exploding under me. I thought we were under terrorist attack. I thought someone was shooting at us.

The explosion knocked Jerry off his feet. Stunned and laying face down, he screamed for help. When he tried to crawl, he immediately collapsed. Within seconds David knew that Jerry had stepped on a landmine. David jumped to safety onto the nearest rock and commanded Fritz to do the same. But as Jerry lay immobile, pleading for help, his friends stepped off their rocks and came to his aid.

Blood poured from Jerry's leg, the skin was shredded and charred, and splinters of bone were covered with dirt and blood. Small toe bones, as if shot from an arrow, impaled his calf.

"I have no foot! I have no foot!" Jerry screamed, again and again. Slipping in and out of consciousness, imagining the fluids draining out his body, Jerry yearned for a cool jug of water. And then, as David and Fritz flipped him onto his back, Jerry was touched by a profound presence.

> I felt something touch me, like God's hand, telling me to shut up. Later I asked my friends if they told me to shut up and they didn't. It seemed like something forceful saying, "Quiet, listen." I stopped screaming ... And then I focused and felt a sense of peace and purpose. I knew I didn't die. This is not how the story ends. I don't die here. And there's a purpose in the Middle East. This focused my brain, like someone gave me a pill that said, "Focus, and be calm."

As Jerry lay in a state of surreal calm, David removed his own shirt, wrapped it over Jerry's stump, and tied a makeshift tourniquet around the injured leg. Fritz searched for Jerry's foot and found the boot but not the foot. ("They never did find my foot, but the boot was intact. It was in good shape. This is what I would call a very good advertisement for Timberland," Jerry would later joke.)

Once the tourniquet began to slow the bleeding, David and Fritz took a cold, hard look at the situation. Their good friend Jerry was bleeding to death, they were many miles from a hospital, and they were standing in the middle of a minefield.

Jerry was 6'3" and weighed 200 pounds. As David and Fritz maneuvered their way through the minefield, Jerry's body became entangled in the thick underbrush and briar patches. They dropped him three times, and each time Jerry hit the ground, he flashed back to the explosion, waited for another blast, and imagined he would die. It took them an hour to reach the edge of the minefield, which was enclosed by a fence with a sign reading "*Muqshim*" – mines. (They were Soviet mines laid by the Syrians in the 1960s.) An Israeli from a nearby Kibbutz had heard the explosion and was standing on the other side of the fence, waiting to see what had happened. As David and Fritz approached carrying Jerry, the Israeli began to cut through the wire fence to come to their aid.

This was Jerry's first serious physical injury. Growing up he had never been forced to deal with substantial physical pain: he had been in good health; had never broken a bone; had never even gotten stitches. This was different. This was far beyond anything he had ever imagined. For seven days, he stayed in a small hospital in Safed, where an Arab surgeon saved as much of the leg as he could. The surgeon performed a relatively risky operation, called the Symes Procedure. Unfortunately, gangrene set in several weeks later, forcing Jerry to undergo a second surgical procedure in which more of the leg was amputated. For several months after the accident, Jerry was unable to walk because his good leg had also been blown open. Bones and shrapnel had to be plucked out, and skin from his back grafted to his legs.

Once stable, Jerry faced a critical decision: whether to return home for further surgery and rehabilitation or to remain in Israel for treatment. Jerry's father was the president of a hospital in the Boston area. If Jerry returned home, he would be treated as a VIP in one of the world's best hospitals by some of the world's best doctors, and he would be surrounded by his loving family and friends. Jerry chose to stay in Israel. There, he thought, "the fellowship of suffering was normal," and Israeli doctors were experts in treating traumatic amputations. If he stayed in Israel, he could spare his family from feeling his pain, sensing his anger, or seeing him cry. Israel was also the place where he felt he could best address the question "Where is God?"

And so Jerry was transferred to the Tel Hashomer rehabilitation hospital outside Tel Aviv. Even though many friends visited him, Jerry felt afraid, isolated, and self-concious. "I was alone in this hospital. Like, here's your room, here are your room-mates; Israelis my age who were doing physical therapy. And everybody is looking at you. Suddenly you're like a freak. 'Oh, here's the American, the dumb tourist, who got blown up camping in Northern Israel.'"

One of his roommates, a soldier who had lost both legs and wanted to die, slept the day away and stashed pills, perhaps intending to kill himself.

> It felt like *One Flew Over the Cuckoo's Nest*, and I suddenly felt sad and alone. I thought that I might be crazy. People were trying to introduce themselves, but they were all missing arms, legs, eyes, or they were burn victims. I felt sick and afraid, and all of these people were like ghosts. And I remember this older guy who was doing rehab and he had this new above-the-knee prosthesis and he said, 'You're gonna get one of these, too,' and he took it off and I saw his stump and his leg, and he was making light of it. And I remember feeling that I hated him, that I hated his stump, that I hated his prosthesis. I hated that he was talking to me, and I felt sick, and all I wanted to do was vomit the baba ganoush that I had just eaten.

When Jerry did go home to Boston, he worried about his friends. Would they feel uncomfortable around him? Would they treat him differently? Would they avoid him? Could they fully accept him as the same old Jerry?

> Some of my closest friends drove up to see me, and I remember how afraid they were. I had been living with this for six months but no one else had; they had only heard the awful news. Was I changed? Was I the same Jerry? How should they act? Should they look really glum and sad? Should they just hug, you know, an extra beat too long? I probably overcompensated by trying to make people feel comfortable. Like asking them if they wanted to see my stump or making fun of it and treating my stump like a puppet and making it bark. I even had a pet name for it – Dino.

Jerry went back to college and completed his studies, then moved to Washington, DC, to look for a job in international affairs. While job hunting, he worked as a substitute teacher and, perhaps surprisingly for someone with an artificial leg, he also worked as a home builder. Jerry's career took a new turn when the Brookings Institution hired him as a research assistant in its Middle East Policy section. This experience led him to a position as Assistant Director of the Wisconsin Project on Nuclear Arms Control, an affiliate of the University of Wisconsin Law School. Jerry grew accustomed to his disability and learned to compensate for the inconvenience. He had married, reaffirmed his Catholic faith, and found a job serving society. He believed that he had fully accepted his disability. He had moved on.

Then in 1995, Jerry got a phone call from a stranger named Ken Rutherford. Ken had met one of Jerry's college friends at a social function, and the friend recommended that Ken call Jerry. Although Ken knew that Jerry was an amputee, he did not know how much the two of them had in common.

> He thought that he was perhaps the only American civilian amputee who had lost a leg to a landmine. Actually, he lost both of his legs in Somalia. And he was like, 'I can't believe it, a landmine survivor, and with your work! Don't you know that landmines are called weapons of mass destruction in slow motion? They've killed more people than nuclear chemicals and biological weapons combined. So with your work experience in non-proliferation and weapons of mass destruction and your personal experience losing a leg to a landmine, you could really be effective. Do you know about the emerging campaign to ban landmines?'

Jerry had read several articles about landmines in arms control magazines but had never made the conscious connection between the two types of weapons. Once he did, he was hooked. Three months later, he and Ken attended a UN-sponsored First International Conference on Landmines in Vienna. There, they both told their story, for the first time, and bore witness before a UN panel, an opportunity that ignited Jerry's imagination.

> I saw immediately how this could tap into my passion for a cause and also how powerful the voices of survivors were in this movement. They were living evidence – the lifeblood of the campaign to end landmines. Vienna was a turning point for me, a philosophical turning point that set me on fire for the advocacy issue.

By working for nuclear non-proliferation, Jerry had already prepared for similar activism. Yet it took years for him to find his way to this new mission.

At first, Jerry's boss allowed him to fundraise for landmine survivors by creating a subdivision of the Wisconsin Project on Nuclear Arms Control. But by 1996, Jerry had become consumed by his new passion, and his boss knew that he would eventually lose his valued colleague. Despite his considerable family responsibilities – by now he and his wife had four children under age six – Jerry left his job, cashed out his retirement plan, and set up an office in his basement. It was a risky move, to put it mildly. But he was committed to the cause. He spent day and night fundraising. Even once the group had achieved a great deal, Jerry was willing to acknowledge that he might fail.

> All along I felt that, even if it doesn't work, even if I fail, it's not failure because, look, we will have helped change the world, drafted a treaty to ban landmines, saved millions of lives, helped thousands of survivors. So, if I fail as a director of a non-profit organization because I'm not a good enough fundraiser or I don't know how to build properly as an entrepreneur, then I still succeeded. The failure would still be glorious.

Twenty years after losing his foot in Israel, Jerry White, along with his good friend and colleague Ken Rutherford, accepted the Nobel Peace Prize, which honored the work of International Landmine Survivors Network (which has since been renamed Survivor Corps).

How did Jerry evolve from feeling sad, alone and sick about the loss of his leg to feeling joyous, passionate, and committed to the welfare of other landmine survivors? How did he progress from victim to survivor – then to what he calls "supersurvivor"? Jerry answers these questions in his book *I Will Not Be Broken*, which outlines five steps to overcoming a life crisis.

- Face facts: accept what has happened.
- Choose life: live for the future, not in the past.
- Reach out: connect with other survivors.
- Get moving: set goals and take action.
- Give back: service and acts of kindness empower the survivor to be an asset rather than a victim. (White, 2008)

Jerry's story is an example of what numerous researchers have found: "Rather than seeing themselves as victims of a terrible and mindless fate, resilient people and groups devise ways to frame their misfortune in a more personally understandable way, and this serves to protect them from being overwhelmed by difficulties in the present" (Campbell *et al.*, 2008, p. 63). This concept appears over and over again in the literature on resilience (Coutu, 2002).

Acceptance

Accepting the reality of our situation, even if that situation is frightening or painful, is an important component of cognitive flexibility. To remain effectively engaged in problem-oriented and goal-directed coping, we must keep our eyes "wide open," and acknowledge, rather than ignore, potential roadblocks. Avoidance and denial are generally counterproductive mechanisms which may help people cope for a while, but ultimately they stand in the way of growth, interfering with the ability to actively solve problems.

Sometimes acceptance involves not only acknowledging the reality of one's situation, but also assessing what can and cannot be changed, abandoning goals that no longer seem feasible, and intentionally re-directing efforts toward that which can be changed. Thus, acceptance is not the same as resignation and does not involve giving up or quitting. Instead, acceptance is based on realistic appraisal and active decision-making.

For Jerry White, as for many trauma survivors, fully accepting his loss took a very long time. It was not until many years after his accident, when Jerry was invited to a conference on landmine survivors in Cambodia, that he experienced what he calls an "emotional turning point." It was August, the temperature was well over 100 degrees with nearly 100% humidity, the streets smelled of putrefied food, and Jerry was drenched with sweat. As he stopped to change the dressing on his stump, a young, one-legged beggar, with a crutch under her arm, approached him saying, "You're one of us."

> First, I was repulsed by her. I thought. "I'm not a Cambodian beggar. I'm not like you. You've lost a leg, but you're begging in the streets. That's not me." Then

> I was repulsed by myself. She was right. How dare I separate myself and turn
> my back on her? How could I turn my back and leave if there was something I
> could do? She showed me that I was a jerk. What I didn't know, at the time, was
> that I was part of a family, the family of landmine survivors.

By seeing himself as a part of that family, Jerry had taken another step toward acceptance, a step that allowed him to more fully embrace his own status as a survivor.

Many of the other resilient individuals we interviewed also cited acceptance as a critical factor in their ability to thrive under conditions of high stress and trauma. Somehow, they learned how to focus their attention and energies on problems or issues that they believed they could solve and rarely wasted time "banging their head against the wall," fighting battles that they could not win. In other words, they were realistic and pragmatic, choosing not to waste energy on hopeless causes.

Colonel William Spencer, another former Vietnam POW, recalls an experience from his survival school training that taught him an important lesson about acceptance.

> One of the things that they did was put us in a little box. And the box was made
> to shrink. If you moved, the box would constrict. It was bad. I could hear other
> guys scream and then they [the instructors] would let them out … When I
> went in, I tried to push against it, and that panicked me. I realized that's not
> the thing to do. So then I just relaxed and I tried to [mentally] play golf and
> occupy my mind with other things. … Because when I fought it, I was losing.
> I stopped fighting it when I realized I couldn't change it and pushing made it
> worse. … The same thing that protected me in that box, I think helped me in
> the environment [prison camp] that I was in later.

Perhaps our most graphic example of acceptance involved another Vietnam POW who, after 15 months in solitary confinement, sensed that he was about to "lose his mind." Each day he struggled to understand how and why his life had taken such a dramatic turn. Less than two years earlier, as a Navy aircraft carrier pilot, he had reached the top of his game. He was highly respected, had the "best job in the world," and was happily married with two children. Now, starved and emaciated, he lay shackled in a rat- and mosquito-infested windowless concrete prison cell, refusing to believe or accept that his life had been reduced to mere survival.

And then, one morning, he heard a loud and distinct voice that startled him.

"This is your life."

And it was true. This was his life, not a dream, not his imagination. There was no denying it, no wishing it away. This was real.

> When I heard that voice, things changed. I don't know where it came from.
> It was pretty loud. I'm sure I heard it. I know it sounds weird but it wasn't my
> voice. It's almost like it lifted this weight off my shoulders, 'cause the voice was
> right. I was in this cell and I wasn't going anywhere. So I guess when I really
> admitted it to myself, I just kind of stopped fighting and things got a lot better.

> I mean, I always knew I was in prison, but after that voice it just changed. I just wasn't as miserable anymore, and I started to take care of business, you know, I started to exercise as much as I could and I tried to stay in touch with some of the guys. … After that voice, I felt a lot better.

These experiences echo the essence of the well-known "Serenity Prayer": "God grant me the serenity to accept the things I cannot change, the courage to change the things I can, and the wisdom to know the difference."

The science of acceptance

In the scientific literature, acceptance has been cited as a key ingredient in the ability to tolerate highly stressful situations among survivors of extreme environmental hardship and threats to life (Siebert, 1996) and among highly successful learning-disabled adults (Gerber & Ginsberg, 1990). It has also been associated with better psychological and physical health in many different groups of people. In a nation-wide survey of individuals shortly after the terrorist attacks of September 11, 2001, researchers found reduced levels of posttraumatic stress symptoms in those who accepted the situation (Silver *et al.*, 2002). In a study of mothers whose children had life-threatening cancer diagnoses and were undergoing bone transplants – a painful and highly invasive procedure – Sharon Manne and colleagues (2002) found that those who accepted their situation reported fewer depressive symptoms. Acceptance has also been recommended as a coping mechanism to be used by families dealing with pediatric cancer (Kazak *et al.*, 1999).

Elsewhere in this book we have mentioned cognitive-behavioral therapy as a means to develop a more positive explanatory style, and as a means to observe the world more realistically. A related therapy called Acceptance and Commitment Therapy (ACT) uses acceptance as a starting point for taking action to address problems. The American Psychological Association describes it this way:

> The goal of acceptance and commitment therapy (ACT) is to increase psychological flexibility, or the ability to enter the present moment more fully and either change or persist in behavior when doing so serves valued ends. Therapists and clients work to establish psychological flexibility through six core ACT processes, including acceptance, the opposite of experiential avoidance; cognitive defusion, in which negative thoughts are observed mindfully instead of avoided or reasoned away; chosen values; and committed action. (American Psychological Association, 2008)

ACT has been used successfully to treat problems ranging from chronic pain to smoking cessation to eating disorders. Research also suggests that it may be useful in the treatment of stress and anxiety disorders (Orsillo *et al.*, 2005).

Cognitive reappraisal

Several years ago, while conducting a study on the psychological and neurobiological consequences of the Holocaust, a close colleague asked an elderly Holocaust survivor if she had ever dreamed about her experiences in the camps.

"Oh yes," the woman replied. "I've never stopped dreaming about those times. I just had a dream the other night. Mostly it's the same horrifying one. It wakes me up in the middle of the night. I'm in a panic. I'm sweating, and it's hard to breathe. Yes, I still dream about the camps."

At that point, our colleague replied, "My Goodness, it must be horrible to still have those nightmares after all these years."

"Oh no," the woman said. "It's OK. It's OK because when I awaken I know that I'm here and not there."

Positive reappraisal requires us to find alternative positive meaning for neutral or negative events, situations and/or beliefs. While this remarkable woman suffered profoundly from her Holocaust experiences, she somehow found a way to reappraise her nightmares cognitively. Although she was unable to control her nightmares, she was able to view them as powerful reminders that she was lucky to have survived and now had the privilege of waking up each morning to a new day.

Like this Holocaust survivor, US Airways pilot Chesley Sullenberger narrowly escaped death, as described in Chapter 9, when his plane's engines were disabled. Although he remained outwardly calm during the emergency, Sullenberger suffered from the experience afterwards. Like many (if not most) trauma victims, he struggled with insomnia, distracted thinking, loss of appetite, flashbacks, and "second-guessing and what-iffing." Soon, however, he was able to reappraise his circumstances and see that his experience could give him power – in his case, to influence aviation policy. In his book *Highest Duty* (2009), Sullenberger explains how he decided to move forward: "I've been asked by colleagues to be a public advocate for the piloting profession and for airline safety. ... I know I now have the potential for greater influence in aviation issues, and I plan to be judicious in how I wield that influence" (p. 275).

Decades earlier, in his groundbreaking work on crisis intervention and prevention, Norman J. Finkel coined the term "strens" to describe life events that were health-promoting or growth-enhancing. Although most of these events were positive in nature, a substantial number were clearly traumatic. After years of crisis-oriented research, Finkel (1974) concluded that some people possess the capacity to convert trauma into growth and that they do so through "some cognitive restructuring mechanism." That is, they tend to reframe the negative, search for opportunity in the midst of adversity, and extract positive meaning from trauma and tragedy. Although the term "strens" never gained widespread acceptance, the concept of cognitive reapprasial has been widely recognized.

In the decades since Finkel made his groundbreaking observations, numerous researchers have found that the capacity to positively reframe and extract meaning from adversity is an important component of stress resilience: resilient individuals often find that trauma has forced them to learn something new or to grow as a person (Park *et al.*, 1996). The reported potential "benefits" of trauma have been numerous and far-ranging: greater compassion for and acceptance of others; closer ties with family and friends; a greater sense of kinship with humanity; an enhanced sense of community; a heightened appreciation of nature; renewed religious faith;

development of more effective coping skills; commitment to a healthier lifestyle; improved self-esteem and self-respect; increased emotional strength; enhanced wisdom and maturity; a shift in values, priorities, and perspective; intensified appreciation of life; and a new sense of meaning and purpose (Tedeschi *et al.*, 1998; Anderson & Anderson, 2003).

As human rights worker Sister Dianna Ortiz writes of torture survivors, "From a position of slowly increasing strength, many of us can then begin to redirect our energies to helping other survivors, raising public awareness about the practice of torture, confronting our perpetrators, or simply learning to live life anew with some sense of hope" (Ortiz, 2001, p. 29).

Gratitude as a form of reappraisal

Perhaps surprisingly, some resilient trauma survivors also express a measure of gratitude, feeling that the ordeal has enriched their lives in some way. "Well, first of all, it makes you very humble," says former Air Force pilot Steve Long, describing some of the effects of having been a POW in Vietnam for over five years.

> A lot of the old axioms that you hear – like, "You never really appreciate anything until you take it away," those axioms exist because they're true. And I think anybody that goes through an experience like this, and even like the World Trade Center, the families that were associated with it, they all come to understand this sooner or later: Life is precious. Appreciate it while you can, while you have it, because it can be taken away very easily.

Over the years, since his return from Vietnam, Captain Long has been invited to speak about his war experiences to many audiences, including, high school and college students. For some people, talking about past traumas can be painful, reactivating old feelings of fear and sadness. However, for Long, it provides a way to educate others about the importance of moral integrity, perseverance, learning from the example of role models, and facing fear with trusted colleagues and friends. It also reminds him what the experience taught him.

> It keeps things fresh in my mind that I want to remember. I want to remember to appreciate the things that we have, the freedoms that were taken away from me. I want to remember to place my family first. I don't want to fall back into taking things for granted. I swore that when I got home I'd never forget to be thankful for that piece of bacon, because that was one of the things that I thought about a lot. Just simple things in life.

In their 2003 book *Emotional Longevity*, Norman and Elizabeth Anderson point out that a surprisingly high percentage of people who survive a major crisis later describe the crisis as having affected their lives positively, at least in some important ways. In addition, they cite research showing that individuals who reframed a crisis positively were less likely to develop posttraumatic stress symptoms after being exposed to combat or natural disasters, and adjusted better after losing a family member. This was also true for survivors of incest. Even medically, patients who had suffered a heart attack were less likely to suffer a second one if they were able to view the crisis as a wake-up call or inspiration to re-evaluate their lives.

In some cases the cognitive reframing that accompanies trauma can actually be life-altering. In her innovative work with trauma survivors, Ronnie Janoff-Bulman (1992) proposed that trauma-related changes in personal psychology and personality result from questioning, shattering, and then rebuilding one's basic assumptions about the world.

And indeed, many of the resilient Vietnam POWs whom we interviewed believed that their imprisonment, while it shattered their previous approach to life, eventually proved meaningful and in some cases even positive. Bill Spencer, for example, believes that life is a test and that our mission here on Earth is to learn lessons that lead to growth and maturity, and that many important lessons are the byproduct of adversity.

> In my view, life is an experiment, a test. I think our Lord puts us here to learn things about ourselves. And we really grow and mature more during trials than during the good times. When things are really going well, we start getting real sloppy and we get gregarious and we waste our time. The job's great, everything's wonderful! But when things really go bad, if we concentrate, we can learn a lot. It's not fun. It's not what we ordered. The fun times are better. But really we mature more when we're under an intense trial.

Quite apart from his POW experience, Spencer also lived through a far greater tragedy. One of his children was physically handicapped and died at a young age, an experience that profoundly affected the family.

> I lost a son. And as he became more and more ill I realized how valuable he was and all he had taught me, all the lessons I learned from him. I learned more from him than from anyone or from any lesson. But his life was full of trial. He died when he was 24. And he was handicapped.
>
> When I was a kid, I was very athletic and everything came easy to me. So I have a son who can't do anything. It's good for me. Bad for him. He was here, I think, to teach me those lessons, and the rest of our family. I learned a lot from him. … You don't necessarily learn that much from a normal child. It sounds funny. … I didn't volunteer for it. But after it's all over you realize I can write down 18 things that I learned from him, more than any other source. So did a lot of other people: my wife, his sisters, people who cared for him.
>
> When we had his funeral, there were hundreds of people there we'd never seen. And they just came and told their stories about all the things that he had taught them, because he was handicapped. We learn a lot when we care for somebody, when they can't do it for themselves, that's when we really learn a lot.
>
> One morning, he was about three or four and we always said prayers around a little chest that we had gotten in the Philippines. We always knelt. And I had two daughters and a son and wife. And the five of us would kneel and I would say prayers and I would usually lead or call on one of them and then I'd go to work. And on this morning I was in a hurry. I failed to get up in time and I was rushed for my schedule. Nobody else was rushed, just me. So I said, "Well, we're just going to say our prayers standing up. I'll give the prayer."

I started saying the prayer and I looked down and my three-year-old was on his knees. So without saying anything I knelt and without saying anything more, the rest of the family knelt. He led us. And that's just one example. He taught me how to pray. You don't say prayers hastily. If you're going to say prayers, do it right. He did a lot of things like that. It was just easy for him. He was never in a hurry. So he didn't take shortcuts on important things.

Despite the grief over losing his son, Bill Spencer continues to search for positive lessons embedded in tragedy. And by reframing the tragic, he finds meaning in suffering, thereby enriching his own life and the lives of those around him.

The science of cognitive reappraisal

Throughout this book we have described studies that have used fMRI and other neuroimaging techniques to measure activity in various brain regions when participants engage in specific behaviors or thought processes. Although neuroimaging studies of cognitive reframing are difficult to design, researchers at Columbia University have conducted a number of such studies.

In reviewing an extensive scientific literature on cognitive strategies to regulate emotions, researchers Allison Troy and Iris Mauss (2011) propose that positive cognitive reappraisal fosters resilience through its effect on negative emotions. More specifically, reappraising the meaning of a stressful event as less negative or more positive changes emotional reactions to the event and results in a more adaptive and resilient response. Studies have shown that individuals who frequently use positive cognitive reappraisal as a mechanism to change their emotional reactions to stress report greater psychological well-being and more positive outcomes compared to individuals who do not use positive cognitive reappraisal as a coping mechanism (John & Gross, 2004).

Recently, neuroscientists have found that reappraising an event as being more negative or more positive changes activation in brain regions associated with emotions. Columbia University researcher Kevin Ochsner and colleagues (Ochsner *et al.*, 2009; McRae *et al.*, 2009) have conducted a series of fMRI studies where subjects were instructed to reinterpret visual stimuli (e.g. neutral or negative images) while being scanned. In some studies, subjects were asked to pay attention and respond naturally to a set of pictures that depicted different situations, some negative in content. Subjects were then instructed to reinterpret these situations so that they felt less negative about them. Overall, Ochsner's research found that reappraisal of negative situations successfully decreased negative emotions, increased activation in areas of the prefrontal cortex related to cognitive control, and decreased activation of the amygdala.

As we have described in Chapter 1 and elsewhere, the prefrontal cortex is the "executive" region of the brain which is involved in planning, directing, and inhibiting; and the amygdala is the "alarm center," where the brain processes emotion and fear outside of conscious awareness. Ochsner's study suggests that conscious efforts to positively reframe or reappraise an aversive situation activates the brain's executive region and inhibits its emotion center.

Cognitive reappraisal of failure

Resilience demands the emotional stability to handle failure, what Admiral James Stockdale referred to as the "ability to meet personal defeat with neither the defect of emotional paralysis and withdrawal nor the excess lashing out at scapegoats or inventing escapist solutions." In our experience, those who are resilient generally meet failure head-on and use it as an opportunity to learn and to self-correct. Stockdale used his knowledge of history to do that.

> The only way I know how to handle failure is to gain historical perspective, to think about men who have successfully lived with failure in our religious and classical past. When we were in prison we remembered the Book of Ecclesiastes: "I returned and saw that the race is not always to the swift nor the battle to the strong … but time and chance happeneth to them all." … Failure is not the end of everything, a man can always pick himself up off the canvas and fight one more round. To handle tragedy may, in fact, be the mark of an educated man, for one of the principal goals of education is to prepare us for failure. (Stockdale, 1984, pp. 56, 73)

There's truth to the cliché "It's not how many times you fall down, it's how many times you get up that counts." Failure can teach us to adjust, to improve, and to find new ways to overcome difficulties. Thomas Edison provided a classic example of reframing: "If I find 10, 000 ways something won't work, I haven't failed." he said, "I am not discouraged, because every wrong attempt discarded is another step forward."

Another popular saying is worth remembering: "Learn from the mistakes of others. You can't possibly live long enough to make them all yourself."

Humor: another form of cognitive reappraisal

In his classic book *Man's Search for Meaning*, Viktor Frankl referred to humor as "another of the soul's weapons in the fight for self-preservation. It is well-known that humor, more than anything else in the human makeup can afford an aloofness and an ability to rise above any situation, even if for a few seconds" (1963, p. 63). For Frankl, humor provided a healthy means to gain perspective. And with perspective comes the capacity to reappraise and generate alternative approaches and solutions to problems.

Like other positive emotions, humor tends to broaden one's focus of attention and thereby foster exploration, creativity and flexibility in thinking. In so doing, humor may incorporate a number of other resilience coping mechanisms such as cognitive reappraisal, active problem focused coping, and infusion of positive meaning into ordinary events. As noted by the philosopher André Comte-Sponville:

> The best or most profound humor plays on meaning that touches important areas of our lives, drawing us into its wake and shaking up larger fields of significance, our beliefs, values, illusions in short our seriousness. Sometimes humor seems to bring about an implosion of thought … Humor can zero in

on the very meaning of our behavior and reactions, shaking their foundations and calling into question, scrambling our values, pretensions, and points of reference. (1996, p. 219)

Humor can also serve as a tool to help us face our fears. Humor provides distance and perspective, but does so without denying pain or fear. Humor manages to present the positive and negative wrapped into one package, and according to a noted Viktor Frankl scholar, Ann Graber, humor combines "optimism with a realistic look at the tragic." Without Pollyanna-like optimism, humor can actively confront, proactively reframe and at times transform the tragic. Consider screenwriter and director Woody Allen musing on mortality. "I'm not afraid of dying," says Allen. "I just don't want to be there when it happens." And, "I don't want to achieve immortality through my work. I want to achieve it by not dying."

Of course, we have all known people who use humor as a form of avoidance, making jokes even when seriousness is called for. This is not what we are recommending. However, the ability to see humor even in tragedy can be an important component in resilience. While it may sometimes appear incongruous, humor can be a creative way to confront and cope with what we fear or find painful.

In this sense, perhaps humor may be viewed as a user-friendly and creative form of exposure. As noted in Chapter 3 on Facing Fear, exposure therapy is a category of treatment for fears that involves facing the feared object or situation. It allows the patient to extinguish or lessen fear by encountering the fear in a safe environment. Humor tends to be safe because it incorporates the feared stimulus in a palatable form, sometimes even belittling it and thereby gaining some control over it.

Jerry White used humor when he endorsed Timberland boots and gave a nickname to his stump. In addition, he recalls,

> We started to play tricks on other amputees in the hospital, like telling new amputees that part of their treatment would be sex therapy with a beautiful psychologist, but that no one really talked about it. [We said] it was the hospital's way of helping you to feel like a man again.
>
> I have always said that humor is everything in recovery, so I'll gravitate to whoever laughs the most. No matter what it's about, even if it is dark humor, it just sort of helps. Once, when lights were going out and I was making some kind of joke, one guy said, "But look at us. Don't you realize what has happened?" And the room went quiet. I thought to myself, stay away from this man, he's toxic to me. I can't not laugh. So, if he's trying to say why are we laughing and trying to take away one of the biggest survival tools I have in life, which is humor, and trying to de-legitimize it as denial, I felt irritated and wanted to say "Shut up, of course we know, but if laughter and joking is one of the ways to muscle your way through, then why would you want to take that away?" And if you do take it away, look at what you become, as sad and depressed as this guy who is really sinking down and not dealing well with his limb loss.

Most of the POWs we interviewed also cited humor as an essential tool in their ability to survive and resist. For example, when Rod Knutson could no longer withstand another day of brutal torture, he "succumbed" to the demands of the North Vietnamese to provide them with information about his personal life. "I told them my dad had a chicken farm and he raised three chickens. I told them that I went to school at Farm District Number One and the only job I ever had was selling peanuts to basketball players." Another POW, Ken Coskey, remembers the nicknames, "Big Ug, Zero, and Rudolf," that he and his fellow prisoners used when referring to their guards. Rudolf was the guard with the large red nose.

Staff Sergeant Bobby Henline was never a POW, but his experience ranks among the most severe traumas survived by military veterans (Ledford, 2008). Henline, now married and a father of three, had enlisted in Operation Desert Storm when he was only 17, then returned to civilian life. After the terrorist attacks of September 11, 2001, he re-enlisted and was deployed to Iraq. By 2007, he was serving his third deployment in Iraq when his luck ran out. Traveling in a convoy, Henline's vehicle struck a roadside bomb; the four other soldiers in his Humvee were killed. Burned over 50% of his body, he lost his left hand and part of the arm. His face and scalp were permanently disfigured; most of his hair, ears, and eyelids are gone.

During the months he spent recovering and undergoing multiple surgeries in Brooke Army Medical Center's burn unit, Henline had such a habit of joking with the staff that he recalls that they told him, "You've got to go do standup." And he thought, "I can't do that." But a year later, he had a new hobby: performing on open mic night at a comedy club in his Texas home town of San Antonio. In a 2009 interview with National Public Radio, Henline provided a glimpse of his routine:

> In case you didn't notice, I'm a burn survivor. I've been extinguished for years now. It's actually a rare birth defect. It's a sad story. My mother had to work in the circus as a fire eater while she was pregnant and she thinks she has the right to complain about her acid reflux. Mom, come on! (Gildea, 2009)

Humor and the brain

Substanial evidence exists for the effectiveness of humor as a coping mechanism. Studies involving combat veterans (Hendin & Haas, 1984), cancer patients (Carver, 1993), and surgical patients (Culver *et al.*, 2002) have found that when humor is used to reduce the threatening nature of stressful situations, it is associated with resilience and the capacity to tolerate stress (Martin, 2003). In patients with depression, humor can sometimes diminish depressive symptoms by reducing tension and psychological discomfort, attracting support from others, and creating a positive perspective on difficult circumstances.

Like positive emotions and optimism, humor has been shown to activate a network of subcortical brain regions that constitute core elements of the dopaminergic reward system. In an event-related fMRI brain imaging study of healthy volunteers, Dean Mobbs and colleagues at Stanford University (2003) found that funny cartoons, in comparison to non-funny cartoons, caused activation of the amygdala and nucleus accumbens. A time series analysis showed that activity in the nucleus accumbens increased as the intensity of humor increased. The nucleus accumbens has repeatedly been linked to psychologically and pharmacologically mediated rewards and the amygdala has been associated with processing positive emotions, laughter and reward magnitude, in addition to its well-known role in fear and fear-related behaviors (Mobbs *et al.*, 2003; Moran *et al.*, 2004).

Our response to humor can be divided into a cognitive component (understanding the joke – or "getting it") and an affective component (enjoying the joke – finding it funny). In a study of jokes, Vinod Goel and Raymond J. Dolan (2001) reported that the two components activated different regions of the brain: the cognitive component of humor was associated with activation of the posterior middle temporal gyrus while the affective component with activation of the ventromedial prefrontal cortex. Like the nucleus accumbens and the amygdala, the ventromedial prefrontal cortex has been implicated in representation and control of reward-related behaviors. Thus, humor is associated with areas of the brain that are involved in cognitive appraisal as well as reward and motivation, capacities that appear to be associated with resilience.

Applying cognitive flexibility in your own life

Recent research on coping has shown that successful adaptation depends less on which specific strategies are used, than on whether coping strategies are applied flexibly depending on the nature of the stressor (Cheng *et al.*, 1999; Bonnano *et al.*, 2001; Whealin *et al.*, 2008). Sometimes it is wise to accept and tolerate a situation, while at other times it is best to change it. Similarly, emotion theorists argue that expression of emotion is not necessarily better than suppression. What helps people cope is having the flexibility to express or suppress emotions in accordance with the demands of a given situation (Barrett & Gross, 2001).

In her *Harvard Business Review* article on resilience, Diane Coutu evokes the concept of *bricolage*, or tinkering, as proposed by the French anthropologist Claude Lévi-Strauss.

> Bricolage in the modern sense can be defined as a kind of inventiveness, an ability to improvise a solution to a problem without proper or obvious tools or materials. … When situations unravel, bricoleurs muddle through, imagining possibilities where others are confounded. … Consider UPS, which empowers its drivers to do whatever it takes to deliver packages on time. Says CEO [Mike] Eskew: "We tell our employees to get the job done. If that means they need to improvise, they improvise. Otherwise we just couldn't do what we do every day. Just think what can go wrong: a busted traffic light, a flat tire, a bridge washed out. If a snowstorm hits Louisville tonight, a group of people will sit together and discuss how to handle the problem. Nobody tells them to do that. They come together because it's our tradition to do so." (Coutu, 2002, pp. 54–55)

This practice has served UPS well even through major disruptions such as hurricanes. Moreover, concludes Coutu, the company's ability to continue making deliveries "gave others a sense of purpose of meaning amid the chaos" (p. 55).

We can summarize the strategies in this chapter as: acceptance, reappraisal, dealing with failure, and generating humor. These are all associated with cognitive and emotional flexibility. Here are some suggestions that may be useful if you wish to further develop your cognitive flexibility.

Acceptance

The well-known Serenity Prayer, which we mentioned earlier in this chapter, captures the essence of the kind of acceptance that contributes to resilience: an acceptance of those things that we cannot change. This type of acceptance is not passive "giving up," but rather a well-considered decision not to waste effort and energy on a fruitless attempt to change the unchangeable. Mindfulness meditation and Acceptance and Commitment Therapy are two modalities readers may explore as part of an effort to increase acceptance and cognitive flexibility.

The Serenity Prayer is, in fact, a key element of 12-step programs such as Alcoholics Anonymous. "The Big Book" of Alcoholics Anonymous says this about acceptance:

> ... acceptance is the answer to *all* my problems. Today. When I am disturbed, it is because I find some person, place, thing or situation – some fact of my life – unacceptable to me, and I can find no serenity until I accept that person, place, thing or situation as being exactly the way it is supposed to be at this moment. (Alcoholics Anonymous, 1976, pp. 449–451)

Once we have accepted that which we cannot change, we can focus our attention on what we can change.

Reappraisal

The technique of reappraisal is at the heart of Cognitive Behavior Therapies, which we have described in various chapters in this book. Whether working with a therapist or practicing self-help, one can always ask, "How else can I think about this? How would someone else think about this? What was it like for the other people involved?" Questions like this help to get us out of our own narrow view of a situation and open up new possibilities for coping and problem solving. In their book *Resilience at Work: How to Succeed No Matter What Life Throws at You*, Salvatore R. Maddi and Deborah M. Khoshaba (2005) outline seven steps for a type of reappraisal they call transformational coping:

- Fully describe the stressful situation.
- How could this situation be worse?
- How could the situation be better?
- Create a story about a worse version.
- Create a story about a better version.
- What can you do to create the better version and decrease likelihood of the worse version?
- Place the situation into perspective.

Learn from failure

Regardless of how resourceful we are, there will be times when we simply cannot attain a cherished goal. In such situations, when an endeavor, big or small, doesn't work out, flexibility can be critical. In their book *Mental Toughness: A Champion's State of Mind* (2005), Karl Kuehl and his co-authors point out, "The ability to make adjustments begins with attitude, and the first attitude is accepting that failure is an education, then learning from the experience rather than becoming engulfed in frustration ..." (p. 198). In her book *Stoic Warriors: The Ancient Philosophy Behind the Military Mind*, Nancy Sherman (2007) writes, "If we fail we can always get up again and try again. To be defeated need not mean we are out of the race. Life gives us new contests and new opportunities in which happiness can prevail" (p. 35).

Humor

Of all the aspects of resilience, obviously humor is the most fun. Humor's value has been recognized for millennia: Proverbs 17:22 tells us, "a merry heart doeth good like a medicine." In his classic book *Anatomy of an Illness as Perceived by the Patient*, first published in 1979, Norman Cousins described his recovery from an arthritis-like illness that involved chronic pain. After pain-relieving medications failed to help him, Cousins decided to surround himself with funny movies, books, and other sources of humor. He reported that "I made the joyous discovery that ten minutes of genuine belly laughter had an anesthetic effect and would give me at least two hours of pain-free sleep" (2nd ed., 2001, p. 43). Cousins's work inspired a new form of therapy known as humor therapy or laughter therapy. There are even "laugh workshops," which some people find helpful. Any of us can imitate these strategies and go out of our way to watch funny movies, read funny books, and choose to hang around with people who have a good sense of humor. In *Toughness Training for Life*, Jim Loehr recommends: "Think nutty, goofy, silly, funny, off-the-wall thoughts. ... In almost every situation, being able to laugh puts you in emotional control" (1993, p. 190).

In sum, people who are resilient tend to be flexible: knowing when to accept that which cannot be changed; knowing how to positively reframe life's challenges and failures; using humor to reframe the tragic and that which is frightening; regulating emotions by sometimes suppressing feelings and at other times expressing them. In many respects, resilience requires creativity and flexibility: creativity to explore multiple viewpoints and flexibility to embrace a positive but realistic assessment, or reassessment, of a challenging situation.

References

Alcoholics Anonymous (1976). *Alcoholics Anonymous Big Book*. New York, NY: Alcoholics Anonymous World Service.

American Psychological Association (2008). Acceptance and commitment therapy (abstract). *Systems of Psychotherapy Video Series*. Accessed 7/8/10 at http://www.apa.org/pubs/videos/4310860.aspx

Anderson, N. B., & Anderson, P. E. (2003). *Emotional longevity: What really determines how long you live.* New York, NY: Viking Press.

Barrett, L. F., & Gross, J. J. (2001). Emotional intelligence: A process model of emotion representation and regulation. In T. J. Mayne & G. A. Bonanno (Eds.), *Emotions: Current issues and future directions* (pp. 286–311). New York, NY: Guilford Press.

Bonanno, G. A., Papa, A., O'Neill, K., Westphal, M., & Coifman, K. (2001). the importance of being flexible: The ability to both enhance and suppress emotional expression predicts long-term adjustment. *Psychological Science*, 15(7), 482–487. Available: https://www.psychologicalscience.org/pdf/ps/bonanno.pdf

Campbell, D., Campbell, K. & Ness, J. W. (2008). Resilience through leadership. In Lukey, B. J., & Tepe, V. (Eds.). *Biobehavioral resilience to stress.* New York, NY: Taylor & Francis.

Carver, C. S. (1993). How coping mediates the effect of optimism on distress: a study of women with early stage breast cancer. *Journal of Personality and Social Psychology*, 65, 375–390.

Cheng, C., Hui, W., & Lam, S. (1999). Coping style of individuals with functional dyspepsia. *Psychosomatic Medicine*, 61, 789–795.

Comte-Sponville, A. (1996). *A small treatise on the great virtues: The uses of philosophy in everyday life.* New York, NY: Henry Holt & Company.

Cousins, N. (2001). *Anatomy of an illness as perceived by the patient: Reflections on healing and regeneration*, 2nd edn. New York, NY: W. W. Norton.

Coutu, D. (2002). How resilience works. *Harvard Business Review, May*, 46–55.

Culver, J. L., Arena, P. L., Antoni, M. H., & Carver, C. S. (2002). Coping and distress among women under treatment for early stage breast cancer: Comparing African Americans, Hispanics and non-Hispanic whites. *Psychooncology*, 11, 495–504.

Finkel, N. J. (1974). Strens and traumas: An attempt at categorization. *American Journal of Community Psychology*, 2(3), 265–273.

Frankl, V. E. (1963). *Man's search for meaning: An introduction to logotherapy.* A newly rev. and enl. ed. of *From death-camp to existentalism*. Translated by Ilse Lasch. Pref. by Gordon W. Allport. Boston, MA: Beacon Press.

Gerber, P. J., & Ginsberg, R. J. (1990). *Identifying alterable patterns of success in highly successful adults with learning disabilities.* Washington, DC: United States Department of Education Office of Special Education and Rehabilitative Services. Accessed 1/15/10 at http://www.eric.ed.gov/ERICDocs/data/ericdocs2sql/content_storage_01/0000019b/80/23/d2/bf.pdf.

Gildea, T. (2009). Wounded vet takes pain of war to comedy club. Texas Public Radio, December 26. Accessed 1/15/10 at http://www.npr.org/templates/story/story.php?storyId=121767614.

Goel, V., & Dolan, R. J. (2001). The functional anatomy of humor: segregating cognitive and affective components. *Nature Neuroscience*, 4, 237–238.

Hendin, H., & Haas, A.P. (1984). *Wounds of war: The psychological aftermath of combat in Vietnam.* New York, NY: Basic Books.

Janoff-Bulman, R. (1992). *Shattered assumptions: Towards a new psychology of trauma.* New York, NY: The Free Press.

Kazak, A. E., Simms, S., Barakat, L., Hobbie, W., Foley, B., Golomb, V., *et al.* (1999). Surviving cancer competently intervention program (SCCIP): A cognitive-behavioral and family therapy intervention for adolescent survivors of childhood cancer and their families. *Family Process*, 38(2), 175–191.

Koerner, P. (2010). Innovation – There's got to be a better way [eZine article]. Accessed 7/2/10 at http://ezinearticles.com/?Innovation- -Theres-Got-to-Be-a-Better-Way&id=1384677. Note: Pete Koerner is the author of *The Belief Formula: The Secret to Unlocking the Power of Prayer* (Bell Rock Press, 2007).

Kuehl, K., Kuehl, J., & Tefertiller, C. (2005). *Mental toughness: A champion's state of mind.* Chicago, IL: Ivan R. Dee.

Ledford, T. (2008). Nonprofit helps wounded vet start over: Home for a hero. OperationHomeFrontOnline, August 4. Accessed 1/15/10 at http://www.homefrontonline.com/article.asp?articleid=1296.

Loehr, J. (1993). *Toughness training for life.* New York, NY: Dutton.

Maddi, S. R., & Khoshaba, D. M. (2005). *Resilience at work: How to succeed no matter what life throws at you.* New York, NY: AMACOM, a division of the American Management Association.

Manne, S., DuHamel, K., Nereo, N., Ostroff, J., Parsons, S., Martini, R., *et al.* (2002). Predictors of PTSD in mothers of children undergoing bone marrow transplantation: The role of cognitive and social processes. *Journal of Pediatric Psychology, 27*(7), 607–617.

Martin, R. (2003). Sense of humor. In Lopez, S. J., & Snyder, C. R. (eds.), *Positive psychological assessment: A handbook of models and measures* (pp. 313–326). Washington, DC: American Psychological Association.

Mobbs, D., Greicius, M. D., Abdel-Azim, E., & Menon, V. (2003). Humor modulates the mesolimbic reward centers. *Neuron, 40*,1041–1048.

Moran, J. M., Wig, G. S., Adams, R. B. Jr., Janata, P., & Kelley, W. M. (2004). Neural correlates of humor detection and appreciation. *Neuroimage, 21,* 1055–1060.

Ochsner, K. N., Bunge, S. A., Gross, J. J., & Gabrieli, J. D. E. (2002). Rethinking feelings: An fMRI study of the cognitive regulation of emotion. *Journal of Cognitive Neuroscience, 14,* 1215–1229.

Ochsner, K. N., Silvers, J. A., Buhle, J. T. (2012). Functional imaging studies of emotion regulation: a synthetic review and evolving model of the cognitive control of emotion. *Annals of the New York Academy of Sciences, 1251,* E1–E24.

Orsillo, S. M., Roemer, L., & Holowka, D. (2005). Acceptance-based behavioral therapies for for anxiety: Using acceptance and mindfulness to enhance traditional cognitive-behavioral approaches. In S. M. Orsillo & L. Roemer (Eds.), *Acceptance- and mindfulness-based approaches to anxiety: Conceptualization and treatment.* New York, NY: Springer.

Ortiz, D. (2001). The survivor's perspective: Voices from the center. In Gerrity, E., Keane, T. M., & Tuma, F. (Eds.), *The mental health consequences of torture.* New York, NY: Kluwer Academic/ Plenum Publishers.

Park, C., Cohen, L., & Murch, R. (1996). Assessment and prediction of stress-related growth. *Journal of Personality, 64,* 71–105.

Sherman, N. (2007). *Stoic warriors: The ancient philosophy behind the military mind.* New York, NY: Oxford University Press.

Siebert, A. (1996). *The survivor personality.* New York, NY: Pedigree Books.

Silver, R. C., Holman, E. A., McIntosh, D. N., Poulin, M., & Gil-Rivas, V. (2002). Nationwide longitudinal study of psychological responses to September 11. *Journal of the American Medical Association, 288,* 1235–1244.

Stockdale, J. B. (1984). *A Vietnam experience.* Stanford, CA: The Hoover Institution.

Sullenberger, C. B. III, with Zaslow, J. (2009). *Highest duty: My search for what really matters.* New York, NY: HarperCollins.

Tedeschi, R. G., Park, C. L., & Calhoun, L. G. (Eds.) (1998). *Posttraumatic growth: Positive changes in the aftermath of crisis.* Mahwah, NJ: Lawrence Erlbaum Associates.

Whealin, J.M., Ruzek, J.I., & Southwick, S. (2008). Cognitive behavioral theory and preparation for professionals at risk for trauma exposure. *Trauma, Violence, and Abuse, 9,* 100–113.

White, J. (2008). *I will not be broken: Five steps to overcoming a life crisis.* New York, NY: St. Martin's Press.

Meaning, purpose, and growth

When philosopher Frederick Nietchze wrote, "He who has a why can endure almost any how," he was referring to the power of meaning. Other renowned scholars have also recognized the powerful effects of meaning; of having a worthy goal or mission in life. As Carl Jung wrote in his classic book *Man and His Symbols*, "[Man] can stand the most incredible hardships when he is convinced they make sense" (1968, p. 76). South African dissident Nelson Mandela stands as an inspiring example: Mandela was able to tolerate 30 years of imprisonment with grace and dignity because his imprisonment symbolized the struggle for equality. Meaning can give us strength and meaning can give us courage. During your own life, when called upon to defend a cherished idea, stand up for a worthy cause, or protect a loved one, perhaps you have been surprised by the reservoir of strength and resilience that lies within.

Undoubtedly the best-known and most influential advocate for finding meaning is holocaust survivor Viktor Frankl, who wrote,

> Deep down, in my opinion, man is dominated neither by the will to pleasure (as proposed by Sigmund Freud) nor by the will to power (Alfred Adler), but by what I call the will to meaning: his deep seated striving and struggling for a higher and ultimate meaning to his existence. (1958, p. 20)

In psychological research, studies have found that having a clear and valued purpose, and committing fully to a mission, can dramatically strengthen one's resilience. Yale School of Management professor Amy Wrzesniewski found that "most people see their work as either a Job (focus on financial rewards and necessity rather than pleasure or fulfillment; not a major positive part of life), a Career (focus on advancement), or a Calling (focus on enjoyment of fulfilling, socially useful work)" (Wrzesniewski *et al.*, 1997, p. 21). In keeping with Frankl's conception of service as a pillar of meaning, the ability to see one's work as a calling may enhance resilience. This holds true even for people performing "dirty work" jobs (e.g. hospital cleaners) and for people who have been prevented from pursuing their chosen career.

Donald Campbell and colleagues in the Department of Behavioral Sciences and Leadership at West Point teach future military commanders that it is critical for their soldiers to understand and embrace the significance of their duty, service and sacrifice. Campbell has found that soldiers who believe in the importance of their mission, even if it is dangerous, derive greater benefits from their work than soldiers who do not believe in the mission. This was borne out by researchers Thomas

Britt, Amy Adler, and Paul Bartone (2001) in a prospective study of 161 US soldiers participating in a stressful peacekeeping mission in Bosnia. The researchers found that soldiers who considered this work to be meaningful later reported greater benefits from the mission compared to soldiers who found the mission to be less meaningful.

Civilian workers who feel a sense of purpose in their work also exhibit strength in the face of work-related stress. In a study of city bus drivers, Paul Bartone (1989) found that those who were high in hardiness (a construct related to resilience) were generally proud of their work and found it to be meaningful. When faced with work-related stressors, these same individuals fared better than those for whom driving a bus was "just a job." Similarly, in a 12-year longitudinal study of employees at Illinois Bell Telephone, Salvatore Maddi (1987) found that workers who reported a purposeful direction in their community, school, and work activities were more resilient during an organizational crisis than were workers who lacked such direction.

In our own clinical work and research, we have looked for ways to help patients derive strength in the wake of their traumatic experiences. Fifteen years ago at the Yale University-affiliated division of the National Center for PTSD, we helped to develop a treatment program for combat veterans with chronic PTSD that was based on logotherapy, an intervention developed by Frankl and several of his students. The literal meaning of logotherapy is "healing through meaning." For years we had worked with veterans who expressed doubts about the meaning of their lives, dominated as they were by guilt and by painful memories and fears. Many of them had experienced the darkest side of human nature and were plagued by feelings of aimlessness. These feelings affected their work, family relations, spirituality, and their desire to fully engage in life.

In a 2006 article that described this treatment program, we wrote that logotherapy directly addresses

> the dialectic of fate and freedom that may be expressed as follows: Even though we as human beings cannot often control the circumstances in our lives (fate), we usually can control our attitudes and responses to those circumstances. As one protégé of Frankl put it, "[T]he meaning of fate lies in our response to it … Chance decides what happens but we decide how to take it." (Southwick et al., 2006, p. 162; quote from Lukas, 2000)

In this article, we described how community service was an integral part of the treatment plan for these veterans. Through community service, patients often discover a sense of purpose through giving to others.

> During orientation to community service, veterans are reminded that they are already experts in many respects: They are experts in fear and psychological trauma, experts in personal and spiritual pain, experts in loss and failure, experts in hopelessness and emptiness, experts in coping with a society that rejects its injured members, and experts in survival and resilience. We next pose the question, "What can you do and what will you do with your expertise?" (Southwick et al., 2006, p. 166)

Each veteran was assigned to a community service site that tapped into his special expertise. For example, if a veteran had been homeless, we recommended that he or she volunteer for Habitat for the Humanity. Another veteran, who had spent years living alone, volunteered with Meals on Wheels, which delivers meals to elderly shut-ins. Like the veteran, the recipient of meals may have felt socially isolated and afraid. Or veterans might tutor underprivileged school children, many of whom had been exposed to violence in their inner-city neighborhoods. As a group, the veterans also initiated their own projects that they felt called to offer.

> For example, the first project – a toy drive and holiday party for children in the foster care system – was meaningful to one veteran who had been abused as a child and wanted "the kids to know someone cares." For another group member, anguished over his inability as a soldier to help children orphaned by war, this work enabled him to effectively help children harmed by their circumstances. And, for a third veteran, the project provided a means for him to confront his regrets of not connecting with his own children, due to longstanding trauma-related emotional numbing, and to work towards connection with his grandchildren. (Southwick *et al.*, 2006, p. 167)

Much of the impetus for the service work was fueled by personal experiences of suffering, guilt, and loss in war.

> One group member, acting on his own, decided to devote a portion of his service-connected disability benefits to fund a partial scholarship in the name of his friend who died in Vietnam. This veteran, who has struggled with survivor guilt over the years, found a meaningful way to honor his friend, who had planned to return to college after Vietnam. (Southwick *et al.*, 2006, p. 168)

The veterans' role in choosing and originating projects aligns with the idea that "chance decides what happens but we decide how to take it" (Lucas, 2000). Similarly, most of the people we interviewed for this book found ways to exercise whatever freedom they had as they searched for meaning in the aftermath of trauma. Elizabeth Ebaugh, the social worker who was abducted and raped, eloquently describes her search.

> I go inside and ask what this is trying to show me about my own life. What is this trying to teach me? The overarching philosophy that's guiding me is in the way I handle it. There's room for getting really angry that I got raped. What's important is where you stay. If I were to stay in that place of anger and "why me?" and "why did this happen?" then I'm only going to be like a hamster in a cage. So … I take it to a more transcendent place, where I think, how can I use this in my spiritual journey? Maybe this didn't have to happen, maybe there is no reason, but if I give it a reason, if I find a reason for how it can better my life, then that makes it a golden nugget in my life, rather than something horrible.

Although she could not control her fate on the night of the horrific incident, she could and did, to a large degree, determine how she *responded* to that fate. Over time,

Elizabeth chose to find value in her trauma, to be strengthened by it, and to use it as a motivation for her own emotional and spiritual growth.

Like Elizabeth, Jerry White chose to find meaning in trauma – in his case, losing his leg to a landmine.

> There are three types of trauma victims: Those people who say why me, and the pity piece that goes with that. Then there's the other Christian martyr thing, why *not* me – with suffering all around, why do I deserve *not* to be in a wheelchair or maimed or burned or whatever? And the third type simply asks, "Why?" This is a healthy question. This question is a search for meaning. For years I never asked the "why" questions, like "Why did I step on that land mine?" Or, "Why were those minefields there in the first place? Who put them there? Why are minefields blowing up people during wars and even years after wars are over?" Now, 20 years later, with perspective and enough living, I understand that the better question is "Why?"
>
> We each have a choice not to be a victim. If someone wants help from me or from the Landmine Survivors Network, they have to make movement toward us because we're not hanging around with the victim club. It's a radical stance. You have to choose to get up, choose life not death. The word "survivor" means to live through it, to refuse to accept defeat. It is a romantic idea and I am still striving to fully achieve it. I won't be defeated.
>
> There is a rescue side to the work, a life-saving side. And that's related to understanding that people get stuck on their victim platforms and that we want to help them get unstuck and we want to prod them forward.

But White asks survivors to do more than to quit "the victim club."

> It's not just moving people from death to life or from victim to survivor, it's an expectation of survivor citizenship, where people move on and become givers to the community. They could become community leaders, change agents, future peer supporters, whatever, but our expectation, all along, for the Landmine Survivors Network was that it be a movement forward that blessed the community, that took shattered lives, offered some tools to overcome, and then encouraged individual survivors to come back and serve as a role model for others, a living example of survivorship.

Jerry White uses the term "super-survivor" to describe the person who successfully moves from victim to survivor and then takes it even a step further. Super-survivors recognize the healing and strengthening value of "paying forward," or giving to others and to the community.

Judith Herman, a well-known trauma researcher, refers to this transformation as a "survivor mission." Trauma survivors who find such a mission recognize "a political or religious dimension in their misfortune and discover that they can transform the meaning of their personal tragedy by making it a basis for social action. While there is no way to compensate for an atrocity, there is a way to transcend it by making it a gift to others" (Herman, 1997, p. 201). That is, these individuals have used their adversity as a catalyst for reaching out to others. In doing so, they try to make life better for their families, their communities, and even for people in societies far beyond their own personal experiences and day-to-day lives. They create foundations and advocacy groups, become tireless volunteers, assume difficult leadership responsibilities, and mentor others.

Survivor mission: shining a light on the Sudan genocide

If the word "survivor" can be applied to anyone, it is to Valentino Achak Deng and the thousands of young men and women like him who endured one of the most horrific – yet little-known – humanitarian crises of the twentieth century.[1] Valentino was born in southern Sudan, a region of rivers, grasslands, and tropical forests where for generations his ancestors, the indigenous Dinka people, have herded cattle and raised millet, sorghum, and other crops. In recent years most Americans have seen headlines about genocide in western Sudan's Darfur provinces, but the outside world is less aware of similar atrocities against the southern half of the country, beginning in the late 1970s when oil was discovered there.

Valentino was 6 or 7 years old in 1988 when he was one of many thousands of children who fled their homes when they were attacked by militias from the north. They had seen their parents killed, entire villages burned, wells contaminated, and cattle and crops laid waste. Hiding among the grasses, roots of trees, and in riverbank swamps, these "lost boys" (girls were more likely to have been killed with the adults or carried off as slaves) eventually made their way across the conflict-ridden region, where raiding militias had destroyed sources of food across the Ethiopian border. Along the way, many boys died of disease and dehydration; others were killed by wild animals or by gunfire from the militia groups, against which they were constantly on alert. Valentino had walked more than 500 miles from his village when he and the others who had not died reached the safety of a United Nations refugee camp.

Life in the camp was comfortable by comparison; the refugees built shelters of sisal bags supported by sticks, and they received regular rations of dried corn and beans, which they cooked in water drawn from the nearby river. Many young boys, Valentino among them, were soon assigned to carry the dead from the hospital tent to the camp's burial area and to dig graves for them. Weeks, months, and years passed as the displaced Sudanese in the camp, now numbering over 40,000, awaited word that they could safely return home. Then, in 1991, the overthrow of the Ethiopian government forced them to flee again. This time they went to Kenya, where first one and then another United Nations refugee camp served as home for Valentino.

More than a decade after he had run away from his village, Valentino was accepted as a refugee immigrant by the United States. A nonprofit organization called the Lost Boys Foundation helped him to settle in Atlanta, where he supported himself with low-wage jobs and enrolled in college. Ironically in the United States he experienced not only the prejudice of white people against blacks, but also of African-Americans against African immigrants, and of different Sudanese groups against one another.

---

[1] Information about Valentino Achak Deng is drawn from http://www.valentinoachakdeng.org/ and Eggers, D. (2006).

He witnessed how alcohol, drugs, compulsive gambling, and violent crime harmed some of his fellow Sudanese immigrants. It would be understandable if Valentino and others like him chose to become hostile, or fearful, or simply alienated from the world. But instead, here are Valentino's thoughts as recorded by the American writer Dave Eggers:

> I will reach upward. I will attempt to do better. I will not be a burden. … I will always be grateful for what pleasures I have enjoyed, what joys I have yet to experience. … I will live as a good child of God, and will forgive him each time he claims another of the people I love. I will forgive and attempt to understand his plans for me, and I will not pity myself. (Eggers, 2006, p. 533)

Valentino had been in the United States for only a short time when the Lost Boys Foundation put him in touch with Eggers, who chronicled his story in the novel *What Is the What* (2006). Valentino's purpose from the beginning of the book project was to draw public attention to the continued suffering in southern Sudan and the political complexities of the fragile peace achieved there in 2005. He continues to accept speaking engagements and to channel profits from the book into the Valentino Achak Deng Foundation. Like other humanitarian groups such as Sudan Sunrise, this foundation builds schools, libraries, and teacher-training facilities in southern Sudan. In 2009 the foundation opened an educational complex with 15 buildings in Valentino's home village, Marial Bai. As he wrote in the preface to *What Is the What,*

> My desire to have this book written was born out of my faith and beliefs in humanity; I wanted to reach out to others to help them understand Sudan's place in our global community. …
>
> I am blessed to have lived to inform you that even when my hours were darkest, I believed that some day I could share my experiences with others. This book is a form of struggle, and it keeps my spirit alive to struggle. To struggle is to strengthen my faith, my hope and my belief in humanity. Since you and I exist, together we can make a difference! (Eggers, 2006, pp. xiv–xv)

There are countless other examples of "super-survivors", individuals who have turned their misfortune into a survivor mission; they include, to name just a few:

- Carolyn McCarthy, who was elected to the US Congress on a gun control platform after her husband was killed in a random shooting on the Long Island Railroad;
- Candy Lightner, Cindy Lamb, and the other women who founded Mothers Against Drunk Driving after their children were injured or killed by drunk drivers;
- Terry Fox, the young cancer patient who founded the Marathon of Hope, an annual run across Canada that has since raised nearly $300 million for cancer research;
- Jim Muller, Charles Kenney, Peggie Thorp, and other Roman Catholics who founded Voice of the Faithful in response to sexual abuse by priests; its goal is to "keep the faith, change the church";

- Eddie Canales and Mike Kipp, who founded Gridiron Heroes Spinal Cord Injury Foundation to help injured high school football players after Canales' son became paralyzed from a football injury;

- John Walsh, host of the TV show *America's Most Wanted*, who began his crusade to bring criminals to justice and to help find missing and exploited children after the 1981 abduction and murder of his 6-year-old son.

Making a "small" difference is better than doing nothing

One of Viktor Frankl's observations is that meaning may be found even in the most ominous circumstances.

> We must never forget that we may also find meaning in life even when confronted with a hopeless situation, when facing a fate that cannot be changed. For what then matters is to bear witness to the uniquely human potential at its best, which is to transform a personal tragedy into a triumph, to turn one's predicament into a human achievement. When we are no longer able to change a situation – just think of an incurable disease such as inoperable cancer: We are challenged to change ourselves. (Frankl, 1963, p. 116)

Frankl referred to the capacity for finding meaning in adversity as "tragic optimism," optimism in the face of human suffering, guilt, and even certain death. Tragic optimism encompasses the human potential to transform suffering into human achievement and guilt into meaningful action.

Lt. Col. Paul Morrissey is a psychiatrist with an emergency medicine background. Since 2008 he has directed the mental health program for the United States Military Academy at West Point. In 2006, he served in Iraq, where his mission was to provide combat stress control services to US soldiers stationed at Forward Operating Base Scania, south of Baghdad. Adjacent to the base, there was a make-shift burn clinic for Iraqi children.

> We had an Iraqi doctor who served as a translator officially, but he was the main person taking care of the kids, and some of our medics would help out too. One thing I push out of my mind is that the "clinic" was a Conex, a shipping container with lights, a primitive table, that's it. These kids would come in after being bounced and tossed over rough roads for hours, and their wounds would be covered with yellow, gooey pus, and flies; kids would be sitting there with flies buzzing all around them. It was a horrific thing to see. Some of the kids would come in on stretchers because they were so malnourished they couldn't walk. We would do what we could to fix them up, and send them out looking good with antibiotics and fresh bandages, and they always left with a few Jolly Rancher candies. We were able to provide at least some comfort which seemed to make a little difference, and increased the odds that they would live another week.
>
> One thing that really got to me was the day two burned Iraqi boys came in, one in the morning and a second in the afternoon. The first was a beautiful 15-month-old boy … He was turning blue and had no palpable pulses because of low blood pressure, in shock caused by a bacterial infection from the burns. We resuscitated him and were so happy to have saved his life. It was the greatest

feeling to win one, and we were all proud and elated. But then the 18-month-old showed up with almost the exact same problem, and quickly coded and died. It was devastating to lose him and we were all despondent, both from seeing this dead kid in front of us, hearing his father's wailing sobs, and knowing that many other Iraqi kids were dying because they weren't getting adequate medical care.

That's combat stress for doctors, watching little kids die of treatable illnesses. There's a sense of powerlessness when you don't have nurses and staff and millions of dollars' worth of equipment supporting you. There you are with 50 Iraqi kids in a shipping container, it's just – whoa – like holy crap, what can we do? When you're here in the US, there's always someone to ask, always someone to help out. There, it's you and a kid – you and your little bag, and someone in deep trouble. It helped us to understand what it was like to be a general practice doctor 100 years ago.

Morrissey explains that most of the children's burns were not related to combat, but occurred instead from open-flame heating in the home, and, in some cases, from abuse. And in addition to burn victims, some children came in with cancer, congenital heart defects, and other life-threatening conditions. For example, one teenage boy arrived with a softball-sized tumor in his neck that impaired his breathing. The diagnosis turned out to be Hodgkins lymphoma – for which, according to Morrissey, the chances of survival in Iraq are slim. One thing most of the patients had in common was that Iraqi doctors had already done all they could for them.

The families had been told, "your fate is in Allah's hands. Now go home," because the care of burns is too labor-intensive and the Iraqi hospitals lacked basic supplies. But some parents still decided to travel four or five hours to reach the American base, which is a very dangerous thing to do in Iraq.

There was a five-year-old boy with about half of the skin on his scalp and face burned off. Somebody in Iraq at some point had tried skin grafts, but it didn't work very well and half of his head was an open oozing wound. Over the course of a few months he was coming in two or three times a week for dressing changes, which was very painful, and he would try to be tough and not cry, but often he couldn't help it. We were all frustrated because we were supposedly "helping" this kid, but what we were actually doing was torturing him. We would give him pain medication, but that made him dizzy for a few hours, so eventually he didn't want any pain medication. I was amazed at his strength and stoicism and courage, but I knew that he needed much more than we could give him in Iraq.

Soon Morrissey was talking with military chaplains and US embassy staff to unravel the bureaucratic logistics of securing passports and visas for the young boy and his father to leave Iraq, raising money for his travel expenses, and finding a US hospital willing to donate care. Many enlisted soldiers at Forward Operating Base Scania made donations, small and large, out of their modest earnings. This was the beginning of the Iraqi Children's Project, a not-for-profit corporation that partners with Boston Shriners Hospital and various other hospitals in the United States – Massachusetts General Hospital, Jefferson Medical College in Philadelphia, SUNY

Upstate Medical University in Syracuse, and others – to provide advanced care for critically ill and injured Iraqi boys and girls. As of 2009, the Iraqi Children's Project had brought 18 children and their parents or guardians to the US.

In organizing the Iraqi Children's Project, Col. Morrissey took meaningful action in the midst of a seemingly impossible situation. Yes, the results are small – 18 kids out of the thousands who need help – but that is 18 better than no kids. Despite the "whoa," the seemingly hopeless circumstances, Morrissey created meaning. This reminds us of the Jewish proverb, "It is better to light one small candle than to curse the darkness." Morrissey has what we referred to earlier as tragic optimism, optimism in the face of human suffering. He and the Iraqi Childrens' Project partners are doing what they can, and not getting discouraged by the darkness.

Col. Morrissey's work illustrates the concept we described in Chapter 4 on moral compass: that we are responsible for what we can control, and not responsible for what is beyond our control. This distinction, central to Stoic philosophy, was also described by World Trade Center survivor Jimmy Dunne, whom we introduced in Chapter 1. Speaking to a business audience in 2004, Dunne distinguished between "the infinite things," which an individual person cannot control – the movements of the stock market, the horror of an airplane smashing into a building – and "the finite things" that we can control: attitude, effort, conduct.

In choosing to turn misfortune into a springboard for helping others, survivors of trauma often discover in themselves unexpected tenacity and strengths, and these qualities become of the foundation for their purposeful living and of their humanitarian efforts. Understanding how great humanitarianism grows out of adversity is related to posttraumatic growth.

It is important to acknowledge that in some cases becoming a "super-survivor" is not an option. For example, a terminally ill patient may be incapacitated to the point of depending upon others even for basic daily activities like eating and bathing. Sometimes the best one can do is to accept and find meaning of a personal nature while living through the last stages of an illness. Accepting that one's own death, or the death of a loved one, is imminent may be one of the most difficult tasks that we face as humans. In his book *Hand to Hand: From Combat to Healing*, former British Royal Marine and PTSD sufferer Nigel Mumford (2000) points out that "cure" is a medical term, and that not everyone can experience cure. However, healing can be spiritual and emotional, and unlike cure, healing may be available to those who have the capacity to choose it. In her book on death and dying, *The Journey Home*, Ann Graber writes,

> As a first step when hospice is invited into the treatment team, the illusion that recovery will be forthcoming has to be given up. Denial of approaching death can no longer be sustained; neither by the patient, nor by the family. Those who can accept this inevitability, in spite of the anguish it may cause, are preparing for a harmonious parting of ways on their journey home. … The transformative process – inherent in unavoidable suffering – makes us realize that tragedy often contains the seeds of grace: We can become more than we were before, by facing the challenges life presents to us. (2009, pp. 31–32)

Posttraumatic growth

To understand how some trauma survivors create new meaning and purpose out of what may seem to be a cruel and meaningless world, Ronnie Janoff-Bulman (1992) from the University of Massachusetts has described two types of meaning: meaning as comprehensibility, and meaning as significance. In the immediate aftermath of a trauma, survivors try to comprehend what has happened. They may have trouble believing and accepting that a loved one is gone forever or that they have lost all of their possessions. Their long-standing assumption that the world is safe and predictable may be shaken, leaving them feeling vulnerable and lost, and they may experience repetitive intrusive thoughts about the trauma. For some survivors, attempts to comprehend the trauma gradually shift to attempts to creating meaning out of the trauma and possibly grow from it.

In recent years, while most researchers have described a self-transcending, functional and constructive side to posttraumatic growth, some have also described a potentially self-deceptive or illusory side (Zoellner & Maercker, 2006). Richard Tedeschi and Lawrence Calhoun developed the Posttraumatic Growth Inventory (PTGI) (1996), which assesses three general domains: changes in the perception of self, changes in the experience of relationships with others, and changes in one's general philosophy of life. Changed perception of self can be summarized by the statements, "I've been through the absolute worst that I know. And no matter what happens, I'll be able to deal with it" and "I am more vulnerable than I thought, but much stronger than I ever imagined." Changes in the experience of relationships with others include feeling a stronger connection with other people and greater compassion for those who suffer. Changes in philosophy often grow out of existential questions about the meaning of life and one's purpose in a world replete with inexplicable suffering. Recognizing that the trauma has engendered growth may give purpose to the trauma, even if unintended.

We have used the PTGI in our own research with veterans of Operation Enduring Freedom (Afghanistan) and Operation Iraqi Freedom as well as with former Vietnam POWs. In a study of nearly 300 Iraq and Afghanistan veterans (Pietrzak *et al.*, 2010), our colleague Robb Pietrzak found that 72% reported growth in at least one of the assessed areas as a result of their service in the Middle East. The most common areas of growth were changing priorities about what is important in life (52.2%) and greater ability to handle difficulties (48.5%). Posttraumatic growth has also been reported in other groups of trauma survivors including, refugees, cancer patients, and veterans of World War II and Korea.

It is important to understand that intense psychological distress does not preclude posttraumatic growth. In fact, like some researchers, we found that individuals who reported higher levels of posttraumatic stress symptoms as a result of their military service in Iraq and Afghanistan also reported more growth than those with lower levels of posttraumatic stress symptoms. Perhaps, for some survivors, in order to promote growth, a traumatic experience must cause enough distress to shake the individual's view of the world and his or her place in it. Perhaps it must be disruptive enough to force the individual to reassess, revise and rebuild fundamental aspects of their psychological, philosophical and/or spiritual life.

Indeed, when we used the PTGI to assess 30 former Vietnam POWs (Feder *et al.*, 2008), 93% described greater appreciation of life as a result of their imprisonment, 80% greater personal strength, and 50% or more described improved relating to others, new possibilities, and spiritual change. There was no difference in growth inventory scores between those with PTSD and those without it. Understandably, not a single former POW said he would choose to repeat the experience. However, most were able, over time, to take a profoundly painful experience and make it meaningful by viewing it as a force that helped to shape their character.

Your own meaning, purpose, and growth

Thinking back to our formative years, many of us were encouraged to envision and strive toward a meaningful adulthood. "What do you want to be when you grow up?" we were asked. Of course, life ambitions change as we grow older and more know-ledgeable about the available options. Hopefully, throughout our lives we will have the freedom to choose a direction that allows us to use our own talents, strengths and interests, and hopefully we will have the option to periodically re-evaluate our talents and strengths, particularly when we encounter a setback or event that shakes our world view. It is through this process that we can, in the words of Ann Graber quoted earlier, "become more than we were before."

In *Man's Search for Meaning* and *The Will to Meaning*, Viktor Frankl (1963) points out that what is meaningful for one person may not be meaningful for another, or for the same person at a different point in time. For Frankl, meaning is not handed or given to us. Instead it must be searched for, found and discovered in the concrete experiences of our daily lives.

Searching for meaning and purpose is often discussed openly in psychotherapy and pastoral counseling. Earlier in this chapter we described logotherapy; unlike many traditional forms of psychotherapy, logotherapy looks to the future rather than examining the past, and it focuses on the patient's areas of strength rather than solely on symptoms of psychopathology. Logotherapy uses several basic techniques: "self-distancing (learning to gain distance from and. observe the self); paradoxical intention (wishing for or doing that which is feared); Socratic dialogue (interviewing designed to elicit the patient's own wisdom); and dereflection (redirecting attention from the self toward other people or meaningful goals)" (Southwick *et al.*, 2006, pp. 162–163).

Another therapy that incorporates the search for meaning and purpose is called Well-Being Therapy, which is based on Carol Ryff's multidimensional model of well-being (Ryff & Singer, 1998; Ryff, in press). These dimensions include autonomy, environmental mastery, personal growth, positive relations with others, purpose in life, and self-acceptance. Well-being therapy is conducted in three phases. In the first phase, the client is asked to identify moments of well-being and to describe the cir-cumstances surrounding those positive experiences. In the second phase, the client learns to recognize how his or her own actions or thoughts may prematurely interrupt a well-being experience. Finally, in the third phase, the therapist orients the patient to Ryff's multidimensional model and discusses how each of its dimensions can be used to maximize well-being in the client's life.

As an everyday example of the power of meaning and purpose, our friend Elsa describes a recent surge of strength and resilience that arose when she wholeheartedly adopted a personally meaningful goal. For most of her adult life, Elsa had been quietly concerned about what she viewed as economic, health and social inequities in our society. However, she felt powerless to effect change and never made these issues a priority in her life. That changed for her when Barack Obama was elected president in 2008.

> When I heard him speak about how his own mother, when she was dying of ovarian cancer, had to argue with her insurance company about whether her illness was a pre-existing condition, I was convinced that this president was not just saying he wanted to see national health care reform – he really meant it. So, within weeks after the election, I started attending and then organizing neighborhood meetings about health care. Standing outside local post offices handing out literature was something I'd never done before, but here I was doing it. Writing letters to the editor of the local newspaper, making announcements in church. I was unstoppable. Because this was something I really believed in. I wasn't sitting around worrying about what people would think of me, good or bad. It was simply, "I want to see this injustice get fixed, and now that there's a chance to get it done, until it is done I am not giving up."

Elsa's resilience surfaced as she campaigned for health care reform because this was an issue she believed in and found meaningful. For the first time in her life, she was willing to take major risks, to have people challenge her, and to tolerate criticism. Her strong belief in the meaning and purpose of this cause helped her persevere.

One of us (SS) recalls listening to a lecture by his sergeant during Army basic training in which the recruits were admonished, "Whatever you do, do *not* call your mother and complain about the way you're being treated here. Do *not* get your mother on our case, because there is only one thing the Army can't handle, and that's an angry mother. Because mothers do *not* care about protocol, they do *not* care about rank, they do *not* care about getting busted; all they care about is protecting Little Johnny." Although the sergeant's sarcasm was not lost on us, my fellow soldiers and I realized there was truth to what he was saying. A mother may be unable to do the 100 pushups required of trainees, but a mother on a mission to protect – or avenge – her beloved child is unstoppable.

President Bush learned this in 2005 from Cindy Sheehan. After her son, Casey, had been killed in Iraq, she spent weeks camped outside his ranch in Crawford, Texas, protesting the Iraq War. As Sheehan wrote in her memoir, *Peace Mom*, the day she was informed that her son was dead, "I had to decide something in my heart and soul. Would I stay here and fall into a depression of grief and regret? Would I voluntarily leave and join Casey through suicide? Or would I stay and fight?" (2006, pp. x, xi). For Sheehan, staying and fighting meant transforming herself from "normal mom" to a "cyclone of peace action" (p. 217); within months she became perhaps the best-known contemporary peace activist in the world, meeting with heads of state and earning nicknames like "Mother Courage" and "Mrs. Hope." Sheehan closes her memoir with a simple observation that "One person can make a difference. I am living proof of that. ... Go now and change the world. It is in us all" (p. 240).

References

Bartone, P. T. (1989). Predictors of stress-related illness in city bus drivers. *Journal of Occupational Medicine*, **31**, 657–663.

Britt, T. W., Adler, A. B., & Bartone, P. T. (2001). Deriving benefits from stressful events: The role of engagement in meaningful work and hardiness. *Journal of Occupational Health Psychology*, **6**(1), 53–63.

Eggers, D. (2006). *What is the what: The autobiography of Valentino Achak Deng, a novel*. New York, NY: Vintage.

Feder, A., Southwick, S. M., Goetz, R. R., Wang, Y., Alonso, A., Smith, B. W., et al. (2008). Posttraumatic growth in former Vietnam prisoners of war. *Psychiatry*, **71**(4), 359–370.

Frankl, V. E. (1958). The search for meaning. *Saturday Review*, **41** (September 13), p. 20.

Frankl, V. E. (1963). *Man's search for meaning: An introduction to logotherapy. A newly rev. and enl. ed. of From death-camp to existentalism*. Translated by Ilse Lasch. Pref. by Gordon W. Allport. Boston, MA: Beacon Press.

Graber, A. (2009). *The journey home: Preparing for life's ultimate adventure*. Birmingham, AL: LogoLife Press.

Herman, J. (1997). *Trauma and recovery: The aftermath of violence – from domestic abuse to political terror*, 2nd edition. New York, NY: Perseus Books.

Janoff-Bulman, R. (1992). *Shattered assumptions: Towards a new psychology of trauma*. New York, NY: The Free Press.

Jung, C. G., von Franz, M-L., Henderson, J. L., Jacobi, J., & Jaffe, A. (Eds.). (1968). *Man and his symbols*. New York, NY: Random House.

Lukas, E. (2000). *Logotheraphy textbook*. Toronto: Liberty Press.

Maddi, S. R. (1987). Hardiness training at Illinois Bell Telephone. In J. P. Opatz (Ed.), *Health promotion evaluation*, pp. 1001–1115. Stevens Point, WI: National Wellness Institute.

Mumford, N. W. D. (2000). *Hand to hand: From combat to healing*. New York, NY: Church Publishing Inc.

Pietrzak, R.H., Goldstein, M. B., Malley, J. C., Rivers, A. J., Johnson, D. C., Morgan, C. A. III., et al. (2010). Posttraumatic growth in veterans of Operations Enduring Freedom and Iraqi Freedom. *Journal of Affective Disorders*, **126**(1), 230–235.

Ryff, C., & Singer, B. (1998). The contours of positive human health. *Psychological Inquiry*, **9**(1), 1–28.

Ryff, C. D. (2012). The role of purpose in life and personal growth in positive human health. In P. T. P. Wong (Ed.), *The human quest for meaning*, 2nd edn. New York, NY: Routledge Publishers.

Sheehan, C. (2006). *Peace mom: A mother's journey through heartache to activism*. New York, NY: Atria Books.

Southwick, S. M., Gilmartin, R., McDonough, P., & Morrissey, P. (2006). Logotherapy as an adjunctive treatment for chronic combat-related PTSD: A meaning-based intervention. *American Journal of Psychotherapy*, **60**(2), 161–174.

Tedeschi, R. G., & Calhoun, L. G. (1996). The Posttraumatic Growth Inventory: Measuring the positive legacy of trauma. *Journal of Traumatic Stress*, **9**(3), 455–471.

Tedeschi, R. G., Park, C. L., & Calhoun, L. G. (Eds.) (1998). *Posttraumatic growth: Positive changes in the aftermath of crisis.* Mahwah, NJ: Lawrence Erlbaum Associates, p. 6.

Wrzesniewski, A., McCauley, C. R., Rozin, P., & Schwartz, B. (1997). Jobs, careers, and callings: People's relations to their work. *Journal of Research in Personality*, **31**, 21–33.

Zoellner, T., Maercker, A. (2006) Posttraumatic growth in clinical psychology – A critical review and introduction of a two component model. *Clinical Psychology Review*, **26**, 626–653

Chapter 12

The practice of resilience

Resilience is more than a concept. Building it requires practice. But where to begin? This is a complex question for which science does not yet have an answer. However, based on our years of experience in the fields of stress, trauma, and resilience, we believe that for most people it is best to begin by choosing one or two resilience factors that align with their personal values, feel natural to them, fit well with their lifestyle, and that seem doable. And then we recommend consistent practice and patience, because building resilience will take time and sustained effort.

Over time, it may be possible to add more resilience factors to your training. As you add factors to your practice, they may interact with one another and enhance your overall resilience. For example, people who become more optimistic often become more likeable – which in turn may open up greater access to social support. Increased social support may then provide the safety net and confidence needed to try out new, more active, creative, and effective strategies for coping with a host of challenges.

Building resilience requires the same commitment and persistence necessary to excel at a sport or succeed at following a fitness regime. The qualities and habits of mind cultivated in athletics – stick-to-itiveness, drive, concentration, dogged commitment, and willingness to tolerate some pain – stand one in good stead when training to increase resilience. The Olympic gymnast Dan Millman, who went on to a career as a motivational speaker, understands that there is no way to wake up one morning transformed. Instead, he says, "Champions form the habit of doing what most people find boring or uncomfortable. The secret of success is no secret at all – it comes from sound preparation, a step-by-step process, and focused effort through the hurdles, peaks, and valleys" (1999, p. 27). *Wishing* to become more resilient is only the first step on a long path that requires sustained effort.

As in any training, there will be successes and failures. If one approach to training fails, try other approaches until you find one that suits you. Remember that even a "failure" doesn't mean that you are out of the race; instead, failure may be an opportunity to re-evaluate and readjust. Six-time NBA World Champion Michael Jordan emphasized this when he said, "I've missed over 9,000 shots in my career. I've lost almost 300 games. 26 times I've been trusted to take the game-winning shot and missed. I've failed over and over and over again in my life. And that is why I succeed" (Goldman & Papson, 1999, p. 49).

In his 2009 book *Got Fight? The 50 Zen Principles of Hand-to-Face Combat*, martial arts champion Forrest Griffin makes an important point: "… you're not meant to get everything right the first time around. If you did, it wouldn't be any fun. ... From my mistakes, I learned that I needed to pace myself better. ... I recommend not biting off more than you can chew" (2009, p. 28). Instead, Griffin focuses on a long-term strategy of learning about your bad habits and then rigorously training to eliminate them, not just for weeks, but for months and years.

It is also important to understand that no one can be resilient at all times and in all areas of his or her life. Psychologist Howard Gardner, author of *Extraordinary Minds* and many other books, is known for identifying various kinds of intelligence, suggesting that we all have areas of strength on which we can build. Other psychologists, notably Martin Seligman (2002), have advocated a similar approach in identifying one's "signature strengths."

Consider, for example, Lew Meyer, the firefighter who was captured in Vietnam and used physical fitness as a way to save himself and others at the Hanoi Hilton. Meyer returned after the war and continued working as a firefighter. He was an expert at putting out fires. When we asked him if he ever felt afraid during a fire, he replied, "No, I love fighting fires. For me, fighting a good fire is like pitching a no-hitter." In this domain, Lew was remarkably resilient. However, as often happens when someone is successful in a career, he was promoted to an administrative position. This post required a whole new set of skills, those needed to construct work schedules, evaluate personnel, write budgets, and enforce safety regulations. Meyer found these tasks much more difficult than putting out fires. In this domain, Lew no longer saw himself as resilient. Does this indicate that Lew was flawed? Had he failed? Not at all. The point is that each of us is stronger in some areas than others.

When we engage in an activity that calls on our strengths, we may experience a state that has been called "flow." This is a concept coined by psychologist Mihali Csikszentmihalyi (1990). When we experience flow, he says we are

> completely involved in an activity for its own sake. The ego falls away. Time flies. Every action, movement, and thought follows inevitably from the previous one, like playing jazz. Your whole being is involved, and you're using your skills to the utmost. (Geirland, 1996)

When Law Meyer fought fires he often experienced something akin to flow or "being in the zone."

How resilience applies to our modern world

In this age of convenience, it may be easier to *think* about resilience than to actually *do* what is necessary to enhance it. Here are some practical suggestions for applying the principles of resilience to everyday life in various domains.

The individual

Much of this book describes ten resilience factors as they relate to the individual.

- Fostering optimism
- Facing fear

- Solidifying moral compass
- Practicing religion and spirituality
- Attracting and giving social support
- Imitating resilient role models
- Physical training
- Mental and emotional training
- Enhancing cognitive and emotional flexibility
- Finding meaning, purpose, and growth

However, resilience is also relevant in broader contexts, such as in the family and parenting, in work and career, and even in society as a whole.

The family

We all need family. Ideally it's one of our most important sources of resilience, the place where we learn what it is to feel safe, loved and accepted. It's the place where we feel protected and defended from threats, and where we are encouraged to be our best. The family is also typically the root of values. For many people, early experiences within their family form the core of what enables them to become and remain resilient.

For others, the early family experience is not so favorable. Some of us may harbor vivid childhood memories of knock-down, drag-out fights with our siblings or shouting matches with our parents. As adults, we may benefit from understanding the struggles that our parents may have faced in raising a family. Perhaps they came from difficult or troubled families themselves; perhaps they were doing the best they could under harsh circumstances. By trying to understand and in some cases "forgive" family members, hopefully we can open the door to rewarding and supportive relationships.

In her autobiography, *And a Voice to Sing With*, the musician Joan Baez (1987/2009) describes the rebuilding of an adult relationship with her younger sister, Mimi Farina.

> We didn't have much to say to each other for some time. When we talked, the conversation was stilted, guarded, or simply fake. She seemed to be always angry, and I'm sure I just went on doing what I've been accused of doing more than once – namely, telling stories about myself. Then one day in the late seventies it dawned on us that we had not even a remnant of the close and special relationship we'd had for so many years, and we decided, mutually, to get together for lunch and "talk." We were both late, and later on, confessed that we had both taken a Valium just to be able to face each other.
>
> What I remember most about that lunch was that Mimi had no idea of her own strength and growth. When I suggested that she had often hurt my feelings, she thought I was bluffing or lying. She still saw me as powerful and untouchable, and herself as powerless and insignificant. There were lots of teary moments and righteous assertions as to who was right and who was

wrong, and not much was settled, but it was a honest effort, and the beginning of the long road back to a close and honest friendship. (pp. 318–319)

This anecdote becomes more poignant with the knowledge that some 20 years after this lunch encounter Mimi Farina died of cancer at the young age of 56.

Sadly, some families may be so toxic that reconnecting with them can only be damaging. When this is the case, it may be best to create a new "family" that provides a healthy source of strength. We may do this in marriage or a romantic relationship, with a group of friends, with fellow members of our workplace, or with a religious congregation.

Whatever our family history contains, it is always wise to surround ourselves with allies; people who like and accept us, who treat us with kindness and respect, and who encourage us to be our best selves. In good times, these people provide a framework for sharing goodwill and resources; when troubles arise, we can count on them to "be there" for us – as we are for them.

In today's society, we often neglect a core source of family strength – ancestry. How much do you know about your parents, grandparents, and other ancestors? What were their lives like? What hardships did they face, and how did they deal with these hardships? How do their challenges compare to those that you face? The Buddhist author Thich Nhat Han suggests that our ancestors are within each of us. They are in our genes and in the way we were raised. They made us who we are. Through meditation or simply through family storytelling, we can learn to draw on the strengths of those who lived before us. In searching for models of resilience, we needn't rely solely on famous historical figures like the "founding fathers," or Martin Luther King Jr., or Helen Keller. We can also look to our own ancestors, our grandparents, aunts, uncles, and parents, as models of strength.

Family dynamics expert Froma Walsh (2002, 2003, 2006) advocates a "family resilience framework" in therapeutic approaches to handling adversity. The Walsh Family Resilience Framework comprises nine key processes that resilient families tend to use when responding to trauma and stress. Family therapists may encourage the use of one or more of these processes when helping a family through a crisis:

- making meaning of adversity,
- maintaining positive outlook,
- fostering transcendence and spirituality,
- practicing flexibility,
- enhancing connectedness,
- drawing on social and economic resources,
- achieving clarity,
- expressing emotions openly, and
- solving problems collaboratively.

If you have read this book from the beginning, you will notice that these resilient-family processes resemble the resilience factors we have observed among individuals in our own research. It appears that many of the principles of resilience that apply to the individual are also relevant to the well-being of the family.

Raising children

Will our children be prepared for the world they will face as adults? To raise a child with resilience as a goal, we must find the right balance between protecting that child and pushing him or her to achieve beyond their present capabilities or level of maturity.

As we noted in Chapter 1, a number of social critics have written about trends toward narcissism and cynicism in today's society. In her 2007 book *Generation Me: Why Today's Young Americans Are More Confident, Assertive, Entitled – And More Miserable Than Ever Before*, psychologist Jean Twenge examines the attitudes and feelings of young people ages 18 to 25. She cites archival results of personality tests over the decades since World War II to document increases in the belief that "I am special," in the feeling that my life is out of control, and in the need for social approval. At the same time, Twenge found that young adults had less capacity to accept criticism, to work toward a goal, and to empathize with others. For example, Twenge and her colleague Keith Campbell (2009) observe, "On a reality TV show, a girl planning her Sweet Sixteen wants a major road blocked off so a marching band can precede her grand entrance on a red carpet" (p. 1).

In recent years, teachers and child development researchers have commented on "helicopter parenting," an overly involved style of interaction in which the parent hovers over the child and swoops in to help whenever the child encounters adversity. In a November 2009 cover story, *TIME* magazine observed:

> The insanity crept up on us slowly; we just wanted what was best for our kids. … But in the 1990s something dramatic happened, and the needle went way past the red line. From peace and prosperity, there arose fear and anxiety; crime went down, yet parents stopped letting kids out of their sight; the percentage of kids walking or biking to school dropped from 41% in 1969 to 13% in 2001. Death by injury has dropped more than 50% since 1980, yet parents lobbied to take the jungle gyms out of playgrounds, and strollers suddenly needed the warning label "Remove Child Before Folding." Among 6-to-8-year-olds, free playtime dropped 25% from 1981 to '97, and homework more than doubled. … By the time the frenzy had reached its peak, colleges were installing "Hi, Mom!" webcams in common areas, and employers like Ernst & Young were creating "parent packs" for recruits to give Mom and Dad, since they were involved in negotiating salary and benefits. (Gibbs, 2009)

As described in a 2008 CNN article, clinical psychologist Nancy Weisman explains why this parenting style is detrimental to resilience, referring to a sense of entitlement that kids acquire when parents rescue them every time they drop the ball. As a result, children don't learn the consequences of their behavior, how to solve their own problems, how to regulate their own emotions, how to manage stress constructively – in short, they don't learn basic coping skills. "It's important for kids to know they're not going to be rescued," Weisman says (Krache, 2008).

Of course, the concern that inspires extreme over-parenting is typically well-intentioned. At the opposite end of the scale from the helicopter parent is the neglectful parent who doesn't have time for the child, or who withholds attention or who leaves a "latchkey" child to his or her own devices before the child has reached an appropriate level of maturity. Researchers have also expressed concern about the authoritarian parent who controls the child with threats and punishment. Educator James Loehr (1993) points out the disadvantages of this approach: "Fearful children become fearful adults. A child who is controlled by fear – fear of making mistakes, guilt, fear of failure, fear of rejection, fear of loving – will inevitably acquire nontough [non-resilient] ways of thinking and acting" (p. 219).

The British pediatrician Donald Winnicott (1958) coined the term "good-enough mother" for one who protects her infant but does not overprotect, and who fulfills the infant's needs but gradually delays gratification as the child grows older and better able to cope with adversity. This style of mothering allows the child to gradually experience and master more and more challenges. The good-enough mother does not intentionally expose the child to stress that the child cannot manage, but she does encourage ample exposure to challenges that the child can master. In this sense, the "good-enough" mother is the best mother. The same is true of good fathers, teachers, coaches, mentors, and bosses.

Journalist and mother Lenore Skenazy has written a practical guide titled *Free-Range Kids* (2010) in which she advocates allowing school-age children to experience the ups and downs of life without constant adult supervision. In her Free-Range Kids blog, Skenazy writes:

> We don't want our kids to fall off a bike. Who does? But we do want them to learn how to ride. So we have two choices: We can hold onto their handlebars … forever. That way they'll never, ever fall. Or we can wish them luck and then – let go.
>
> Chances are, if we do that, they will, at some point, fall. When they get up again, they'll have two huge things going for them:
>
> - They'll know they can fall and get back up again. If that's not a life lesson, what is?
> - They'll be learning how to actually ride a bike. (Skenazy, 2009)
>
> Most things in life take some tumbles before we get it right.

In *Toughness Training for Life*, James Loehr echoes many of the same thoughts:

> Teaching children how to solve problems, how not to panic, and how to think things through clearly before acting, can make a substantial difference in their ability to control negative arousal. Kids need to know how thinking and acting impacts feelings and emotions. Being prepared for tough times simply means a code of acting and behaving that reinforces personal control. Obviously, parents who model tough [resilient] thinking and acting during tough times become the most powerful teachers. … Parents who impart a love of life, a

> passion for living, send a powerful message to their children. No matter how tough life is, there is joy and happiness to be found. (1993, p. 221)

In the late nineteenth and early twentieth centuries, a number of organizations were founded with the goal of increasing resilience in young people. Among them were the YMCA and YWCA, the Woodcraft Indians, the Sons of Daniel Boone, and the Boy Scouts and Girl Scouts (Macleod, 1983). These organizations focused on mental, physical, social, and religious development. Even today the mission of the Boy Scouts of America is to provide "a program for young people that builds character, trains them in the responsibilities of participating citizenship, and develops personal fitness," and the mission of Girl Scouts of America is to "build girls of courage, confidence, and character, who make the world a better place."

Other programs promote specific aspects of resilience in children. One example is the Penn Resiliency Project (http://www.ppc.sas.upenn.edu/prpsum.htm) for teachers in elementary and middle school. Headed by Jane Gillham and Karen Reivich, this project offers a series of lesson plans designed to help students challenge negative beliefs and learn "assertiveness, negotiation, decision-making, social problem-solving, and relaxation." As another example, in their book *Raising Resilient Children*, Robert Brooks and Sam Goldstein (2001) describe a classroom exercise that any teacher can use to encourage cognitive flexibility. Teachers ask the class on the first day, "Who feels they are going to make a mistake or not understand something in class this year?" (p. 279). Then, before any students raise their hands, teachers raise their own hands, and they begin a class discussion about the value of making mistakes and learning from them. A third example of a program that can enhance resilience in children is the Giraffe Project, which we described in Chapter 4 on moral compass. The Giraffe Project asks each child to "stick your neck out" to do what is right.

Work and career

Many of us have faced – or will face – difficult situations at work – receiving a negative performance review, being passed over for a promotion, or even losing our job. In the book *Firing Back: How Great Leaders Rebound After Career Disasters*, Jeffrey Sonnenfeld and Andrew Ward (2007) acknowledge that "... career distress can be one of the greatest sources of life stress. Being fired, for example, has been ranked ... among the most stressful events in life, just after death of family members, jail, and personal injury or illness" (p. 6). However, as devastating as job loss can be, the authors recommend facing up to the reality of what has happened, and using it as a platform for recovery. "Leaders should not be measured by how they bask in the gratification of their accomplishments," they argue. "Rather, they should be measured by how they respond when fate deflates the joys and hard-earned triumphs. How well do they pick themselves up and get back in the race?" (p. 3).

Sonnenfeld and Ward also point out that business leaders who are now household names, like Michael Bloomberg and Steve Jobs, were fired from firms before they started their own enterprises; and that Jimmy Carter, despite failing to be re-elected in 1980, "...

continued tirelessly in his humanitarian, public health, and diplomacy missions, heavily promoting democratic reform around the world and was eventually recognized as a Nobel laureate for peace" (p. 3).

While not everyone can be a Steve Jobs or a Jimmy Carter, most of us can bolster our careers by learning to face fear, cultivate realistic optimism, learn from role models, and give and receive social support. The work environment is sometimes viewed as a dog-eat-dog world where one has to "go along to get along," but resilience comes from staying true to one's values and moral compass, even if it means passing up an opportunity for career advancement. And surely cognitive flexibility, humor, and finding meaning and purpose are as valuable at work as they are in personal life.

Indeed, many researchers and business experts have recognized the importance of finding meaning in tasks performed at work, no matter how humble. As an example, The GoodWork Project was developed by psychologists Mihaly Csikszentmihalyi, William Damon, and Howard Gardner in order to advocate and promote "work that is excellent in quality, socially responsible, and meaningful to its practitioners." Employees who understand the significance of their mission at work are more likely to give their full effort, to "go the extra mile." This was the finding of organizational behavior researchers Michael Cole, Heike Bruch, and Bernd Vogel (2006); workers were less cynical and more resistant to the stresses of organizational crises if their supervisor helped them to understand the significance of their efforts.

There are many fine books about career success that incorporate a variety of the resilience factors we have identified. Among these are *The Seven Habits of Highly Effective People* by Steven Covey, and *The Pyramid of Success: Buiding Blocks For a Better Life* by the famed UCLA basketball coach John Wooden. Wooden was a renowned and beloved basketball player and coach who was inducted into the Basketball Hall of Fame as both player and coach. With Wooden as head coach, the UCLA men's team won 7 consecutive NCAA national championships and 10 championships in 12 years. Wooden based his formula for success on fundamental building blocks that he described in his Seven Point Creed and his Pyramid of Success. He was given the Seven Point Creed by his father, Joshua, when he graduated from grammar school:

- Be true to yourself.
- Make each day your masterpiece.
- Help others.
- Drink deeply from good books, especially the Bible.
- Make friendship a fine art.
- Build a shelter against a rainy day.
- Pray for guidance and give thanks for your blessings every day. (2004, p. 25)

Wooden spent over a decade constructing his Pyramid of Success. He believed that real strength began with building a strong foundation. In his words, "The first two blocks of the pyramid are the two cornerstones because to be strong, you have to have a strong foundation. The cornerstones of success to me, in anything, are hard work and enjoy what you are doing. So, one cornerstone is industriousness and the other is enthusiasm. The other elements of the pyramid include: Friendship, Loyalty, Cooperation, Self-Control, Alertness, Initiative, Intentness, Condition, Skill, Team Spirit, Poise, Confidence, Competitive Greatness" (2011).

Society on the large scale: community resilience

Most of us live in communities where we share with others a wide variety of resources and services. As noted by Dartmouth professor Fran Norris, community members are dependent on one another both in good times and in bad. For example, some traumatic events, such as natural disasters or wars, are experienced simultaneously by a large number of people. Norris writes,

> ... we must recognize that survivors are connected and dependent upon one another's coping strategies. ... They help each other but also compete for scarce resources. Household preparedness is vital, but one household can no more prepare for disaster than it could, on its own, protect itself from crime or disease, educate its children, or keep the roads safe. Thus an individual's resilience is inextricably linked to the community's ability to prepare for, respond to, and adapt to adverse conditions. Simply put, when problems are shared, so must be solutions. (Norris *et al.*, 2010, p. 1)

Norris believes that community resilience relies on effective sharing of resources. In her model, community resilience depends on four primary resources: economic development, social capital, information and communication, and community competence. The first resource, economic development, is influenced by the diversity and distribution of resources in addition to the volume of resources. Communities are more vulnerable and less resilient when they rely on a narrow range of resources (e.g. a city dependent on one large automobile plant) or when distribution of community resources is markedly unequal (e.g. the poorest neighborhood may suffer the most in natural disasters).

Social capital refers, in part, to relationships between the individual and his/her neighborhood, community organizations, and community at large. Elements of social capital that foster community resilience include citizen participation, emotional connection to the community mutual concerns and shared values, and the receiving and giving of social support.

Community resilience also depends on communication and the effective sharing of information. For example, during emergencies information that is shared accurately to community members can save lives. Finally, Norris describes the need for meaningful intentional action. Resilient communities work together with creativity and flexibility to solve problems.

Activities that incorporate multiple resilience factors: a few examples

As we have pointed out earlier, resilience factors tend to build upon one another and sometimes operate synergistically. Here are just a few examples.

Become a volunteer

Volunteering to join with others in the pursuit of a worthy goal has many potential benefits. First and foremost, it can provide aid to an organization, to a cause, or to people in need. But it can also strengthen the volunteer him- or herself, by enhancing one or more of the resilience factors.

After giving a talk on resilience to a Yale Medical School Alumni group, one of us was approached by a board member from the Hole in the Wall Gang Camp, a no-fee outdoor retreat for children with cancer and other serious illnesses that was founded by the actor and philanthropist Paul Newman. The board member felt that the principles of resilience were strongly related to the camp's mission. The following summer I volunteered to serve for a week as a camp counselor at The Hole in the Wall Gang Camp in Ashford, Connecticut. Following the success of the Hole in the Wall Gang Camp, other sister camps have opened throughout the United States and overseas, all serving children with serious illnesses.

> As I drove to Ashford, I didn't know exactly what to expect. I had been a camp counselor at age 20, but that was a long time ago, and the kids I counseled were not sick. I did know that I would be sleeping on a bunk bed in a cabin with twelve-year-old boys.
>
> When I entered the grounds, I was impressed with the beauty of the place: a compound of sturdy, well designed but rustic looking buildings set near a pristine New England lake. The camp was equipped with an infirmary staffed by expert medical personnel, a theater where the kids had a chance to perform, a building devoted to arts and crafts, a boathouse, a horseback riding stable, a gymnasium, and a grand hexagonal dining hall that resembled a huge American Indian lodge with multicolored banners hanging from its vaulted ceiling.
>
> During the weekly orientation for new volunteers, I was introduced to my two new bosses, college age counselors, who had both worked at the camp for several years. They made me feel right at home.
>
> When I first walked into the cabin, six or seven boys were playing a game of some sort, and one of the counselors was helping another boy unpack his clothes. I said hello and was directed to one of the upper bunks, which had my name taped on it. I unpacked my gear and then stepped into the bathroom. Looking into the mirror, I was startled to see this old guy with white hair staring back. "That can't be me," I thought. I must look like a frail grandfather to these kids. Somehow, before coming to the camp, I had convinced myself that I was still that "cool" 20-year-old counselor who loved to challenge campers to running races and games of basketball, and who was up on the latest in pop culture and hip music. Now I began to wonder if the Hole in the Wall Gang campers would have any interest in listening to my cassette tapes of The Byrds, Three Dog Night and Peter, Paul and Mary. I began to feel uneasy, a little anxious, pretty irrelevant.
>
> Now what? Why would these kids want to hang out with an old guy like me? Maybe signing up to be a volunteer counselor wasn't such a good idea.
>
> Just then, one of the boys walked up to me and asked, "Steve, would you like to be on my team?"

"Sure," I replied. "But, I don't know the rules, and I don't know if I will be any good at it."

"Don't worry," he said. "We'll teach you. You'll be OK. It's not that hard."

And, indeed, with his invitation, I was now OK. I was now a member of the team.

The mission of the Hole in the Wall Gang Camp is to give children suffering from major medical illnesses the chance to spend time in a rural setting where they can just plain have fun. That's what Paul Newman wanted for all children, no matter how ill. He wanted them to have a relatively carefree week of fun.

> Even though all of the kids had a serious medical illness, and in some cases a major physical disability, they knew how to have fun; they invented games, cracked jokes, and made friends in a matter of minutes. They were not entitled, narcissistic, Me-generation types. Instead, they were fun-loving, generous and kind. Over the course of the week, I don't remember hearing a single complaint from any of the kids about his illness.
>
> When I look back on this week and think about resilience, a number of factors stand out. Serving as a volunteer counselor helped – and at times forced – me to step out of my comfort zone, increase my flexibility, contribute to a worthy goal, receive and give social support, and look more closely at my own purpose and mission in life. However, the most powerful boost to my own resilience came in the form of role models: the devoted, sturdy and self-less men and women on the staff, and, most important, the boys in my cabin. I continue to be impressed by the degree of resilience, bravery, and grace that I witnessed in these young gentlemen, and try my best to imitate them.

There are an unlimited number of ways to volunteer your time and energy. You can serve at a soup kitchen, join a choir, tutor a child, teach an adult to read, help build a house for the homeless, clean up a neighborhood park, or work for world peace. As an example, our friend Martha is a retired nurse who volunteers with the Red Cross in her community. One weekend a month she is on call. If an event such as a fire, a flood, a water main break or a gas leak occurs in her community and people need to be evacuated, Martha is the nurse on duty at the Red Cross evacuation site. Another friend, Paul, is an experienced businessman who volunteers with Service Corps of Retired Executives (SCORE) to help people prepare tax returns. Gladys, who has always enjoyed painting and sewing, volunteers at her local senior center by teaching classes in fabric painting. Dorothy, who was widowed several years ago, volunteers with a local hospice by facilitating a weekly grief support group. And George, a junior in college, started a drop-in tutoring service for students who needed help with their course work.

Depending on the organization, volunteering may also provide us with opportunities to deepen our religious or spiritual practice (e.g. participating in a religious-based mission), to exercise moral courage (e.g. joining a group that fights against a perceived injustice), to improve physical health (e.g. participating in a bike ride to raise funds for cancer research), and/or to boost brain fitness (e.g. becoming a tutor or volunteer consultant). And for anyone, the experience may foster cognitive and emotional flexibility. This results, in part, because volunteering typically involves stepping out of one's normal routine and sometimes out of one's social, geographic or cultural comfort zone. In addition, volunteer organizations often bring together a heterogeneous group of individuals from different work and family backgrounds, and they typically operate within a structure or hierarchy that differs from the one the volunteer is accustomed to at work or at home.

Athletic competition

Physical exercise, as we've described in Chapter 8, is associated with both physical and emotional resilience. Although we can build resilience by exercising alone, exercising with a friend adds social support, and by joining a competition we actively seek to challenge and test ourselves. Even better, competition involving team sports provides us with camaraderie and opportunities to find new role models. Finally, competing for a cause – for example, a 10k run for cancer – adds the dimension of altruism. Whether consciously or not, we may put to work at least five resilience factors by participating in such an event. Opportunities abound: as just one of countless possible examples, the Team in Training (TNT) program organizes marathons, half-marathons, bike rides, ski marathons, and other athletic events to raise money for the Leukemia & Lymphoma Society.

In the United States today, some teachers and parents believe that competition is destructive to the emotional well-being of children, and they try to create an alternate world where everyone is a winner, where everyone wins a trophy. However, competition is unavoidable. It permeates modern life: we compete in athletics, for entrance into college, for jobs, even for mates. Sometimes we win and sometimes we lose.

Jeff Gruen, the father of Deborah, the remarkable young woman born with a potentially disabling condition whom we met earlier in the book, learned about the value of competition from both of his daughters. Until his daughters joined the local swim club, Gruen believed that competition was bad, that it undermined confidence, camaraderie, and the sheer joy of learning. To protect his children, he enrolled them in a "kinder" and "gentler" alternative private school

> Competition is bad. That was my basic premise in life. We sent our kids to a little hippie school where there was no competition. They would have gym class but they wouldn't keep score, that kind of stuff, and I ate that up. I thought, "Yeah, that's the way kids should live."

But Jeff's older daughter, Michele, didn't see it that way.

> When Michele was about seven or eight, she started swimming more competitively, and one day we were driving home from a meet, she couldn't have been more than first or second grade, and she says, "Well, how did I do, Dad?"
>   Honestly, she did terribly. She came in dead last. But I said, "You did fine."
>   "No Dad, how did I do?"
>   "You did very well. Your time was really very good."
>   "No Dad, did I beat that other girl? Did I come in third?"

> And I remember thinking, "Wow, I don't get this. I send you to hippie
> school where they have no competitive sports and you ask, 'How did I do, Dad?
> I want to know. I have a right to know.'" I just wasn't getting it at all.

Gradually both Michele and her sister Deborah taught their father to rethink competition. Later, their example proved helpful to Gruen as he came to understand the value of tolerating and even embracing competition at the medical school.

> I learned an incredible amount about how to professionally survive [as a
> pediatric researcher] and about my academic career through their sports. Part
> of the reason I didn't do sports growing up was that I didn't understand them.
> If I can't win, I don't want to play, and that was really my attitude for years and
> years. And with my children, [they weren't big winners] but they loved it. It
> took me a long, long time to learn that they didn't have to win the race to be
> happy. … For them, their P.B., their personal best, became really important,
> and I didn't understand it. If I couldn't get the big paper published, do the big
> experiment, get the big grant, it made me very angry and very upset, which is
> a tough way to conduct a professional career, especially if you are constantly
> comparing yourself with people at Yale, which we all naturally do. So it took
> me a long time to learn this.

Many of the resilient people we interviewed like to compete in various ways. They recognize that competition, when kept in perspective, can bolster feelings of self-efficacy and bring out our best. It can enhance performance and propel us to heights that we would not otherwise reach.

Become a mentor

Mentoring takes the concept of role models and turns it around. As a mentor, you serve as a model for someone who needs skill building and encouragement. In the process, you also develop your own skills, because when we teach we learn. In addition, mentors typically embrace an optimistic outlook (believing that their mentee's life will get better), practice altruism (giving of their time and talents), give and receive social support (from program coordinators, fellow mentors, and their mentee), and so forth.

Perhaps the most widely known mentoring program is Big Brothers Big Sisters of America (BBBS; http://www.bigsnyc.org/v-stories.php#annette), which matches children ages 6 through 18 with adult mentors. BBBS also has programs devoted to special populations such as children whose parents are in the military or in prison. The minimum time commitment is one hour per week. Volunteers can meet their little "brother," or "sister," in the community or at school, and the emphasis is on friendship. In an impact study published in 2000, Joseph P. Tierney and colleagues found that, compared to a control group, children who had been BBBS mentees for at least 18 months were less likely to start using drugs and alcohol and less likely to hit someone; they also showed improved school attendance and performance, improved attitudes toward completing schoolwork; and better relationships with peers and family members.

While Big Brothers Big Sisters mentoring is structured as a long-term relationship – many BBBS pairs stay together for 5 years or more – other programs provide opportunities for mentoring that are one-time commitments. The National Foundation for Teaching Entrepreneurship (NFTE), for example, teaches low-income high school students how to start a business. Adults with business experience present a lesson in their areas of expertise, take students on a field trip, or sit on a panel that evaluates students' business plans.

Survivor mission: go ahead, be a Bob Woodruff or a Jerry White

In Chapter 9, on mental and emotional training, we told the story of Bob Woodruff, the ABC journalist who suffered a traumatic brain injury when he was wounded by a roadside bomb in Iraq. With his wife Lee, Bob co-wrote the book *In an Instant: A Family's Journey* (Random House, 2007) chronicling his injury and the process of rehabilitation.

The Woodruffs also founded The Bob Woodruff Foundation to help other survivors of combat-related injuries. According to its website, ReMind.org, the foundation "provides resources and support to service members, veterans and their families to successfully reintegrate into their communities so they may thrive physically, psychologically, socially and economically." Like Jerry White, who founded the International Landmine Survivor Network, Bob and Lee Woodruff have chosen to use their traumatic experience as a platform for helping others.

One need not be wealthy or famous to embrace a survivor mission. Just look at Valentino Achak Deng and his Lost Boys Foundation, or remember the women who started Mothers Against Drunk Drivers. While funding can certainly help, passion, a clear mission, and persistence are essential.

Resilience: it's your responsibility

Ultimately, resilience is about understanding the difference between fate and freedom, and learning to take responsibility for one's own life. Human beings are free, but with freedom comes responsibility, the responsibility to find and imitate resilient role models; to cultivate positive emotions and optimism; to face one's fears; to solve rather than avoid problems; to learn from failure; to constructively reframe unpleasant, stressful, and traumatic events; to seek out and to attract social support; to keep one's body in the best physical shape possible through exercise, good nutrition, and sleep; to use whatever strengths we have and to cultivate those strengths; to devote time and energy to spirituality and religion for those so inclined; to assist others who are in need; to search for, extract and create meaning; to acquire the knowledge and skills necessary to achieve goals through training; to accept that achievement rarely comes without enormous work and hardship; to find and embrace a survivor mission when appropriate; to persist when it would be easier to give up; to search for opportunity in adversity; to accept what cannot be changed; to do our best to bear unavoidable physical and psychological pain with grace and dignity; and to learn and to grow from the hand that fate deals us, even when that hand is a bad one. These are the choices that each of us faces, repetitively, throughout life.

"When should I begin to train?" you might ask. The answer: now. As John McCain writes in *Why Courage Matters*,

> If you do the things you think you cannot do, you'll feel your resistance, your hope, your dignity, your courage, grow stronger every time you prove it. You will someday face harder choices that very well might require more courage. You're getting ready for them. (McCain & Salter, 2008, p. 205)

Next you might ask, "How will I know if I have succeeded in my training?" Who should I compare myself to? Forrest Griffin in his book *Got Fight?* has a good answer.

> Although it can be depressing to admit to yourself that you will never be the best, it is liberating at the same time. Instead of trying to be better than everyone else, which is existentially arrogant, you can focus on being the best that *you* can be. … you can take pride in the fact that you did the most you possibly could with what you were given. You can take pride in every accomplishment. What more can you ask for? (2009, p. 84)

Our friend Willie tells us of his experience volunteering with the Special Olympics, the competitive athletics program for those with intellectual disabilities. Willie has been a volunteer for the past 10 years because he likes to "see all those smiling faces. Everybody tries so hard. They don't hold back."

This year Willie remembered one contestant in particular. He was a small teenager who wore a metal brace on his right leg. Willie first noticed him because he was wearing a blue-and-gold uniform, the same colors that Willie himself had worn years earlier when he played saxophone in his high school band. As Willie watched the young man hobble to the starting line with six other contestants, he wondered why these Special Olympians were so eager to compete. What drove them to push themselves to their limit? And Willie also worried about the young man with the leg brace. How in the world could he compete with the other contestants? Would he even have the strength and coordination to complete the 100-yard race?

When the starting pistol fired, everyone began to shout and cheer: the crowd, the parents, the coaches, the contestants. The excitement again reminded Willie of his high school days when the fans erupted with excitement as his band marched onto the football field for their half-time show. Now the cheers were for these Special Olympians. A tall, lean red-headed girl came in first, followed by a short muscular boy with Down syndrome. As the others finished one by one, Willie noticed that the young man with the braces was far behind the pack. His neurologic disorder made his body movements appear spastic and irregular. He swerved from right to left and from left from right as he slowly made his way down the track.

Eventually the young man joined the other racers at the finish line. His coach immediately shook his hand and patted him on the shoulder, a job well done. Then, one of the other contestants, a petite teenage girl, approached the young man, and in a loud voice said, "You came in last."

"Tha, tha, that's OK," he stuttered, as he faced the girl and looked her in the eye. "I came in."

And perhaps that is the essence of this book: we need not be the swiftest or the strongest. What counts instead is that we "come in" – that we develop our talents, put forth our best effort, and commit ourselves to a life of purpose, growth and resilience.

References

Baez, J. (1987, 2009). *And a voice to sing with: A memoir.* New York: Simon & Schuster.

Boy Scouts of America (2010). Statement at http://www.scouting.org/ accessed 11/1/10.

Brooks, R., & Goldstein, S. (2001). *Raising resilient children: Fostering strength, hope, and optimism in your child.* New York, NY: McGraw-Hill.

CNN online article by Donna Krache, How to ground a "helicopter parent" (2008, August 19). Accessed 7/2/10 at http://www.cnn.com/2008/LIVING/personal/08/13/helicopter.parents/index.html.

Cole, M. S., Bruch, H., & Vogel, B. (2006). Emotion as mediators of the relations between perceived supervisor support and psychological hardiness on employee cynicism. *Journal of Organizational Behavior, 27*(4), 463–484.

Csikszentmihalyi, M. (1990). *Flow: The psychology of optimal experience.* New York, NY: Harper and Row.

Geirland, J. (1996). Go with the flow. *Wired* magazine, September, Issue 4.09. Accessed 5/7/10 at http://www.wired.com/wired/archive/4.09/czik_pr.html.

Gibbs, N. (2009, November 20). The growing backlash against overparenting. *TIME* Magazine. Accessed July 2, 2010 at http://www.time.com/time/nation/article/0,8599,1940395,00.html.

Griffin, F., & Krauss, E. (2009). *Got fight? The 50 Zen principles of hand-to-face combat.* New York, NY: William Morrow.

Goldman, R. & Papson, S. (1999). *Nike culture: The sign of the swoosh.* Thousand Oaks, CA: Sage.

Loehr, J. (1993). *Toughness training for life: A revolutionary program for maximizing health, happiness and productivity.* New York, NY: Dutton.

Macleod, D. L. (1983). *Building character in the American boy: The Boy Scouts, YMCA and their forerunners, 1870–1920.* Madison, WI: University of Wisconsin Press.

McCain, J., & Salter, M. (2008). *Why courage matters: The way to a braver life.* New York, NY: Ballantine Books.

Millman, D. (1999). *Body mind mastery: Training for sport and life,* 3rd edn. Novato, CA: New World Library.

National Foundation for Teaching Entrepreneurship (NFTE), available at http://www.nfte.com/Volunteer/.

Norris, F. H., Sherrieb, K., & Pfefferbaum, B. (2010). Community resilience: Concepts, assessment, and implications for intervention. In Southwick, S., Charney, D., Friedman, M., & Litz, B. (Eds.), *Resilience: Responding to challenges across the lifespan.* Cambridge: Cambridge University Press.

Seligman, M. E. P. (2002). *Authentic happiness: Using the new positive psychology to realize your potential for lasting fulfillment.* New York, NY: Free Press.

Skenazy, L. (2009). Free-Range Kids blog post. Accessed 7/2/10 at http://freerangekids.wordpress.com/faq/#7.

Skenazy, L. (2010). *Free-range kids: How to raise safe, self-reliant children (without going nuts with worry).* Hoboken, NJ: Jossey-Bass.

Sonnenfeld, J., & Ward, A. (2007). *Firing back: How great leaders rebound after career disasters.* Cambridge, MA: Harvard Business Press.

The GoodWork Project: Excellence, ethics, and engagement in the professions. http://www.goodworkproject.org/

Tierney, J. P., & Grossman, J. B., with Resch, N. L. (2000). *Making a difference: An impact study of Big Brothers Big Sisters*. Phildelphia, PA: Public/Private Ventures.

Twenge, J. M. (2007). *Generation me: Why today's young Americans are more confident, assertive, entitled – and more miserable than ever before*. New York, NY: Free Press.

Twenge, J., & Campbell, W. K. (2009). *The narcissism epidemic: Living in the age of entitlement*. New York, NY: Free Press.

Walsh, F. (2002). A family resilience framework: Innovative practice applications. *Family Relations*, **51**(2), 130–137.

Walsh, F. (2006). *Strengthening family resilience*, 2nd edn. New York, NY: Guilford Press.

Walsh, F. (Ed.) (2003). *Normal family processes: Growing diversity and complexity*, 3rd edn. New York, NY: Guilford Press.

Winnicott, D. W. (1958). Mind and its relation to the psyche-soma. In Collected papers, through paediatrics to psychoanalysis (pp. 243–54). London: Tavistock Publications. (Reprinted from *British Journal of Medical Psychology*, **27** (1954), 201–209.)

Wooden, J. The Pyramid of Success. Accessed 4/4/11 at http://www. coachwooden.com/index2.html. See also http://sports.espn.go.com/espn/eticket/story?page=wooden.

Wooden, J., & Tobin, J. (2004). *They call me coach*. New York, NY: McGraw-Hill.

Appendix: Further Information about Posttraumatic Stress Disorder

For those desiring further information, we offer these additional details about posttraumatic stress disorder (PTSD).

What is Posttraumatic Stress Disorder?

Although PTSD has existed throughout human history and can be found in all cultures throughout the world, it has only been formally recognized in the medical and psychological professions since the 1980s. Initially it was primarily associated with Vietnam combat veterans, but soon many other categories of trauma were recognized as potential causes of PTSD, including (but not limited to) rape, sexual molestation, robbery and other violent crimes, accidents, terrorism and torture, natural disasters, and witnessing the same.

Survivors who suffer with PTSD re-experience their traumatic event again and again in the form of intrusive and distressing memories, nightmares and flashbacks (i.e. acting or feeling as if the traumatic event is occurring again in the present). And many become psychologically distressed and/or physiologically aroused when they are reminded of the event. PTSD is also characterized by avoidance of people, places, activities, conversations, feelings and thoughts that remind the survivor of the trauma. A detachment from others and a restriction of emotions is common. Finally, individuals with PTSD typically complain of increased arousal, marked by hypervigilance, difficulty sleeping, irritability, exaggerated startle, and in some cases outbursts of anger (American Psychological Association, 2010).

Guilt, shame, and the inability to trust others are not formally part of the PTSD diagnosis but are common among trauma sufferers. Survivors often feel guilty for having lived when others died and/or believe that they could have or should have done more to prevent the trauma or to help others during the event – even when intervening was not possible. For example, several of Jimmy Dunne's colleagues at Sandler O'Neill spoke of feeling "haunted, wondering who else they could have saved. 'I feel guilty because I left. … Why didn't I tell them to get out? I should have told them to leave'" (Brooker, 2002, p. 60). Feelings of self-blame can become overpowering, sometimes to the point that the individual contemplates suicide. Indeed, along with a rise in PTSD among military veterans, there has been increasing concern about suicides of active duty personnel deployed in Iraq and Afghanistan (Dao, 2010).

Feelings of powerlessness and of being permanently changed by the trauma are also common. Human rights worker Sister Dianna Ortiz quotes a torture survivor who expresses how the memory of trauma continues to permeate daily living:

> Once I was safe, I thought I was free of my torturers. I actually believed that I would never see them again, that I would never have to smell them or hear their voices. But what I soon realized was that they were within me; they literally had made their home inside my soul. ... I felt so dirty, so contaminated by evil. (Ortiz, 2001, pp. 18–19)

To deal with their symptoms, survivors with PTSD often self-medicate with substances of abuse hoping to calm their hyper-active nervous system, improve sleep, and suppress traumatic memories. Those who become exhausted from night after night of sleeplessness and nightmares may experiment with whatever substances they can obtain. Alcohol, benzodiazapines (Valium, Xanax, Ativan), and opiates (codeine, heroin) each suppress the central nervous system and have a quieting effect that counters the hypervigilance typical of PTSD. These substances can be so effective that survivors with PTSD may develop a substance abuse disorder (Jacobsen *et al.*, 2001). In fact, nearly 50% of PTSD patients meet criteria for alcohol dependence at some point during their life (Jacobsen *et al.*, 2001). In addition, trauma survivors may develop one or more related psychological disorders, such as major depression or panic disorder. In-depth descriptions of these related disorders are beyond the scope of this book, but we mention them to underscore the complexity of psychological reactions to trauma.

It is easy to see how PTSD symptoms can be debilitating and can interfere dramatically with daily life. These symptoms can derail careers, marriages, family relationships and friendships. In a 1999 study, Mary L. Malik and colleagues found that PTSD impaired quality of life more severely than either major depression or obsessive-compulsive disorder (Malik *et al.*, 1999).

How is PTSD assessed?

Researchers have developed a number of instruments to assess PTSD; these include the Clinician-Administered PTSD Scale (CAPS), the Posttraumatic Stress Diagnostic Scale (PDS), and the PTSD Checklist (PCL), among others (see Blake *et al.*, 1995; Foa, 1995, 1997; Friedman *et al.*, 2007; Weathers *et al.*, 1993). The CAPS is administered by a trained mental health professional; it focuses on two factors: frequency of symptoms and intensity of symptoms. Sample CAPS questions are, "Have you ever had unwanted memories of [the traumatic event]? What were they like? What did you remember?" and "How much distress or discomfort did these memories cause you? Were you able to put them out of your mind and think about something else? How hard did you have to try? How much did they interfere with your life?" The PDS and the PCL similarly assess the symptoms listed by the American Psychiatric Association, but are in the form of self-report scales in which patients rate their own level of symptoms and distress. The PCL comes in several versions, including one for military personnel and one for civilians. Like the CAPS, it asks patients to rate the level to which they were bothered in the past month by phenomena such as "Suddenly acting or feeling as if a stressful experience were happening again (as if you were reliving it)"; "Having physical reactions (e.g. heart pounding, trouble breathing, sweating) when something reminded you of a stressful experience"; and "Feeling emotionally numb or being unable to have loving feelings for those close to you."

How prevalent is PTSD?

Estimates vary as to the prevalence of PTSD (Friedman *et al.*, 2007). A well-designed study in 1995 found that roughly 8% of all Americans experience PTSD at some point in their life, with 5% of men and 10.4% of women meeting criteria for the disorder. Survivors of certain kinds of trauma are more likely than others to be affected (Kessler *et al.*, 1995). Some 30–50% of female rape victims develop PTSD, and the incidence among male rape victims is even higher: up to 65%, according to some estimates (Rothbaum *et al.*, 1992). About 12% of motor vehicle accident survivors experience PTSD (Norris, 1992), and among combat veterans the rate is 15–30% (National Center for PTSD, 2009). There are varied estimates of the rate of PTSD in US veterans returning from Iraq and Afghanistan. The World Health Organization (2006) reported 11.2–17.1%, compared with a baseline rate of 5% before deployment. A Rand Corporation study in 2008 found that 19% of these veterans experienced symptoms of either PTSD or major depression (Alvarez, 2008).

As we have said earlier in this book, most people who undergo a trauma will not develop PTSD; of course, the more intense, severe and overwhelming the trauma, the more likely it is that symptoms of PTSD will follow. Fortunately, treatment techniques that can be effective in helping individuals to recover from PTSD and other anxiety-related problems are now widely in use. Some of these techniques have been briefly discussed at various junctures in the book.

References

Alvarez, L. (2008). Nearly a fifth of war veterans report mental disorders, a private study finds. *New York Times*, April 18. Accessed 2/15/10 at http://www.nytimes.com/2008/04/18/us/18vets.html.

American Psychiatric Association. (1994). *Diagnostic and statistical manual of mental disorders* (4th ed.). Washington, DC: Author.

American Psychological Association (2010). *The road to resilience.* Washington, DC: American Psychological Association, http://www.apa.org/helpcenter/road-resilience.aspx (accessed June 25, 2010).

Blake, D. D., Weathers, F. W., Nagy, L. M., Kaloupek, D. G., Gusman, F. D.,

Charney, D. S., *et al.* (1995). The development of a clinician-administered PTSD scale. *Journal of Traumatic Stress*, 8, 75–90.

Brooker, K. (2002). Starting over. *Fortune*, January 21, 50–68.

Dao, J. (2010). At War: Notes from the front lines: Presidential condolences and troop suicides. *New York Times*, February 1. Accessed 2/15/10 at http://atwar.blogs.nytimes.com/2010/02/01/presidential-condolences-and-troop-suicides/.

Foa, E. B. (1995). *The Posttraumatic Diagnostic Scale (PDS) manual.* Minneapolis, MN: National Computer Systems.

Foa, E. B. (1997). Psychological processes related to recovery from a trauma and an effective treatment for PTSD. In R. Yehuda & A. McFarlane (Eds.),

Psychobiology of post-traumatic stress disorder (pp. 410–424). New York, NY: New York Academy of Science.

Friedman, M. J., Keane, T. M., Resick, P. R. (eds.) (2007). *Handbook of PTSD: Science and practice.* New York: The Guilford Press.

Jacobsen, L. K., Southwick, S. M., & Kosten, T. R. (2001). Substance use disorders in patients with posttraumatic stress disorder: A review of the literature. *American Journal of Psychiatry*, **158** (August), 1184–1190.

Kessler, R. C., Sonnega, A., Bromet, E., Hughes, M., & Nelson, C. B., (1995). Post-traumatic Stress Disorder in the National Comorbidity Survey. *Archives of General Psychiatry*, **52**, 1048–1060.

Litz, B.T. (2005). Has resilience to severe trauma been underestimated? *American Psychologist*, **60**, 262.

Luthar, S.S. (2006). Resilience in development: A synthesis of research across five decades. In D. Cicchetti & D.J. Cohen (eds.), *Developmental psychopathology, Vol.3: Risk disorder, and adaptation*, 2nd edn (pp. 740–795). New York: Wiley.

Maguen, S., Lucenko, B. A., Reger, M. A., Gahm, G. A., Litz, B. T., Seal, K. H., Knight, S. J., & Marmar, C. R. (2010). The impact of reported direct and indirect killing on mental health symptoms in Iraq War veterans. *Journal of Traumatic Stress*, **23**(1), 86–90.

Malik, M. L., Connor, K. M., Sutherland, S. M., Smith, R. D., Davison, R. M., &. Davidson, J. R. T. (1999). Quality of life and posttraumatic stress disorder: A pilot study assessing changes in sf-36 scores before and after treatment in a placebo-controlled trial of Fluoxetine. *Journal of Traumatic Stress*, **12**(2), April, 387–393. DOI 10.1023/A:1024745030140

McEwen, B.S. (2007). Physiology and neurobiology of stress and adaptation: Central role of the brain. *Physiological Reviews*, **87**, 873–904.

National Center for PTSD, Department of Veterans Affairs (2009). How common is PTSD? Accessed January 2009 at http://www.ptsd.va.gov/.

Norris, F. H. (1992). Epidemiology of trauma: Frequency and impact of different potentially traumatic events on different demographic groups. *Journal of Consulting and Clinical Psychology*, **60**, 409–418.

Norris, F. H., & Slone, L. B. (2007). The epidemiology of trauma and PTSD. In Friedman, M. J., Keane, T. M., & Resick, P. A. (Eds.), *Handbook of PTSD* (pp. 78–98). New York, NY: Guilford Press.

Ortiz, D. (2001). The survivor's perspective: Voices from the center. In Gerrity, E., Keane, T. M., & Tuma, F. (Eds.), *The mental health consequences of torture.* New York: Kluwer Academic / Plenum Publishers.

Rothbaum, B. O., Foa, E. B., Riggs, D. S., Murdock, T., & Walsh, W. (1992). A prospective examination of post-traumatic stress disorder in rape victims. *Journal of Traumatic Stress*, **5**(3), 455–475.

Weathers, F. W., Litz, B. T., Herman, D. S., Huska, J. A., & Keane, T. M. (1993). The PTSD Checklist (PCL): Reliability, validity, and diagnostic utility. Paper presented at the Annual Meeting of International Society for Traumatic Stress Studies, San Antonio, TX, October, 1993.

World Health Organization (2006). Report of a workshop on tracking health performance and humanitarian outcomes. Accessed 11/22/09 at http://www.who.int/hac/events/benchmarkmeeting/en/index.html.

Index